Making Room
at the Table

Making Room at the Table

AN INVITATION TO MULTICULTURAL WORSHIP

*Edited by Brian K. Blount
and Leonora Tubbs Tisdale*

Westminster John Knox Press
Louisville, Kentucky

Scripture quotations, unless otherwise indicated, are from the New Revised Standard Version of the Bible, copyright © 1989 by the Divison of Christian Education of the National Council of the Churches of Christ in the U.S.A., and are used by permission.

Book design by Sharon Adams
Cover design by Pam Poll

First edition
Published by Westminster John Knox Press

This book is printed on acid-free paper that meets the American National Standards Institute Z39.48 standard. ∞

PRINTED IN THE UNITED STATES OF AMERICA
01 02 03 04 05 06 07 08 09 10 — 10 9 8 7 6 5 4 3 2 1

Library of Congress Cataloging-in-Publication Data

Making room at the table: an invitation to multicultural worship / edited by Brian K. Blount and Leonora Tubbs Tisdale.—1st ed.
    p. cm.
Includes bibliographical references.
ISBN 0-664-22202-1
    1. Worship. 2. Multiculturalism—Religious aspects—Christianity. I. Blount, Brian K., 1955– II. Tisdale, Leonora Tubbs.

BV10.2 .M25 2001
264—dc21   00-040416

For Our Children

Joshua and Kaylin Blount
Leonora and William Tisdale

With hopes for a day
when all God's children
will be welcomed at Christ's Table

Contents

viii Contents

Introduction

*O*ne of the most powerful places for building community is the Table. The meal is frequently the place where families gather, where reunions are held, where great moments are celebrated, where community itself is shaped and formed. But as anyone who has frequented a school lunchroom knows, meals can also be places where families separate themselves from other families, where divisions of race and culture are most visible, where differences are accented and global community is fractured.

Unfortunately, such divisions are manifest not only around meals in the broader culture, but also in the church. The Lord's Table, which should be the meal that unites us, is frequently the place where cultural divisions among us are most manifest. In many congregations of our day wars are being fought over issues related to culture and worship such as the shape of the liturgy, the choice of music, the style of prayer and preaching, the nature of congregational mission, and the matter of who is invited and welcomed to the Table. Despite our profession of faith that the Table can break down all barriers that divide us, it is still the case that Sunday morning worship is one of the most culturally segregated moments in our broader communal life.

Making Room at the Table is a collection of essays that wrestle with issues of culture and worship in the light of the biblical and theological foundations of the Christian faith. We are using "culture" to mean the social, linguistic, national, ethnic, and theological realities that locate and identify who we are and what we believe and value. When we talk of culture we do not intend a static location but rather shared patterns of meanings that emerge from our particular locations and shape our identity. Our hope is that we might envision new ways for diverse cultures to gather, converse, and celebrate at Table together as one community in Christ without in the process forsaking their own unique identities or leaving behind the bounty that they uniquely contribute to the feast.

This book includes a series of essays written by members of the faculty of Princeton Theological Seminary. It is the third volume in a series of books our faculty has written addressing critical issues facing the church today. (The other two are *Homosexuality and Christian Community*, edited by Choon-Leong Seow, and *Women, Gender, and Christian Community*, edited by Jane Dempsey Douglass and James F. Kay.) Its primary objective is an exploration of the multicultural challenges facing the contemporary church. In it we address questions such as: For whom should worship be structured? According to whose cultural perspective should music and other liturgical elements be chosen? How do we become all things to all people while still maintaining our unique and particular cultural identities? How do we make worship more relevant to and inclusive of groups that have often been excluded such as youth, minorities, and other marginalized peoples? How do we keep tension between worship that is faithful to our own theological and liturgical histories and worship that at the same time is open to the transformation that can come through the engagement with many cultures?

There are three sections in the book, reflecting the perspectives from which we will wrestle with these issues: Biblical Foundations for Multicultural Worship; Theological Foundations for Multicultural Worship; and Toward Multicultural Worship Today.

Part 1, "Biblical Foundations for Multicultural Worship": This section includes essays by Old and New Testament scholars that focus on issues of cultural interpretation of the scriptures and the significance of such interpretation for contemporary worship life. One of the first things we discover is that these issues are not new. They have been a source of challenge and opportunity for the people of God since the formation of the Hebrew faith community at Sinai. Although the covenant the ancients made with God bound them together as one people, that sense of oneness did not eliminate the reality of cultural difference and division. Israel continued to wrestle with issues of class, gender, and nationality in the multicultural context in which they found themselves.

Jacqueline Lapsley looks specifically at the issue of gender and the ways in which it shapes cultural perspective. She examines the worship practices of Hebrew women and how they were considered suspect by the dominant priestly hierarchy of the day. Using Hannah and Eli as examples, she explores how Hannah's ways of worshiping were directly related to the work patterns of women of the time. While for Hannah such practices were a natural way of extending work into worship, for Eli they represented a challenge. His understanding of proper worship was connected to the gendered assumptions of the male priesthood. In the messy encounter of these two faithful ones we catch glimpses of how tensions within the one body can enrich the church today.

These messy tensions certainly continue in the New Testament as well. According to Brian Blount, in the Gospel of Mark, Jesus preaches that the kingdom of God has broken down all boundaries that divide. Jesus therefore heightens cultural tensions by insisting that all people are God's people. This message has dramatic implications for cultural relationships inside the covenant community; for Jesus, issues of purity and holiness no longer determine who can and cannot participate in the worship of God. The poor, the sick, the broken, and the downtrodden are to be embraced and welcomed in community and in worship. Jesus' teachings also have implications for the way in which the covenant community relates to other peoples; God's temple is to become a house of prayer for all nations. The boundaries that once divided Jew and Gentile are now demolished. So too, Blount argues, must comparable boundaries be demolished today.

The early church, in its struggles to become a house of prayer for all nations, finds that there are no easy answers. Indeed, Beverly Gaventa notes that multiculturalism was as hot a topic in the first century as it is now. Nor was the church uniform in its address of such issues. By looking at three examples of Paul's multicultural encounters in the book of Acts, she argues that the church errs today if it thinks there is a "one size fits all" answer to the challenges that face it. Rather the scriptures themselves show us that the contexts in which the cultural encounters occur should shape the ways in which they are addressed. In Acts we see that varying locations and populations require different strategies.

Donald Juel shifts the discussion from a consideration of the church's proclamation of the gospel to those outside the faith, to a consideration of how all those who have put on Christ through baptism live and worship together in their newfound unity. Paul insists that in Christ there is no longer Jew or Greek, slave or free, male or female. But what does that reality mean for Christian worship then and now? For Juel it does not mean denying the individual differences we bring to the worship act. A multicultural community is not one where otherness is obliterated. Rather, it is a community of hospitality in which the richness of individual gifts and the mystery of the other are celebrated.

Part 2, "Theological Foundations for Multicultural Worship": This section includes essays by scholars in theology and ethics that examine how cultural assumptions shape and influence theological and spiritual formation. The first essay takes up where the last New Testament essay left off. Richard Fenn argues that the contemporary Christian church frequently performs the very act of obliteration Don Juel's essay warned us against. Rather than respecting the mystery of the other, the church, in an effort to preserve its institutional life, has drawn marginalized communities in, absorbed them, and wiped out their uniqueness. In the name of "diversity," church leaders have domesticated liturgy and used worship rituals as a form of social control. Fenn warns marginalized groups and communities to be careful, therefore, before accepting the church's offer to allow them to celebrate their identity within a so-called shared liturgical context.

Peter Paris provides a good example of what happens positively when an oppressed community has an opportunity to craft its own theology apart from the worshiping community of its oppressor. In the forced segregation of American slave communities, African American Christians retranslated the gospel into their own linguistic idiom. In the process, they not only contributed new forms for worship, such as the spirituals, but they also laid the foundation of a theology that would enable them to resist oppression. This recontextualization was not simply a reformulation of the oppressor's theology or worship, but was a subversive reconstruction of it.

Sang Lee, writing as a Korean American, wrestles with the issue of worship in a context where a community lives between two cultural identities: Korean and American. Rather than viewing this state of in-betweenness as a negative reality to be avoided in worship life, Lee celebrates it as a positive opening for community formation and transformation. He encourages Korean Americans to embrace the creative potential inherent in their in-between state. He recognizes, however, that Korean Americans, like most humans, resist the ambiguity of that in-between reality. The result of such resistance is either a rejection of the American way of life or too facile an assimilation to it. Genuine worship is the place where both are challenged and neither is blessed. Genuine multicultural worship also requires white Americans to relinquish some of their status and control in order to meet Koreans or other ethnic cultures in that place of betweenness.

For Mark Taylor that place of in-betweenness can be literally drummed into the church through the introduction of Caribbean polyrhythms that deconstruct the ordinary and institutionalized patterns of its worship life. True Christian worship of God in the world has to encompass a matrix of adoration which includes not only collective celebration and the remembrance of the story of Jesus (the predominant foci in most Western worship contexts), but also the resistance of empire and the experience of social liberation. Because polyrhythmic praise is embodied praise it resists the separation between the material and the spiritual in worship, and facilitates Christian adoration of God in all four spheres of the matrix. It also presses the church to become more genuinely multicultural in its worship life, opening itself to embrace musical forms and rhythms (such as rap and reggae) it once considered to be secular, not sacred.

Part 3, "Toward Multicultural Worship Today": This section includes essays by scholars in practical theology that focus on contemporary cultural issues facing the church today. Kenda Creasy Dean moves us into the "now" quickly with her essay, which explores the youth culture as a context for worship. Her frame of reference is the "mosh pit," an embodied experience common to youth who attend rock concerts, but alien to much adult culture. The mosh pit is a place of intense togetherness where something is always happening, where youth are moved about bodily, and where they experience a sense of being part of something bigger than they are. That something is a "happening" that provides youth with a sensation of self-transcendence and ecstatic release. She contends that youth seek a similar experience in worship. While not wanting to fall prey to naked emotionalism, Dean does think that the church needs to take affect and feeling more seriously. She advocates liturgy that incorporates elements of transcendence, abandonment, and passion that correspond to a God whose nature is characterized as much by playfulness and ecstasy as by suffering.

Geddes Hanson argues that before we can have a fruitful discussion on the matter of multicultural worship we must first clear the ground of confusion surrounding the terms "culture" and "worship." For him a definition of culture must take into account not only social traditions that are common to all groups, but also those traditions which are distinctive to particular groups. Those distinctive traditions are the ones that pose a problem for multicultural worship. Because these worshiping traditions and the values that undergird them are deep-rooted and pervasive, they cannot be blended. Hanson therefore questions whether genuinely multicultural worship is either possible or desirable.

The last two essays deal with the worship wars that plague many local congregations today. Martin Tel initiates his conversation by focusing on music: the "universal" language that's dividing the church. One of his concerns is that when we battle over whose tastes will predominate in worship musically, truth is the first casualty. In order to keep the church more truthful about its worship, Tel presses us to ask questions related to excellence (Are there any criteria we can use to evaluate excellence in music cross-culturally?) and relevance (Does our music have significant meaning for those who are worshiping?). He expresses concern that our quest for unity in multicultural worship may preclude the genuine dialogue that can take place when we listen attentively to the musical voice of the other. He also also warns that multicultural worship can become a vehicle for injustice if we substitute worship in diverse forms for active engagement in the struggles of the world.

Using the image of the church as a ship sailing the narrows, with shoals on either side of the channel, Leonora Tubbs Tisdale is concerned that what is often sacrificed in contemporary worship wars is theological depth. In the battles over whose cultural styles and tastes will predominate, which order of worship will be used, whether worship should focus primarily on evangelistic outreach or the ongoing nurture of believers, or how "traditional" or "contemporary" our worship should be, Tisdale is concerned that we fail to provide theological channel markers that keep us from running aground. Insisting that worship be concerned with both the praise of God and the edification of the worshiper, that worship be genuinely Trinitarian in nature, be eschatological in the fullest sense of the term, and address the whole person (heart, soul, mind, and strength), she provides us with guidance that can help us steer the deep.

While the voices in this volume are not uniform, we believe the multiple perspectives brought to bear on this critical issue facing the church today can be enriching to our ongoing conversation. We have been gratified by the eager willingness of our colleagues on the Princeton faculty to write about these issues so close to the heart of the church's life, and to reflect on them in light of their various disciplines. To them we owe a tremendous debt of thanks. We are also grateful to our able editorial assistant, Raewynne Whiteley, for her excellent work on this project, and to our editor, Stephanie Egnotovich, for her support and encouragement each step of the way. Our hope is that this volume will stimulate the kind of multicultural conversation that will expand our horizons and open us to new worship possibilities. The ultimate goal is that the church will be enabled through its worship practices to eat together at the one Table of Christ, where the gifts of all are welcomed and the uniqueness of no one is denied.

Brian K. Blount
Nora Tubbs Tisdale

Contributors

BRIAN K. BLOUNT is Associate Professor of New Testament. He is an ordained minister of the Presbyterian Church (U.S.A.).

KENDA CREASY DEAN is Assistant Professor of Youth, Church, and Culture. She is an ordained minister of the United Methodist Church.

RICHARD K. FENN is the Maxwell M. Upson Professor of Christianity and Society. He is an ordained priest in the Episcopal Church.

BEVERLY ROBERTS GAVENTA is the Helen H. P. Manson Professor of New Testament Literature and Exegesis. She is a member of the Presbyterian Church (U.S.A.).

GEDDES W. HANSON is the Charlotte W. Newcombe Professor of Congregational Ministry. He is an ordained minister of the Presbyterian Church (U.S.A.).

DONALD H. JUEL is the Richard J. Dearborn Professor of New Testament Theology. He is an ordained minister of the Evangelical Lutheran Church in America.

JACQUELINE E. LAPSLEY is Assistant Professor of Old Testament. She is a member of the Episcopal Church.

SANG HYUN LEE is the Kyung-Chik Han Professor of Systematic Theology, and Director of the Asian American Program. He is an ordained minister of the Presbyterian Church (U.S.A.).

PETER J. PARIS is the Elmer G. Homrighausen Professor of Christian Social Ethics, and Liaison with Princeton University African American Studies Program. He is an ordained Baptist minister.

MARK TAYLOR is Professor of Theology and Culture. He is an ordained minister of the Presbyterian Church (U.S.A.).

MARTIN TEL is the C.F. Seabrook Director of Music, and Lecturer in Church Music. He is a member of the Reformed Church in America.

LEONORA TUBBS TISDALE is the Elizabeth M. Engle Associate Professor of Preaching and Worship. She is an ordained minister of the Presbyterian Church (U.S.A.).

PART 1

Biblical Foundations
for Multicultural Worship

Chapter 1

Pouring Out Her Soul Before the Lord

Women and Worship in the Old Testament

JACQUELINE E. LAPSLEY

> As she continued praying before the LORD, Eli observed
> her mouth. Hannah was praying silently; only her lips
> moved, but her voice was not heard; therefore Eli thought
> she was drunk. So Eli said to her, "How long will you
> make a drunken spectacle of yourself? Put away your
> wine." But Hannah answered, "No, my lord, I am a
> woman deeply troubled; I have drunk neither wine nor
> strong drink, but I have been pouring out my soul before
> the LORD."
>
> *1 Sam 1:12–15*

Hannah at Worship

*D*ifferences in forms of worship, and how they relate to the unity
of our faith in God, pose a particularly complex theological problem. But it is not a new problem. The Old Testament witnesses to
the classic difficulty of relating diverse worship practices to the bib-
lically central idea of faith in the one living and sovereign God. This
chapter is an effort to reflect on the types of worship with which
women are especially associated in the Old Testament, and to further reflect on how Christian readers might appreciate those worship
practices without losing sight of the core beliefs that have shaped,
and continue to shape, the Judeo-Christian tradition.[1] This discussion of women and worship in the Old Testament will, I hope, add
to our present reflections on multiculturalism and worship by offering an Old Testament basis for thinking about the ways in which
these twin poles—diversity of worship practices and unifying core
beliefs—may be simultaneously valued as strengthening our life
in God.

We do not know for sure that Hannah's silent (perhaps ecstatic?) prayer is a form of worship especially associated with women; the text is not clear on this point, but it may well have been the case.[2] Yet the fact that Hannah is a woman, and that the way she is praying provokes a negative reaction in Eli, is suggestive: it may be, for example, that the central sanctuaries were primarily identified with men only, and that women's worship practices were consequently little known there.[3] Eli's misunderstanding of, and hostility toward, the way Hannah is praying reflects a more general problem of how to understand the way women worshiped in ancient Israel, especially as reflected in the primary witness of the Old Testament.[4] On the one hand, the evidence that the Old Testament provides about women and worship is sparse and difficult to interpret. On the other hand, much of the clearest evidence is polemical in nature. The paucity of texts dealing with women and worship is in part a reflection of the nature of the material: the Old Testament is largely concerned with official, public, and urban religion, and much of women's religious activity takes place in the home or at local shrines and sanctuaries.[5] Yet based on literary, anthropological, and archaeological evidence, a picture is emerging that suggests that women led vital and dynamic religious lives, even if we can only catch glimpses of those lives.[6]

Women's Worship Practices Considered Legitimate in the Old Testament

Before examining women's religious practices that meet with resistance in the Old Testament, it is worth exploring those worship practices associated with women which are presented as acceptable and legitimate practice. Phyllis Bird has outlined the very limited roles that women had to play in the official cult of Yahweh in ancient Israel, although the intensity of restriction on women's cultic activity varied according to the historical period.[7] Most of the biblical witness suggests that women had more freedom to engage in sanctioned cultic worship before Israel began to be ruled by kings, especially during the "period of the Judges," around 1200–1000 B.C.E., which is the setting for the books of Judges, Ruth, and the beginning of 1 Samuel. This freedom progressively decreased when kings began to rule (around 1000 B.C.E.), and continued to decrease once the last king was deposed and Israel as a separate nation, that is, the southern part known as Judah, had come to an end in 587 B.C.E.[8]

The biblical material relating to the period before Saul began to reign as the first king of Israel (around 1000 B.C.E.) presents women engaged in various religious activities, even filling leadership roles. Miriam's victory song at the sea (Ex. 15:20–21), for example, suggests an important role for women's singing and dancing in worship contexts (cf. the women dancing at Shiloh [Judg. 21:21]), as well as the importance of her status as a prophet alongside Moses and Aaron (cf. Num. 12:2–8). Women are also found to be "ministering" at the tent of meeting in Exodus 38:8 and 1 Samuel 2:22. As prophet and judge, Deborah leads the people in holy war, and the song associated with her (Judg. 5:1) again suggests the importance of women's singing in religious contexts such as victory in holy war.[9] In Hannah's story mentioned above, Hannah and Peninnah accompany their husband to Shiloh for the annual pilgrimage,[10] and share in the communion meal.[11] Bird suggests, using cross-cultural evidence, that Hannah's visit to the sanctuary (cited above) may be viewed as an example of "the way in which women use general or male-dominated religious institutions and occasions for their own purposes to suit their own peculiar needs, investing them at times with their own rituals and meanings."[12] This might help explain why Eli finds Hannah's behavior alien and disturbing. Other examples could be cited, but the general picture is clear: a number of roles in "legitimate" worship were open to women in this period, including some leadership roles.[13]

This situation changed considerably however, during the course of the monarchies in Israel and Judah. The biblical evidence (primarily in the books of Kings and in the prophets) portrays most women's religious activity as unorthodox and therefore unacceptable to the biblical writers (e.g., queens and queen mothers introducing foreign cults [1 Kings 15:13; 18:19; 2 Kings 11:18]). The increasing restrictions on women's participation in the official cult appear to be related to the move toward centralization of worship and specialization of religious functions during this period. In other words, when worship was forbidden in the smaller towns and villages, and priests (always male) began to take over roles previously assumed by the general populace, women had many fewer opportunities to participate in official worship (Huldah the prophetess [2 Kings 22:14] is a notable exception to the general decrease in religious opportunities for women).[14] In part the restrictions on women's participation in worship were due to conflicts between their social roles (such as reproduction, care of children, domestic responsibilities) and religious obligations (e.g., making pilgrimages to major cultic centers, being free of menstrual impurity).[15] Yet these conflicts arose only because worship was created and defined to accommodate the social obligations of men, which should not surprise us.

At any rate, the tightening of definitions of orthodox worship practices while the kings ruled parallels the increasing power of royal circles in religious matters. And with power consolidated in centralized cults, women had virtually no legitimate outlet to express their piety. Why did so much of the religious activity that went on before kingship was established come to be considered unacceptable under the kings? It is possible that times of decentralized power and relatively more social dysfunction (for example, during the "period of the Judges") are more conducive to religious freedom, and therefore to increased opportunities for women to engage in religious life.[16]

Women and Unacceptable Worship Practices

The first commandments of the Decalogue ("You shall have no other gods before me. You shall not make for yourself an idol . . ." [Ex. 20:3–4a; Deut. 5:7–8a]) capture the prevailing view of much of the Old Testament on the question of worship. Those persons responsible for the final versions of Deuteronomy, Joshua, Judges, 1 and 2 Samuel, and 1 and 2 Kings (often called the "Deuteronomistic writers") were especially concerned to urge the sole worship of Yahweh on these terms (e.g., Judg. 2:13–14; 1 Sam. 7:3–4; 2 Kings 21:3–5). The enormous influence and the theological power of this insight into the reality of God should not be underestimated. Indeed, these fundamental tenets of Yahwistic worship not only suffuse and pervade much of the Old Testament, they constitute the foundation of Jewish and Christian belief in the one living God. That these particular texts with their unifying belief in the oneness of God were so carefully preserved and transmitted over millennia speaks to the enormous power of the claim they assert.[17]

Yet it appears that worship in ancient Israel was more complex than these prohibitions imply, in that the use of religious symbols ("idols") and the worship of other gods either in connection with worship of Yahweh or in a separate context, appear to have been not only prevalent but *standard* and *legitimate* worship practices outside of the Deuteronomistic circles responsible for significant portions of the Old Testament.[18] For those whose views of Israelite worship have been deeply shaped by the perspective of Deuteronomy (as is the case for most Jews and Christians because of the importance of this biblical book), it is not difficult to imagine that such unorthodox, illegitimate worship was taking place in Old

Testament times (indeed the Deuteronomists' polemic itself acknowledges the problem).[19]

To see these unorthodox practices as perfectly acceptable, and even normative, in the official cult of Israel (not to mention in "unofficial" contexts), however, seems strange indeed. The reason for this, I believe, is that we have quite unconsciously made the Deuteronomistic view of worship the standard by which all worship at all times is to be judged in ancient Israel. Yet the influence of this particular understanding of worship did not span as much historical time as the Old Testament texts lead one to believe (it appears to have been at its apex of influence in the seventh and sixth centuries B.C.E.). Since women are often associated with these worship practices that so concerned the Deuteronomists,[20] but which may well have been quite normal and acceptable practice at various times, it is worth considering what evidence we have for those practices and how they might illuminate our thinking about multicultural worship.

The authors of Deuteronomy, and the other "historical" books of Joshua–2 Kings, were especially concerned about two types of illegitimate worship: first, the worship of gods other than Yahweh (e.g., Baal, Astarte) and, second, the worship of Yahweh in ways that the Deuteronomists opposed (principally at local sanctuaries and by the use of idols, such as at Dan and Bethel). The ambiguous nature of the available archaeological and biblical evidence makes it difficult to distinguish consistently between these two issues. For example, it is often difficult to determine whether the word *asherah*, in the Bible and in archaeological inscriptions, refers to the goddess of that name (thus potentially a consort of Yahweh) or to a kind of stylized handcrafted tree (probably feminine in its imagery) that was used as a cult object in the worship of Yahweh. Neither of these scenarios was acceptable to the Deuteronomists, yet it is quite likely that women and men who worshiped in these ways saw themselves as faithful worshipers of the God of Israel (and many others probably saw them this way as well). We will consider first the ways in which women are associated with forms of Yahwistic worship not considered permissible, and then reflect on women's participation in the worship of other gods.

Given their limited opportunities in the official cult, it is not surprising that women might be drawn to unofficial forms of worship. Indeed, there is significant evidence to suggest that women engaged in forms of Yahwistic worship that were quite different from the standards set by the Deuteronomic legislation.[21] Nonetheless, this evidence comes in fragmentary form and must be pieced together like pieces of a jigsaw puzzle in order to approximate a picture of women's worship of Yahweh. Anthropological studies, for example, suggest that "visits to local shrines, pilgrimages, and individual acts of petition and dedication related to particular needs were favored by women and better suited to the general rhythms and exigencies of their lives."[22] Yet the "local" and "private" nature of these types of worship practices would have rendered them unacceptable to the Deuteronomists. Disturbingly, the line between orthodoxy and unorthodoxy seems to coincide with the line between male-defined religious practices and those practices favored by women.[23]

The evidence from archaeology adds to the picture of women's worship practices: the two inscriptions found at two separate sites in the Middle East (which include the phrase "Yahweh . . . and his *asherah*") are suggestive, but their significance is still much debated. Whatever the meaning of this phrase (cult object, or Asherah, consort of Yahweh, for example), the Bible itself tends to associate women with the *asherah* (e.g., Maacah, Jezebel). Thus it may have been that women were especially drawn to forms of Yahwistic worship that permitted and even encouraged the inclusion of feminine imagery. While this type of worship was completely unacceptable to the Deuteronomists, it appears to have been quite usual and legitimate in Israel prior to the rise in influence of the Deuteronomists.[24] In addition, a number of small figurines depicting a female form have been found throughout ancient Israel, both in domestic sites and in sanctuaries. We do not presently know how these figurines are related to women's (or men's) religious practices in ancient Israel—their significance remains mysterious. Nonetheless, their presence in a variety of contexts hints at the diversity of the forms of worship actually practiced in ancient Israel. Finally, one wonders whether the singing and dancing that characterized women's Yahwistic worship before 1000 B.C.E., when there were no kings, did not disappear during the monarchies, but rather continued to find expression in "unofficial" worship of Yahweh.[25]

But what about the worship of gods other than Yahweh? The Bible offers glimpses of women as worshipers in non-Yahwistic cults, and women appear to have had a special relationship to some of these cults. The "[p]eculiarly or predominantly female forms of ritual and worship are suggested in the canonical sources only in reference to heterodox [i.e., unorthodox] cults."[26] In Jeremiah 7:18 and 44:15–19, for example, women are depicted as ardent worshipers of the Queen of Heaven (a goddess of uncertain identity), baking cakes to offer to the goddess.[27] Women apparently also fulfilled a cultic function by weaving for the *asherah* in the Jerusalem Temple (2 Kings 23:7).[28] And in Ezekiel 8:14 women act as professional mourners for the god Tammuz (mourning is elsewhere also associated with women [Jer. 9:17; 2 Chron. 35:25]). The fact that these women were worshiping gods other than Yahweh is less interesting than the *ways* in which they worshiped. Baking and weaving—the very domestic skills that women developed in the home—became their modes of worship. Thus the worship practices associated with these women came directly out of their social experience: to weave and to bake became, in the context of worship, holy experiences for these women. It should not be too surprising that women were drawn to forms of worship that allowed them to express their religious experience through skills and gifts they already possessed.[29]

Unity and Diversity

A number of issues arise out of this discussion of women, worship, and the Old Testament and its relevance for thinking about inclusive worship practices today. First, what do we as Christians do with the recognition that the forms of worship presented in the Old Testament are almost exclusively a male creation, and that women's religious experience and the worship nurtured by that experience are either absent or polemically derided (especially during the monarchical period and following)?[30] Second, how can we value the particular ways that women found to express their religious impulses while at the same time affirming the central beliefs of the Deuteronomists concerning the exclusive sovereignty of Yahweh? Finally, how can Christians who are trying to be faithful to scripture read and interpret the polemical style characteristic of much of the Old Testament, such as the Deuteronomistic portions?

To say that we should condemn women's religious practices in the Old Testament because the Deuteronomists do is not a very sound or compelling theological position. To accept the Deuteronomistic position unreflectively means perpetuating ways of thinking that equate "orthodoxy" with male-defined worship while condemning women's religious expression as "unorthodox" (though men are not excluded from illegitimate worship practices in the Bible, of course). Such a position would also implicate us in a literalism that is not only difficult to sustain as a consistent method of interpreting the Bible, but also produces static theological results. It might be helpful instead to engage the New Testament as a lens for reading the Old. After all, Jesus had some unorthodox ideas about what should be considered normative religious practice and faithful worship. Furthermore, Jesus appears to have been particularly interested in peripheral and despised figures, including women. His attitude toward them suggests that we might make room for more critical reflection about the peripheral and despised religious practices associated with women in the Old Testament.

While still fragmentary and sometimes difficult to interpret, the evidence from anthropology, archaeology, and the Bible suggests that non-Yahwistic cults seem to have better served the religious needs of women. This observation might lead, and in the past has led, to an androcentric interpretation: What is wrong with women that they are drawn to foreign cults? But it might also lead us to ask instead, What did these cults offer women that the Deuteronomistic stipulations for worship did not? In the Bible, women transform daily domestic activities, like baking and weaving, into worship practices, but apparently it was only in non-Yahwistic cults that this was possible. Illegitimate cults do not seem to have presented women with the same types of irreconcilable conflicts between social responsibilities and religious life that the Deuteronomistic view of proper worship did. In short, women found ways to worship that both made use of their skills and gifts and were adaptable to the constraints of their lives as they lived them. This provides us with a model for reflecting on our own worship practices and, specifically, on the foundations that undergird them. What constitutes worship and who defines it? On what basis do we make distinctions between appropriate and inappropriate forms of worship?

In sum, in embracing the Deuteronomistic insight into the reality of God, we have also unreflectively embraced the forms of worship they espoused as normative. Yet these forms catered to specifically male needs, in that they were urban, centralized, and entailed male leadership roles, ideal for men who enjoyed more mobility than women. This fact should not lead us to caricature the Deuteronomists as the wicked oppressors of women; the evidence does not permit such facile characterizations. Indeed, Bird notes that in other areas outside of worship the Deuteronomistic legislation is responsible for bringing "women more fully and directly into the religious assembly so that the congregation is redefined as a body of lay men and women."[31] In an important sense, then, we must be deeply indebted to the book of Deuteronomy for its emphasis on the equality of persons before God. Nonetheless, Bird also argues persuasively that it is important to see the way in which the Deuteronomistic vision of worship is gender-defined: "To speak of the faith of Israel's daughters means at the very least to reexamine the boundaries of the religion we have reconstructed and to make room for more differentiated forms of piety than we have hitherto imagined—with attention to hierarchies of power in a gender-differentiated system of roles and offices."[32]

Moreover, as an exercise to expand the boundaries of our thinking, it is useful to consider what types of worship might have suited *women's* particular needs and skills in ancient Israel (their ties to children and childbearing; their domestic artisanry). Worship that catered to the particular situation of women might occur at local sites and utilize the domestic arts more centrally, and include singing and dancing also as central features. There is no inherent reason why such practices must be "unorthodox."

I am not suggesting that we simplistically and unreflectively map these modes of worship onto our modern context. The point here, rather, is to suggest that our thinking about worship (among other areas) often labors under the weight of cultural frameworks of which we are largely unaware. What is gained from the knowledge that orthodox worship in the Old Testament is largely a male-defined cultural construct? It suggests that there are other categories—race, class, ethnicity, for example—that shape our ways of thinking about worship of which we are equally unaware.[33] Because they are so much a part of our traditions, we do not see the ways in which they exclude on the basis of cultural distinctions that are often rooted in historical imbalances of power.

Also arising from this discussion of women and worship in the Old Testament is the more general issue of how to read polemic in the Bible. The Deuteronomists' views of what they considered inappropriate worship forms are most often couched in polemical terms, which complicates how we read them. To take scripture seriously does not mean unreflectively equating polemic with truth. Polemic relates to the *form* of a message, not the content.[34] Thus, an important interpretative skill in reading scripture involves affirming what is crucial to our identity as Christians (we worship the one living God who creates and liberates, for example), while distancing ourselves from forms of polemic that belittle or satirize other religious traditions or worship practices. While polemic can be quite effective rhetorically, one is ultimately on firmer theological ground, in showing respect for all human beings, for example, by finding ways to affirm one's own identity without belittling the identity of others.

Thus, in the case of the Deuteronomistic polemic against the worship of other gods and idols, one might affirm the core insight of the exclusive sovereignty of God at the root of the Deuteronomists' teaching (we have our own "foreign gods" now, of course—such as consumerism or extreme individualism), while rejecting their style of argumentation. In terms of the present effort to open the eucharistic Table to a variety of multicultural worship practices, this suggests that we should not neglect to affirm our common identity. Yet we must also sensitize ourselves to the ways in which *forms* of worship, while often embodying identity in positive ways (to be celebrated), can also function negatively to shape identity through the often subtle denigration of what is different.

Eli, when he confronted Hannah in the sanctuary, had certain expectations about how one should worship in the sanctuary, and Hannah did not fulfill those expectations. His response is initially hostile—he suspects that her behavior might be disrespectful of the sanctuary and therefore of God. Yet when Hannah responds that she has not been drinking, but has been pouring out her soul to the LORD, Eli realizes that she is worshiping out of faithfulness to God, even though he is not familiar with the form of her worship. He announces to Hannah what amounts to an oracle of salvation—a promise that God will respond to her prayers (1 Sam.1:17). In due course Hannah's form of worship, her silent prayers, are vindicated by God in the story when she bears Samuel.

The story serves as a model for how we might think about multicultural worship practices: not in terms of whether they are familiar to us (as Eli does at first), but whether they emerge as a faithful response to the power of God's working in people's lives. Our affirmation of central biblical principles that bind us together as Christians must not deter us from a genuine openness to the working of God's Spirit within forms of worship that seem strange to us. We are called to live in the midst of that sometimes difficult and messy, but often beautiful and inspiring, tension between the unity of our faith in the one, holy, and living God and the diversity of forms that the expression of that faith inevitably takes.

NOTES

1. Some might question using women as a category for reflecting on multicultural worship. Are women sufficiently definable as a cultural minority with respect to worship in ancient Israel? The evidence, I believe, tends to suggest that they are, as Phyllis A. Bird argues: "[T]here is sufficient evidence to suggest that women's religion did represent a significantly differentiated form of religious expression within Yahwism" ("Israelite Religion and the Faith of Israel's Daughters: Reflections on Gender and Religious Definition," in *Missing Persons and Mistaken Identities: Women and Gender in Ancient Israel*, Overtures to Biblical Theology [Minneapolis: Fortress Press, 1997], 120).

2. Cross-cultural studies may provide some corroborating evidence of this. See Bird, "Israelite Religion and the Faith of Israel's Daughters," 118, n. 41.

3. Ibid.

4. For the purposes of this discussion I understand "worship" to include prayer in a sanctuary, such as Hannah's prayer (I will touch on both private and public worship practices).

5. Phyllis A. Bird, "The Place of Women in the Israelite Cultus," in *Missing Persons and Mistaken Identities*, 87; and Carol Meyers, "Women and the Domestic Economy of Early Israel," in *Women's Earliest Records from Ancient Egypt and Western Asia*, ed. Barbara S. Lesko, Brown Judaic Studies 166 (Atlanta: Scholars Press, 1989), 267.

6. For a history-of-religions approach to the religious lives of the women in Judges, see Susan Ackerman, *Warrior, Dancer, Seductress, Queen: Women in Judges and Biblical Israel* (New York: Doubleday, 1998), esp. 89–117.

7. This part of the discussion closely follows Bird's important chapter, "The Place of Women in the Israelite Cultus" in *Missing Persons and Mistaken Identities: Women and Gender in Ancient Israel*, 81–102. Bird carefully and appropriately distinguishes "cultus" from more generalized religion in ancient Israel (p. 84, n. 12), but that distinction is less important here, since all types of worship practices are relevant to this discussion.

8. Tamara Eskanazi has offered a strong challenge to this view, proposing that women in the postexilic era enjoyed rights that may be comparable to those enjoyed by women in the premonarchical period, following Meyers's argument. (See "Out from the Shadows: Biblical Women in the Postexilic Era," *JSOT* 54 [1992]: 25–43.)

9. It is too narrow to view the singing and dancing associated with victory celebrations as "secular." See Bird, "Women's Religion in Ancient Israel" in *Women's Earliest Records*, 283–298, n. 28.

10. Carol Meyers sees 1 Samuel 1 as revealing the "private, personal piety of Elkanah and his family and should not be considered an early version of the pilgrimage festivals" ("The Hannah Narrative in Feminist Perspective," in *"Go to the Land I Will Show You": Studies in Honor of Dwight W. Young*, ed. Joseph E. Coleson and Victor H. Matthews [Winona Lake, Ind.: Eisenbrauns, 1996], 123).

11. All cited in Bird, "Women in the Israelite Cultus," 91.

12. Bird, "Israelite Religion and the Faith of Israel's Daughters," 109.

13. Carol Meyers argues that women achieved a certain measure of equality with men during the premonarchical period, although some have criticized her methods. See *Discovering Eve: Ancient Israelite Women in Context* (New York: Oxford, 1988).

14. Bird, "Women in the Israelite Cultus," 92. These tendencies also significantly restricted men in their worship roles (as in tightening the requirements for the priesthood).

15. Ibid., 88. Meyers also makes this point (*Discovering Eve*, 163).

16. Jo Ann Hackett, "In the Days of Jael: Reclaiming the History of Women in Ancient Israel," in *Immaculate & Powerful: The Female in Sacred Image and Social Reality*, ed. Clarissa W. Atkinson et al. (Boston: Beacon Press, 1985), 25–33.

17. See Patrick D. Miller, "The Absence of the Goddess in Israelite Religion," in *Hebrew Annual Review*, vol. 10, ed. Reuben Ahroni (Columbus: Ohio State University, Dept. of Judaic and Near Eastern Languages and Literatures, 1986), 239–40. The Deuteronomists were not the only ones polemicizing against foreign gods—this is a

dominant theme in the prophetic tradition, of course—but the Deuteronomists artic-
ulated especially forcefully the exclusive sovereignty of Yahweh.

18. Susan Ackerman puts it quite strongly: "A more nuanced reconstruction of the religion of ancient Israel . . . would suggest that despite the biblical witness neither the
priestly nor prophetic cult was normative in the religion of the first millennium"
("'And the Women Knead Dough': The Worship of the Queen of Heaven in Sixth-
Century Judah," in *Gender and Difference in Ancient Israel,* ed. Peggy L. Day [Min-
neapolis: Fortress Press, 1989], 109). Saul M. Olyan makes this point in connection
with the *asherah* in *Asherah and the Cult of Yahweh in Israel,* SBL Monograph
Series 34 (Atlanta: Scholars Press, 1988), 9.

19. "Orthodox" and "heterodox" must always be defined from a particular perspective.
For the purposes of this discussion I understand these terms from the point of view
of the Deuteronomists.

20. Women appear to be especially associated with local, not centralized, worship forms
and with "folk" practices, as opposed to "official" or learned religion. See Bird,
"Israelite Religion and the Faith of Israel's Daughters," 111.

21. Bird, "Israelite Religion and the Faith of Israel's Daughters," 120.

22. Ibid., 112. See also Karel van der Toorn, *From Her Cradle to Her Grave: The Role
of Religion in the Life of the Israelite and the Babylonian Woman,* Biblical Seminar
23 (Sheffield: *JSOT,* 1994), 96.

23. Bird, "Israelite Religion and the Faith of Israel's Daughters," 113.

24. For a summary of the evidence and the difficulties in its interpretation, see Judith M.
Hadley, "Yahweh and 'His Asherah': Archaeological and Textual Evidence for the
Cult of the Goddess," in *Ein Gott Allein?: JHWH-Verehrung und biblischer
Monotheismus im Kontext der israelitischen und altorientalischen Religions-
geschichte,* ed. Walter Dietrich and Martin A. Klopfenstein (Fribourg, Switzerland:
Universitatsverlag; Göttingen: Vandenhoeck & Ruprecht, 1994), 235–68.

25. Singing by women was apparently permitted in the context of mourning rituals (2
Chron. 35:25; Jer. 9:17).

26. Bird, "Women in the Israelite Cultus," 100.

27. Some have even argued that women were especially drawn to the worship of goddesses, but there is simply not enough evidence to suggest such a trend (remember
that *asherah* in the Bible and in the inscriptions mentioned above may well refer to
an object used in *Yahwistic* worship).

28. As mentioned above, how this is understood, whether as a reference to the deity or
simply to a cult object, is not clear, but in this context it may well signify the former.
For discussion see John Day, "Yahweh and the Gods and Goddesses of Canaan,"
184–85, and Susan Ackerman, *Under Every Green Tree: Popular Religion in Sixth-
Century Judah,* HSM 46 (Atlanta: Scholars Press, 1992), esp. 65–66.

29. Patrick D. Miller makes this point in "Imagining God," in *Women, Gender, and
Christian Community,* ed. Jane Dempsey Douglass and James F. Kay (Louisville,
Ky.: Westminster John Knox, 1997), 8.

30. See above, however, on women in the premonarchical period, and see Carol Meyers
on Hannah's presentation of her sacrifice in 1 Samuel 1:24 ("The Hannah Narrative
in Feminist Perspective," 117–26).

31. Bird, "The Place of Women in the Israelite Cultus," 102.

32. Bird, "Israelite Religion and the Faith of Israel's Daughters," 120.

33. Consider, for example, that other classes of persons were also excluded from the priesthood: eunuchs, disabled men, and non-Jews. Yet the Bible itself offers a more inclusive view in Isaiah 66:21, where foreigners are claimed as priests and Levites.

34. I am aware of the ways in which form and content are deemed inseparable in literary theory, and I even subscribe to this view with regard to much narrative and poetic art. But polemic strikes me as being in a different category, and somewhat more separable from content.

Chapter 2

(Kivgdom)

The Apocalypse of Worship

God's desived Veality

A House of Prayer for ALL the Nations

BRIAN K. BLOUNT

*I*n the Gospel of Mark, Jesus is a preacher of multicultural worship. He envisioned a future that was radically different from the one espoused by the Temple leadership of his present Jerusalem. The Temple presided over a world where non-Jewish ethnicities were condemned by the theological motifs of holiness and purity, and demonized by the myopic fever of messianic nationalism. Mark's Jesus offered a counter kingdom proposal: he foresaw a time when every people of every nation would call God's Temple their house of prayer. He saw the apocalypse of worship, the revelation of its end-time reality. God's reality. And so Mark wrote to rally his people. He wanted them to bring into the present what Jesus had foreseen of the end. This is why Mark wrote an apocalypse. It is also why one of the key moments in his apocalyptic drama is Jesus' act of "cleansing" the Temple.

Mark as a Historical Apocalypse

An apocalypse is a revealing of something that was previously hidden. The future, of course, is hidden from human eyes. We cannot see it. We often fail even to anticipate it. We therefore need assistance from someone who can clue us in, someone like Jesus in the Gospel of Mark.

With his very first words, Jesus declares that the present time has filled itself to the brim of historical reality; the future, God's future, is at hand (Mark 1:14–15). And though he identifies this future by calling it the kingdom of God, he also declares that it is a near-unfathomable mystery (4:10–12). Clarification is required; Jesus is the one person who can deliver it. Identified as God's divine agent and son (1:1–11), he is the one who will represent the reality of that future in the midst of the present. That is to say, his campaign of teaching, miracle, and exorcism re-presents on the ground, in the present of those actual preaching moments, the heavenly reality of God's future incursion of divine power and transformation. This is what Mark's apocalypse reveals.

And yet, Mark's Gospel is not what most contemporary readers expect of an apocalypse. It reveals the future, the kingdom of God, through its presentation of Jesus, but that revealing is not one of extraordinary creatures, end-time calculations, mythological number puzzles, or deterministic countdowns. It has no otherworldly journey where a seer escapes the conflicts of the present age by warping forward into a future where God has taken vengeance on all his enemies and raised him to the vindicated status of divine offspring. Mark's apocalypse is historical.

Like other historical apocalypses of its time[1] its most pressing interest is in the problems that occur within human history. The historical apocalypse promotes the determined assurance that God will mount a real-time, historical, and transformative intervention. As opposed to the cosmological dualism of the otherworldly apocalypse, where this world is totally unredeemable and will therefore be destroyed, the historical apocalypse operates from the foundation of an eschatological dualism. Here, though the present and future remain two distinct ages, the future brings its power to bear in such a way that it not only salvages the present, it also transforms it.

An Apocalyptic Challenge to Purity and Holiness

Daniel is the most notable *pre-Markan* apocalypse in the Christian corpus. Interestingly enough, its reflections on the future are primarily historical in orientation. No wonder, then, given Mark's own very historical concerns, that he would depend so heavily on Daniel's work as he crafts his own.[2] But there is a critical distinction. Like the Qumran apocalyptic materials, Daniel uses apocalyptic imagery to shore up Israelite codes of purity.[3] Mark does not.

The cultic premise of purity rests on the theological foundation of holiness. "The notion of holiness is rooted in two concepts: wholeness and set-apartness."[4] Not only does this create an external boundary between those considered to be the people of God and those who are not; it also establishes internal boundaries that separate those people of God who are whole from those who are in some way broken. Things that are broken, like leprous skin, whose lesions permit the flow of mucous where it ought not to be, or things that are out of place, like spilled semen, blood, or spit, whose place is within and not outside the body, are also unholy. People tagged by such unholy traits are also branded by the unholiness they bear. In such a context worship is a very monochromatic affair. Only those who are whole and set apart are welcome in the holy places where worship is itself set apart.

The purity codes set the cultic categories of clean and unclean. With the categories come boundaries. And with the boundaries comes the reinforcement of division: some are in; others, regrettably, but necessarily, are out. "The prime activity of a group with a strong purity system will be the making and maintenance of these lines and boundaries."[5]

The boundaries were of practical as well as theological importance.

> This system of holiness served Israel well throughout its history, preserving a minority culture from absorption into dominant cultures. At the time of Jesus, the culture and religion of the Jews were threatened with absorption into the dominant Greek culture and the imperialism of the Roman Empire. The Jewish structures of purity protected the people from these threats of cultural domination. By keeping themselves separate from the Gentiles, the Jews maintained their beliefs and practices.[6]

Observance of the codes was, therefore, a matter of national as well as religious survival. Accordingly, a centralized infrastructure was geared up to protect and administer them. In Jesus' time, the locus of that centralization was the Jerusalem Temple. "The temple system [was] a major mediation or replication of the ideal of order and purity established in creation."[7] It maintained the boundaries that preserved the "set-apartness" that provided for the continuation of the people. This explains the severity of the warnings posted at the entrances to the Temple sanctuary; Gentiles moved through under a threat of death. It is therefore not surprising that a challenge or threat to the Temple would be considered a threat to the overall social and religious fabric of Jewish society.[8]

Nor is it any longer surprising that someone like the author of Daniel, writing from within the faith perspective of Israel, would use apocalyptic imagery to declare that participation in God's future hinged on allegiance to God's desire for holiness and purity in the present. A people who would worship with a holy God in the future must, necessarily, worship "set-apart" from the impure and unholy in the present. And since every culture and people but God's people of Israel were by definition unholy, worship was itself, by definition, always monocultural.

But what Daniel's story builds up, these very codes of purity and holiness, Mark's Jesus tears down. He is a transgressor of boundaries and a transformer of thought right out of the apocalyptic gate. In his very first act of public ministry, he marches into the local repository of the holy and pure, the Capernaum synagogue (1:21–28). There is irony here. In the monochromatic clean room of worship, Jesus' principle engagement is with a force of *uncleanness*. He must cleanse what is allegedly already clean.

His oddly ironic journey is just beginning. His narrative ministry not yet a chapter old, in this world governed by codes of purity and principles of holiness, he embarks on what can only be described as a quest for contamination. He finds it in a hurry, in the impure touch of a leper (1:40–45). Having discovered the dirt, he lays hands on forbidden, broken skin. Miraculously, instead of becoming impure himself, he heals the skin and makes the leper whole.

Sinners are next. Having engaged one directly, Jesus proclaims that he holds the power of future forgiveness (2:1–12). The protectors of the present condemn this brazenness as blasphemy. He has appropriated to himself a power of cleansing reserved only to God, and, not insignificantly, administered by the Temple infrastructure over which they wielded control. Jesus is not only moving into impure realms where he ought not to be, he is claiming God's power to transform them. And when Mark presents Jesus as the Son of God whom his readers should follow, he is saying something extraordinary. "[I]n contrast to the view that people are to attain holiness by separation from the threatening force of impurity, Mark presents the view that people are to overcome uncleanness by spreading wholeness."[9]

Pressing the point, Jesus moves immediately into a table fellowship with the most impure folk he can find, tax collectors and sinners (2:13–17). He even calls one of them to follow him! When challenged by the purveyors of purity, he replies that those who represent God's future must bring their healing power not to those who are whole, but to those who are broken. Two broken Sabbath laws later, he proclaims himself to be God's future kingdom representative (2:23–3:6). As such, he has the power to interpret God's present commands, even those as sacrosanct as the Sabbath. He interprets that human wholeness is more important than cultic observance and ritual rightness.

The response is predictable. If the future looks as Jesus says it looks, if the boundaries that protect the present are in as much jeopardy from Jesus' kind of future as he proclaims that they are, the protectors of the present must find a way to preclude that future from coming. They must find a way to stop the man who wants to initiate it. They must do what they can, ally themselves with whomever they must, to destroy him (3:6).

An Invitation to Gentiles

Still, Jesus does not stop. According to Mark, it is not enough for the man who represents God on the ground to challenge Israel's internal boundaries; he also goes after the external boundaries that separate the holy people of God from the most unholy compilation of communities there is, the Gentiles. In chapter 5, Jesus enters the unclean territory of the Gerasenes. There, he engages a man whose possession by a legion of unclean spirits has exiled him to the compounded unholiness of a life in the tombs (5:1–20). How does Jesus "cleanse" him? He sends the unclean spirits into the almost laughably unclean pigs. In the transfigurative world of Jesus' mythological mathematics, uncleanness plus more uncleanness equals wholeness.

If a reader missed the point here, it is highly unlikely he or she would miss it for long. At 7:24–8:10, Mark cycles together a virtual Jesus Gentile mission. And it is centered on imagery of the table. An inclusive table.

Mark 7:1–23 sets our place. Here, once again, Jesus appears to be at odds with the holiness and purity codes that structured Israelite life. This time he is challenging the food laws. The first-century, Palestinian table symbolized much more than a meal; it was a representation of community. Jesus' challenges led Mark to the conclusion that the Son of God believed all foods to be clean (7:19). This is a crucial point that could not have been lost on his readers. Such a ruling would mean that all Gentiles and all the food they consumed had a place at the table of God's kingdom people. They too could become a part of God's "holy" community.

Mark narrates the point by immediately sending Jesus into Gentile territory and into the path of a Syrophoenecian woman (7:24–30). Her encounter with the Son of man demonstrates that the bread of life Jesus brings from the table of the future is available to Gentiles in the present. Jesus follows up by offering that "bread," symbolized in the story by healing, to Gentiles in the coagulation of Greek cities known as the Decapolis (7:31–37).

For the obtuse, Mark hammers home the point by concluding this Gentile mission section with the repeat story of another meal miracle, the feeding of the thousands (8:1–10; compare 6:35–44). This time loaves are multiplied for four thousand Gentiles; it is they who eat, with the table language of the Last Supper rippling through the story, until they are satisfied. The future, turning back on the present, has altered the entire narrative of life in the kingdom community. Jesus has offered the bread on God's table to people of all the nations.

"Cleansing" a Fruitless Temple

Jesus underscores Mark's point in chapter 11 when he moves on the very bastion of Israelite holiness and purity, the Jerusalem Temple (11:12–25). On his way to it, Mark explains that Jesus is hungry. Having seen leaves on a fig tree nearby, even though it is not the season for figs, he goes to it in search of fruit. The language here is symbolic: the fig tree was often used by the prophets as a representation of Israel.[10] From both, God expected fruit. In both, God is disappointed. Mark envisions the response. In chapter 11, Jesus curses the fig tree to its death. Just after his Temple action, when he and his disciples are leaving the scene, Peter recognizes the tree and declares that it has withered, right down to its roots. Because Mark has surrounded the story of the Temple action with the cursing of the fruitless Tree, Mark's readers cannot help but get the point that the fruitless Temple will suffer the same God-directed fate.[11]

But exactly how is the Temple fruitless? I would submit that it failed to become—no, it *refused* to become—what the prophets thought God had always intended it to be, a house of prayer for *all* the nations. The Temple *appears* to be bearing the fruit of God's future kingdom; the leafy traditions, cultus, and codes of holiness are all in their proper worship places. And yet the hunger that Isaiah prophesied (Isa. 56:7), a divine craving for a place of prayer and worship where all were welcome, remained unsatisfied.[12]

I climax my case by pointing to the Temple "cleansing" story (11:15–18) that Mark has been cultivating since that first "cleansing" in the Capernaum synagogue. It begins with the language that characterizes most of Jesus' "cleansing" exorcisms, the language of casting out. Jesus casts out the sellers and buyers in the Temple in the same way that he expelled unclean spirits from possessed, tortured souls. This is the apocalyptic language of God's kingdom force breaking through the boundaries of human history, shattering the dominant power of Satan that has occupied it and unleashing a healing, future-directed kingdom transformation (esp. 3:20–27). In other words, in Mark's scenario "The temple is possessed and Jesus is performing an exorcism."[13]

Jesus explains his "exorcism" with the clarifying prophetic word that is Mark 11:17:

> "Is it not written,
>   'My house shall be called a house of prayer for all the nations'?
>   But you have made it a den of robbers."

It is from this interpretative teaching that we finally get a sense of the problem Mark has been narratively condemning throughout his Jesus story up to this point.

For Mark the future should exist in the present; the Temple should be a house of prayer for all the nations. That's why he begins with the prophecy from Isaiah 56:7, "[T]he climax to an oracle that is perhaps the fullest Old Testament vision of an inclusive Israel."[14] The historical context is the crisis that surrounds the so-called Trito- or Third Isaiah (chaps. 56–66). It is the postexilic return of the people from Babylon. Conflicts erupted between those coming home and those who had never left. The matter was one of identity: "[T]he inescapable theological question was: who are the people of God?"[15] Isaiah's inescapable answer was that it could be anyone, even the foreigner.[16] God's house was everyone's house. And, as was the case in Mark 3:31–35 and 7:1–23, God's acceptance is based on the doing of God's will, not on the ritualistic acceptance of cultic codes of holiness and purity. "The verse [Isaiah 56:7] is part of a promise to the 'eunuch' and to the 'foreigner' who have kept justice, done righteousness (v.1) and kept the Sabbath (v.2), that they will have a share in the promises soon to be fulfilled for God's people. They too will have a place on God's 'holy mountain' (v.7); their sacrifices too will be accepted (v.7)."[17]

So says God in Isaiah; so says Jesus in Mark. God's house has become anyone's and everyone's house of worship and prayer. When the leaders, the priests and the scribes, refuse to allow this to happen, they refuse to let the Temple bear the fruit it has always been intended to bear. Jesus' "casting out" in the Temple, then, was as potent a symbolic strike against the Temple as his exorcisms were against the kingdom of Satan. "The Jewish leaders know that God resides on earth in the Temple, and they protect God from what is unclean. Jesus condemns the Temple as holy space because the leaders use it to set boundaries and prohibit Gentile nations from worshiping there (11:17)."[18]

This point is clearly made in the second half of Jesus' teaching statement. The Temple that should be a house of prayer for all the nations has become a cave of bandits. On the surface the language suggests a problem of commercialism.[19] Many have argued that it was simply the act of buying and selling on the holy grounds of the Temple itself that bothered Jesus. Others have suggested that this could not be the case since the exchange of money and the buying and selling were necessary components of the sacrificial system that had been established by Torah. The proper slaughter of animals without blemish or payment of the half-shekel Temple tax could not have occurred unless pilgrims acquired such animals after their long and sometimes arduous journeys to Jerusalem, or could exchange foreign currency into the kind accepted by the Temple.[20] The problem, then, must have been exploitation. The Temple exchange system had become an unjust one that accrued profits for the priestly leaders at the expense of the pilgrim poor.[21]

Still others, however, following I. Abrahams, have pointed out that there is little evidence of widespread abuse in the Temple system.[22] Abrahams argues that only selective periods of abuse occurred during the last decades of the Temple's existence.[23] He has a point. Neither of the suggested concerns appears to be Jesus' worry in the Markan narrative. He is not principally focused on exploitation; he drives out the buyers as well as the sellers. And, apparently recognizing the necessary nature of the exchange and selling process, he enters the Temple on the day after the "cleansing" without any effort to continue his challenge to its system of commerce.

There are, therefore, those who make the case that while Jesus recognized the necessity of the commercial activity, he was dismayed that it had so overwhelmed the Court of the Gentiles, where it took place.[24] Angry that the one place where Gentiles could find a place at the Temple was no longer a place of prayer, he overturned the tables, drove out the sellers and buyers, and prevented any movement of vessels through the Temple in a show of solidarity with them. The problem with this view is that if Jesus recognized the necessity of the commercial enterprises to the sacrificial system, he must also have realized that the activity had to take place somewhere, and wherever that happened worship would be disrupted. Thus, while I do not believe that this concern represents Jesus' concern in Mark's Gospel, I do think its interest in the Gentiles points us in the right direction.

The answer to Jesus' concern in Mark's Gospel lies in the language itself: *cave of bandits*. The Old Testament reference this time is Jeremiah. His temple sermon in chapter 7 (esp. 7:11) is "one of the bitterest attacks upon the temple state in the Hebrew Bible."[25] The prophet rails against his people because they use their religious observances to cover up their sinful behavior; they've come to believe that in spite of their conduct God will overlook their evil if their subsequent observances and sacrifices look appropriate.[26] The prophet's concern is also Mark's. Ritual righteousness is on grand display at his first-century Temple. Pilgrims are in town; buying, selling, and money exchanging are at a high. The business of the faith is good.

But it is the business of bandits. Mark is particular here about his vocabulary. For bandit, he does not use the word *kleptes*, from which we derive the modern terminology "kleptomaniac." *Kleptes,* then as now, refers to a dishonest person who absconds, usually in secret, with someone else's property. Instead, Mark uses the word *lestes,* the same word he uses at 14:48 and 15:27, the same word that Josephus uses some forty-two times and New Testament writers use some fifteen times to refer to armed bands of marauders and insurrectionists, who generally traveled in gangs and secured their objectives through violence.[27] Caves were their hiding places of choice.

It is particularly interesting that the term eventually attached itself to the many revolutionary groups whose opposition to the Roman occupiers of Palestine and their Herodian overseers eventually led to the Jewish-Roman War of 66–70 C.E. Eventually called Zealots by Josephus, they used every means at their disposal to combat what they considered to be the profane presence of Gentiles in their holy land. They meant particularly to use the Temple. Intended to be a house of international prayer, by 70 C.E. it had become a nationalistic front for armed revolution.[28]

Apocalyptic imagery fueled the fire of their resistance. According to the various bandit leaders, God's Davidic kingdom was on the verge of exploding once again onto the scene of human history. God was ready to initiate the process; the people had only to act in concert with the prophetically published plan. Join the revolution. Help usher in God's kingdom. The time, 66 C.E., is now! The launchpad is the Temple. The target is the complete repudiation of Gentile presence on Jewish soil. The Temple had become, in other words, a staging ground for the purification of the people from Gentile presence and the subsequent inauguration of God's holy, and necessarily *monocultural,* reign.

According to Mark, though, these very actions supposedly on *behalf* of the temple were actually the deeds of *bandits* who had made the Temple a *cave* of militant operations. Their very attempt to purify the people by laying claim to the Temple instead becomes the "desolating sacrilege" that Jesus denounces at Mark 13:14.[29] "Mark tells his community . . .

that the revolutionary purge is actually a defilement, [and] that it will precipitate divine judgment."[30]

Since the Temple has become an institutional symbol of nationalist exclusivism, it must be destroyed before the inclusive kingdom vision that Jesus preaches in Mark can take root and bear fruit. Ironically, impurity occurs as the result of a zealous preoccupation with purity; wholeness could only have come if the Temple had been what it was always meant to be, a place where all peoples from all nations joined together in worship. In Mark's revelation of the future in the midst of the present, then, kingdom worship is multicultural worship. And the Temple, because it has become a symbol opposed to that worship, must be destroyed; another temple, not made with hands, will take its place (14:58; 15:29). And that temple will gather its elect from everywhere (13:27).

Multicultural Discipleship

The creation of such a temple, and the multicultural worship housed in it, is not, however, only Jesus' work, according to Mark. It is also the work of the Jesus disciple. Mark makes the case by pointing to the strange words Jesus uses in response to Peter's recognition that the cursed fig tree has withered and died. Jesus appears to go off subject; instead of responding about the fig tree, he talks to Peter about faith and the casting of *this* mountain into the sea. I would submit that Mark wants his readers to know first of all that a believing disciple can do the transformative things that Jesus does. Already, at 3:15 and 6:13, Mark records that Jesus teaches his disciples to exorcise as successfully as he himself does. But do they also have the power to transform fruitless institutions like the Temple? Apparently they do. According to Mark's Jesus, a faithful disciple will be able to say to *this* mountain, "Be taken up and thrown into the sea," and it will happen. *This* mountain will be destroyed.

The only mountain within the story's frame of reference is the one on which the holy city and its Temple are fixed. It therefore has to be the mountain to which Jesus refers. Just as Jesus has the power to curse the unfruitful fig tree, so do his faithful disciples have the power to curse *this* mountain. In both cases, the imagery points directly at the Temple.[31]

Jesus does not, however, stop with the promise of the power to curse what is unfruitful; he also promises that faith will enable the believer to do anything. In this context, to what else could that anything refer than the realization of what Isaiah had long ago prophesied? To this same faithful disciple, *whatever* you ask, even something outrageous, even something as outrageous as a house of prayer for all the nations, *in a place and time where many are warring against exactly that vision,* will occur.

But that prayer is as hard now, in the twenty-first century, as it was then in the first. There is a correspondence between Mark's *holy* cave of banditry and our contemporary centers of monochromatic, monocultural worship. Lamar Williamson is right to point out that this text is easy fodder for anti-Jewish thought, where the fruitless Temple of the first century is equated with current Judaism.[32] Such a worthless equation can only be achieved when one improperly removes the story from its context; Mark's Jesus is making an internal challenge to fellow believers. He is not condemning Judaism as a faith, but appealing for a renewal of the Jewish prophetic hope envisioned by Isaiah, where worship's end-time reality would occur in the present time and a cave of banditry would yield way to a house of prayer for *all* the nations.

It is that internal challenge of Mark's day that corresponds to the situation of our own day, where the oft-quoted observation of the civil rights era remains as true now as it was when it was first proclaimed: eleven o'clock on Sunday morning is the most segregated hour in American life. Williamson is right to point out that Mark's apocalypse of worship speaks most provocatively against this spiritual barrenness of the so-called new temple of Christendom. "It is not hard to see how denominational headquarters, middle-judicatory offices, and local church staff resemble the chief priests and scribes of Jesus' day; nor is it hard to see how our busy, prosperous churches are like leafy, fruitless fig trees."[33]

Like the leaders of Mark's Jerusalem Temple, we have mastered the techniques of a busy religion with all the appearances of success and growth. Worth billions in assets, numbering millions in congregants, contemporary Christian communities appear to be delivering on the Markan hope that the gospel would be preached to all the nations (13:10). And yet our worship remains the kind of worship Mark's Jesus so disdained, a worship of the set-apart, where our Christian community is people just like us. A homogeneity principle rules our contemporary communities as fiercely as Mark believed the purity and holiness codes ruled the lives of cultic, first-century Israel. To be sure, church growth and thus church success are enhanced when churches reach out to folk who come from the same ethnic, racial, and political backgrounds. Visitors are more comfortable and likely to join when they are with others of their kind. Programs are easier to develop when that similarity of orientation encourages a similarity in theological and political perspective. There are, to put it simply, in the present, as there were in the past, practical reasons why a pre-occupation with monocultural worship is desirable. Survival itself—as survival depends on evangelism, and evangelism appears more successful when the homogeneity principle is practiced—depends on it. Just as the survival of the entire people appeared to depend on strict adherence to the holiness and purity codes of the first century. And yet Mark's Jesus stood against those very codes and condemned the Temple because it stood as their fruitless embodiment. If Jesus could combat them then, there is no doubt that we who follow him should combat the principles they represent today. Jesus called for the apocalypse of worship, the realization of its end-time, multicultural reality. In the first century it meant a Temple where Jews and Gentiles could worship as one; in the twenty-first century it surely must mean churches desegregated along lines of race, ethnicity, and culture, and integrated toward the vision of inclusive communities of faith. In such communities, when the bread of the Lord's Table is broken, it will be divided among a culturally heterogeneous fellowship of believers.

The hope lies in what the destruction of the fruitless institutions of homogeneity will bring—not death, but new life, a transformed life whose future is so unlike the present that the present must die before it will yield. Mark's Jesus calls for a discipleship community willing to bring that present to its end. He calls for a community willing to envision the apocalypse of worship, and then work to make that future their present reality. He calls for a community willing to create a world where the principle of homogeneity gives way to a house of prayer for all the nations.

NOTES

1. Cf. Daniel, Apocalypse of Weeks, Animal Apocalypse, 4 Ezra, 2 Baruch.
2. Howard Clark Kee, "The Social Setting of Mark: An Apocalyptic Community," in *SBL Seminar Papers* (1984), 251.
3. Kee, "The Social Setting of Mark," 251. "For both groups, the essential requirement for participation in the eschatological fulfillment is the maintenance of purity."
4. David Rhoads, "Social Criticism: Crossing Boundaries," in *Mark and Method: New Approaches in Biblical Studies,* ed. Janice Capel Anderson and Stephen D. Moore (Minneapolis: Fortress Press, 1992), 151.
5. Jerome Neyrey, "The Idea of Purity in Mark's Gospel," *Semeia* 35 (1986): 99–100.
6. Rhoads, "Social Criticism," 148.
7. Neyrey, "Purity," 94.
8. Cf. Josephus, *Jewish War* 6.5.3, #300–309. Josephus speaks of a certain Jesus ben Ananias who preached against the Temple, was turned over to Albinus, scourged, and

let go. However, because he continued his preaching he was deemed worthy to be put to death. J. R. Donahue comments, "The important thing about the story of Jesus is that it indicates that in Jerusalem there was prophetic activity against the temple, and that this activity was summarily suspect in the eyes of Jewish officials" ("Are You the Christ?" in *Are You the Christ? The Trial Narrative in the Gospel of Mark* [Missoula, Mont.: Society of Biblical Literature, 1973], 219).

9. Rhoads, "Social Criticism," 154.

10. Deborah Krause, "Narrated Prophecy in Mark 11:12–21: The Divine Authorization of Judgment," in *The Gospels and the Scriptures of Israel,* ed. Craig A. Evans and Richard Stegner (Sheffield: Sheffield Academic Press, 1994), 235–48.

11. Craig A. Evans, "Jesus' Action in the Temple: Cleansing or Portent of Destruction?" *Catholic Biblical Quarterly* 51 (1989): 239; Mary Ann Tolbert, *Sowing the Gospel: Mark's World in Literary-Historical Perspective* (Minneapolis: Fortress Press, 1989), 193; Krause, "Narrated Prophecy." It is a point given further weight by the language of destruction that attaches to the Temple, ostensibly at Jesus' direction, at 13:1, 2; 14:58; 15:29.

12. Tolbert, *Sowing the Gospel,* 193. "To Jesus' hunger the fig tree offers nothing except leaves (11:12–13), just as for the spiritual hunger of the nations the temple offers not a 'house of prayer' but a 'den of robbers' (11:17)."

13. Douglas Cunningham, "God's Order Versus the Jewish/Roman Social Order: An Exegesis of Mark 11:15–19," *Tugōn* 8, no. 3 (1988): 318.

14. Ched Myers, *Binding the Strong Man: A Political Reading of Mark's Story of Jesus* (Maryknoll, N.Y.: Orbis Books, 1988), 302.

15. Paula Fontana Qualls, "Mark 11:15–18: A Prophetic Challenge," *Review and Expositor* 93 (1996): 398.

16. P. M. Casey, "Culture and Historicity: The Cleansing of the Temple," *Catholic Biblical Quarterly* 59 (1997): 311–12.

17. Donald Juel, *Messiah and Temple: The Trial of Jesus in the Gospel of Mark* (Missoula, Mont.: Scholars Press, 1977), 131–32.

18. Rhoads, "Social Criticism," 155.

19. Hans Dieter Betz, "Jesus and the Purity of the Temple (Mark 11:15–18): A Comparative Religion Approach," *Journal of Biblical Literature* 116 (1997): 455–72. Betz actually refers to a kind of commercialism which he dubs "monumentalism," whereby the Temple is adorned with the same kinds of lavish accoutrements as the Greek and Roman temples. It was a profaning process that made it impossible for the pious peasants and other "little people" to worship in the way that the law demanded.

20. E. P. Sanders, *Jesus and Judaism* (Philadelphia: Fortress Press, 1985), 63–66.

21. Myers, *Binding the Strong Man,* 299–300.

22. I. Abrahams, *Studies in Pharisaism and the Gospels* (New York: KTAV Publishing House, 1917); David Seeley, "Jesus' Temple Act," *Catholic Biblical Quarterly* 55 (1993): 263–83; David Catchpole, "The 'Triumphal' Entry," in *Jesus and the Politics of His Day,* ed. Ernst Bammel and C. F. D. Moule (Cambridge: Cambridge University Press, 1984), 333.

23. Evans, "Jesus' Action in the Temple," 256–57.

24. D. E. Nineham, *Saint Mark* (1963; New York: Penguin Books, 1979), 302.

25. Myers, *Binding the Strong Man,* 303.

26. Lamar Williamson, Jr., *Mark* (Atlanta: John Knox Press, 1983), 207.

27. Brian K. Blount, "The Social World of Bandits," in *The Good Samaritan (Luke 10:25–37): An American Bible Society Interactive CD-ROM for Windows* (New York: American Bible Society, 1996).
28. Joel Marcus, "The Jewish War and the Sitz Im Leben of Mark," *Journal of Biblical Literature* 111 (1992): 441–62.
29. Ibid., 447–56; Donahue, "Are You the Christ?" 217–22; George Wesley Buchanan, "Symbolic Money Changers in the Temple?" *New Testament Studies* 37 (1991): 288–89.
30. Marcus, "The Jewish War," 455–56.
31. Robert H. Gundry, *Mark: A Commentary on His Apology for the Cross* (Grand Rapids: William B. Eerdmans, 1993), 648; John Paul Heil, "The Narrative Strategy and Pragmatics of the Temple Theme in Mark," *Catholic Biblical Quarterly* 59 (1997): 79; Myers, *Binding the Strong Man*, 305.
32. Williamson, *Mark*, 208.
33. Ibid., 210.

Chapter 3

Traditions in Conversation and Collision

Reflections on Multiculturalism in the Acts of the Apostles

BEVERLY ROBERTS GAVENTA

Were the evangelist Luke to wander into a contemporary discussion of multiculturalism in the church, he would surely be amused to hear Christians talk as if multiculturalism were a development of the late twentieth century.[1] He might even wonder whether his second volume had survived.

Even the most casual stroll through the book of Acts would explain Luke's wonderment at the shortsightedness of contemporary talk about multiculturalism. The place names as early as the second chapter signal the adventure that lies ahead: Judea, Asia, Egypt, Cappadocia, Parthia, Libya, Crete, Arabia. Those are not way stations on Paul's missionary journeys, but simply the homes of the Jews gathered in Jerusalem for Pentecost. Still to come are Paul's travels to Antioch, Corinth, Ephesus, Philippi, Malta, and, of course, Rome. This diversity is not simply a matter of travel, however. Among the characters who enliven Luke's story is Barnabas, a Jew whose home is the island of Cyprus, but who apparently lives in Jerusalem and preaches around the Mediterranean. Then there is the eunuch from Ethiopia who ventures up to Jerusalem to worship and who reads Greek. Apollos, a Jew from Alexandria, appears in Ephesus teaching and then moves on to Corinth. And, of course, Luke tells the story of Paul, a native of Tarsus in Cilicia, a citizen of Rome, and educated in Jerusalem.[2] In short, Luke's world abounds with places, languages, and traditions.

These multiplicities must have created conflicts about the proper ways of worship, yet Luke gives us little indication of those conflicts. In fact, Luke has little to say about worship. He does portray the Jerusalem community continuing in temple practice. And his important summary characterizations of that community refer to prayer, to shared meals, baptism, and the laying on of hands. None of these practices does Luke introduce or explain, presumably because he assumes that his audience knows what they are. And he says nothing about how differences of practice might have been negotiated.

When interpreters concerned about contemporary challenges of multiculturalism go to the Acts of the Apostles, then, the question most often becomes one of Jews and Gentiles in community together. We ask the same question the first generations of disciples asked: "What must Gentiles do to be accepted into the church?" or "On what terms did Jewish Christians receive Gentiles into their midst?"[3] And the texts that serve to focus our interest are most often the conversion of Cornelius (Acts 10:1–11:18) or the Jerusalem Council (Acts 15:1–35). What is at stake here is what the *Gentile outsiders* must do. Although that is a question of much theological importance, there is a sense in which it sheds little light on our own cultural clashes within the church.

But what happens if we frame the question differently? What happens if, instead of asking what Gentiles must do to be acceptable to the Jewish majority within the *ekklēsia*, we ask what that same *ekklēsia* must do in order to make the gospel intelligible to the outsider? On what terms does the *ekklēsia* engage peoples of other cultures?[4]

Three different stories in Acts, set in three strikingly different locations, provide compelling conversation partners for this reflection. The first, Paul's sermon on the Areopagus (Acts 17), shows us Paul engaged in proclamation to an audience deeply influenced by the popular philosophical schools of the day. The second, the riot of the craftsmen in Ephesus (Acts 19:23–41), depicts reaction to Christian preaching in a city that is entrenched in the service of its central deity. The third, the sojourn of Paul and his companions on the island of Malta (Acts 28:1–10), places Paul in the middle of a barbarian population, where neither he nor the locals meet with the reception they expect.

The hermeneutical moves I make here differ from those sometimes made when the church turns to Acts for instruction. Because Luke writes about the church and in the form of history, Christians often read Acts to identify historical traditions and then project those traditions into the present as binding on the church. Acts then becomes something like blueprints for the church's life, an incipient book of order or of canon law. Luke writes a narrative, however, and like most narratives, it creates a world that we as readers may enter, comparing our world with his, noting differences, comparing our own situations and responses with those of the characters, at once engaging and distancing ourselves. Reading Luke as a narrative of the astonishing persistence of the Word of God and of the equally astonishing resistance to it, we look less for church rules than for ways in which Luke's story alternately challenges the way in which we think, comforts us in our griefs, encourages us in our despair, and sustains us in our labors.[5]

Philosophical Seekers in Athens (Acts 17:16–34)

Paul's sermon on the Areopagus is the *locus classicus* for discussion about the proclamation of the gospel in a non-Jewish world. The setting, however, is not that of a generic Gentile audience (as if such a thing were possible), but a debate with Stoic and Epicurean philosophers, two of the most prominent philosophical schools of the first century. And the setting is Athens, the cultural jewel of the ancient world, even if the jewel has faded somewhat by the middle of the first century.

The sermon comprises three sections. In the brief introduction, Paul acknowledges that the Athenians are very religious people, as is evident in the great number of idols (vv. 22–23a).[6] The second and lengthiest section of the sermon consists of a critique of idol worship, a critique that is carefully and diplomatically worded (vv. 23b–29). The final section declares the need for repentance from such idol worship and indicates that there will be a time of judgment and that God has established the certainty of that judgment by raising "a man" from the dead (vv. 30–32).

To those who have been reading Luke's story from the beginning of Acts (or from Luke 1), this sermon initially looks odd indeed. Unlike the early sermons of Peter, Stephen's defense speech, or Paul's initial sermon in Acts 13, the Areopagus speech makes no reference to the history of Israel (cf., e.g., 2:29; 7:2–47; 13:17–25) and quotes not a solitary word of scripture (cf., e.g., 2:17–21, 25–28; 3:22–23; 4:11; 13:33). Even the one reference to Jesus here is indirect, and nothing is said of Jesus' death by crucifixion (cf. 2:32; 3:15; 4:10; 13:30, 37). Athens, it seems, knows little and cares less about the traditions of Jerusalem.

As Paul Schubert demonstrated, however, this initial impression may be deceptive.[7] Although the Areopagus speech *omits* a number of elements that have been prominent in earlier speeches, its affirmations are entirely consistent with the remainder of Luke-Acts. That God is creator (17:24) is not only a presupposition of Luke's thought but pivotal to the prayer in 4:24–30 (see also 14:15). The claim that God does not live in "houses made with human hands" has been made already by Stephen (7:48). God's control over seasons echoes the words of the risen Jesus in 1:7. And the need for repentance figures prominently in earlier sermons (e.g., 2:38–40; 3:19; 11:18).

Yet what we less often acknowledge is that virtually nothing in this speech would come as news to the audience. Instead, the sermon begins quite literally where the audience *is*: in Athens there *are* all these shrines to gods and goddesses. That much makes sense, but we could put that point more sharply still: not only the beginning but *most* of the sermon consists of things with which the audience of sophisticated unbelievers itself would almost certainly have agreed. They also taught that God does not need anything from human beings and that God does not live in buildings made by humans. They also enjoyed the apt citation from earlier generations of poets and philosophers.[8]

What Paul's sermon does, then, is to take basic presuppositions of Christian teaching and recast them in language available to the audience. In this instance the gospel is genuinely translated, even if some crucial elements never appear. Like all translations, much has been lost. Recognizing that God "is not far from each one of us" is remote comfort when compared with the psalmist's song:

> The LORD is near to all who call on him,
>   to all who call on him in truth.
> (Ps. 145:18)

And the sermon's vague reference to "a man whom he has appointed" seems a bland substitute for stories of Jesus healing the sick. So successfully does the sermon speak in the voice of the philosophers that it makes some readers anxious, concerned that Paul may have been cheated by the exchange rate in the marketplace of Athens.

In this one important venue, then, Luke shows us Christian preaching that is not the least bit hesitant to translate the story of Jerusalem into the propositions of Athens. Much earlier, the believers gathered in Jerusalem and prayed for boldness of speech (4:29), and boldness becomes for Luke a characteristic of apostolic labor (e.g., Acts 9:27–28; 13:46; 14:3; 18:26; 19:8; 28:32).[9] In the story of Paul's sermon in Athens we see that the boldness of faithful proclamation of the gospel may require radical translations that invite the outsider in even as they seem a "clanging cymbal" to those already inside.

The Defenders of Artemis
in Ephesus (Acts 19:23–41)

Most discussions of Luke and interreligious dialogue begin and end with Paul's sermon on the Areopagus. Far less familiar, although perhaps far more disturbing, is the scene in which Ephesian craftsmen riot in reaction to Christian preaching. Here Luke shows us that there are "languages" into which the gospel will not translate.

As elsewhere in Luke's story of Paul's mission, Paul's initial activity in Ephesus takes place in the synagogue (as is the case also with Priscilla, Aquila, and Apollos; see 18:24–28).[10] Eventually, however, a sharp dispute prompts Paul to leave the synagogue "taking the disciples with him" and to speak "daily in the lecture hall of Tyrannus" (19:9). The narrator explains that this activity "continued for two years, so that all the residents of Asia, both Jews and Greeks, heard the word of the Lord" (19:10). The power of the gospel Paul preaches is confirmed in Ephesus not only by miraculous healings but also by the dramatic defeat of exorcists who attempt to capitalize on the power of Jesus' name. Again the narrator reports that these events became known to "all residents of Ephesus, both Jews and Greeks," with the result that "everyone was awestruck" (v. 17).

For one particular Ephesian by the name of Demetrius, preaching of the good news was bad news. Luke introduces Demetrius as "a silversmith who made silver shrines of Artemis, [who] brought no little business to the artisans" (v. 24).[11] When Demetrius speaks to the artisans, he reports again what the narrator has already indicated, namely, that Paul has been persuasive not only to Ephesians but throughout the province of Asia. Demetrius characterizes Paul's teaching as "that gods made with hands are not gods" (v. 26). In Paul's sermon on the Areopagus, this same statement has generated no opposition (17:24). The philosophers would have agreed with it. Unlike the Athenians, however, the artisans in Ephesus earned their living by virtue of devotion to Artemis.

Many stories in Acts depict the peril of false attachment to possessions (e.g., 1:18; 5:1–11; 8:14–24; 16:16–24), and it is tempting to interpret Demetrius's outcry merely as a crass attempt to manipulate others in order to protect his own income. We need not read so cynically. Abundant historical evidence suggests that the city of Ephesus was deeply intertwined with the cult of Artemis. Worshiped in Ephesus as early as the eleventh century B.C.E., Artemis served as a protector of the young, of those who sought sanctuary in her temple, and of the city itself. Her temple was a cultural symbol that ranked as one of the wonders of the ancient world; it served also as the financial and banking center of Asia. For obvious reasons, then, the citizens of Ephesus took great pride in the care and administration of the cult of Artemis.[12] A comment by Pausanias may sum up her standing beyond Ephesus: "All cities worship Artemis of Ephesus, and individuals hold her in honor above all the gods."[13]

From the vantage point of the late twentieth century, it is easy to underestimate the importance of devotion to gods and goddesses. Particularly because citizens of a place such as Ephesus would have offered service to more than one deity, we tend to think that any single god is relatively unimportant for them (an ironic reversal of the error of those ancients who regarded Judaism, and later Christianity, as atheistic because those faiths served only one god). Yet this story reminds us that respecting a number of gods can coincide with extreme devotion to one of them. In keeping with the religious sensibilities of the age, the Ephesians recognized other deities, but to threaten the premier standing of Artemis in their city would meet with sharp resistance.[14]

The long-standing and thoroughgoing marriage between the goddess Artemis and the city of Ephesus makes the riot that follows entirely understandable. Demetrius is right. He speaks as a responsible citizen when he insists that this rival to Artemis threatens not only the income of the craftsmen, but the status of Artemis and the piety and well-being of her city. Hearing Demetrius, the populace at first grows wild, so that some Christians are seized and others hustle Paul away from the scene. Later the crowd settles into unified homage: "Great is Artemis of the Ephesians!" The cry is probably not a shout, as in a cheer at an athletic event, but a hymnic cry intended to invoke the power of the goddess herself.[15]

The town clerk manages to restore order (vv. 35–41). Commentators often dwell on his implied defense of Paul and company: they are not temple robbers, they are not blasphemers. Such a public riot will bring on the Roman authorities, who do not look kindly on spontaneous demonstrations—suggesting that it is not Christians but their opponents who threaten public order. Yet the town clerk's opening line also deserves notice: "Citizens of Ephesus, who is there that does not know that the city of the Ephesians is the temple keeper of the great Artemis and of the statue that fell from heaven? Since these things cannot be denied, you ought to be quiet and do nothing rash" (19:35–36).

Luke gives us very little detail regarding the response of Christians to this uproar. We learn that Paul was prevented from going into the crowd by some "disciples" and some local officials (vv. 30–31), but nothing of what he wanted to say or do there. Some Ephesian Jews push forward an otherwise unknown Alexander,[16] but he does not manage to speak and no clue indicates what he would have said. Immediately after the riot stops, Paul leaves Ephesus for Macedonia (20:1). Such silence regarding the Christian response may simply be a function of realistic narration: the situation described would permit no opportunity to speak. Yet the silence extends to the narrator's own voice; nothing here reassures the reader that a Christian community managed to survive in Ephesus.

Arguments from silence are notoriously weak, yet this silence merits at least a pause, especially in light of the larger topic at hand. Neither Paul nor any other believer in Ephesus makes an effort to calm these troubled waters, to reassure Demetrius that his fears are unjustified, to assuage the deep anxieties of the crowd. There is, in short, no attempt to compromise with Artemis, and no Artemisian form of Christian theology issues forth from this story.

A brief excursion into fantasy will sharpen the point here. If we transplant this story to any contemporary North American city where Christian proclamation has, for some reason, compromised the local economy, we may imagine how the evangelists would respond. They would almost certainly attempt to create an economic and social alternative to the latter-day Artemis. Something like the following response almost writes itself:

> "Folks, there is no need to panic. We have no intention of disrupting your industry. Give up manufacturing these miniature temples of Artemis, and we will grant you an exclusive license to make and sell Jesus-trinkets instead. Imagine a full line of miniature mangers, crosses, mustard-seed jewelry. Our Jesus group will triumph finally, and you will lose everything unless you retool your industry. What we are offering is your salvation!"

If Paul's sermon on the Areopagus shows that the gospel can speak in the language of a non-Jewish environment while still speaking a word consistent with its own tradition, the clash at Ephesus shows that the gospel does not speak simply whatever the world wishes to hear. Although toleration in religious practice was the norm in the Greco-Roman world, Christianity here stands as something subversive, not only to a particular group of people but to their goddess and even to their city itself.[17]

The Barbarians of Malta (Acts 28:1–10)

The third text presents the gospel neither translating nor colliding; instead, we find an elusive exchange between Paul and the residents of Malta. The story of Paul and the inhabitants of the island of Malta plays a negligible role in most studies of Lukan theology. Following the high drama of the storm and shipwreck, this tiny episode is anticlimactic, and compared with the world-famous cities of Athens and Ephesus, the island of Malta is distinctly third-rate. One telling indication of the obscurity of this story is that much scholarly investigation of the Malta episode continues to ask on exactly which island the shipwrecked Paul arrives.

Two distinct vignettes constitute the story. First, in a doubly ironic scene, the inhabitants of the island wrongly conclude that Paul is a murderer when a viper threatens his life, and then they wrongly conclude that Paul is a god when the viper does not kill him (vv. 1–6). Second, the leading figure of the island, Publius, hosts the company. Paul then heals Publius's father and others who are ill. The whole episode concludes with the islanders providing generously for the ship as it readies for departure (vv. 7–10).

Odd as the story may seem to contemporary readers, it teems with what Luke's readers would have recognized as utterly predictable elements, as predictable as the car-chase scene in an action adventure movie or the final courtroom revelation in a murder mystery. The storm itself is a stock feature, for shipwrecks and other perils at sea appear frequently in Greco-Roman narratives. The generosity of strangers in such circumstances is another stereotypical element in the story.[18] Many of Luke's contemporaries would have regarded the attack of the viper as divine judgment, and stories of the fickle judgment of barbarians are also common.[19]

Why include such an account? Richard Pervo is surely right, at least in part, when he claims that one of Luke's aims is to entertain.[20] Beyond that, the story offers yet another indication of Paul's innocence. More than innocent, however, Paul now emerges from his long imprisonment and journey as the person in charge of events. The healings confirm not just his innocence but his ability to call on God's power for healing.[21] With this restoration in place, he can go on to Rome where he will preach and teach boldly.

For all its predictability, however, certain features of this story come as a surprise, and perhaps as a disturbance, to someone who has been reading Luke's account from the beginning. When the islanders interpret Paul as a god, we expect him to offer an emphatic correction just as he and Barnabas did in Lystra in a similar situation (14:8–18). Herod, who did not refuse the title of god, was struck down by God for his hubris (12:20–24). Yet Paul says nothing to correct the islanders.[22] Equally striking is the absence of any reference here to preaching or teaching. To be sure, the healings reflect Paul's access to some power, but the ancient world knew of many healers, so the connection with healing in Jesus' name remains implicit rather than explicit. To put the matter sharply, especially if read in isolation from the larger Lukan narrative, this story displays no connection with the gospel of Jesus Christ.

One way of understanding the several unusual features of this story is to look again at the reciprocity manifested here. In Luke's world, as in many cultures, the bestowing of a gift or favor carries with it the expectation of a reciprocal gift or favor.[23] This scene displays a kind of double reciprocity. Publius hosts Paul and the others, and in return Paul heals Publius's father. Paul then heals all the inhabitants who are ill, and the inhabitants in turn supply not only "honors," but the provisions needed for continuing the voyage to Rome. That reciprocity creates a bond between the two parties, Paul and his companions on the one side, Publius and the islanders on the other. Luke is content to allow these gifts and the connection they forge to speak for themselves, hinting ever so slightly that this connection may have a future.[24]

Conclusions

When we ask of Acts the question, On what terms does the *ekklēsia* engage people of other cultures, the answer turns out to be complicated. If we are reading for some consistent rule that may be excised from Luke's narrative and applied in our own communities of faith, we will come away frustrated. Luke is telling a story, however, not formulating a set of laws, and we need to ask what his story might suggest for us. These three very different stories at least suggest that Luke understands that varying locations and populations require differing strategies. In Athens, where intellectual inquiry is expected and public address is a common mode of cultural exchange, Paul plays by the house rules. He offers a discourse that the Stoics and Epicureans would recognize, but it consists of themes that are necessary (if not sufficient) for Christian preaching. Athens is a marketplace for ideas, and Paul could enter that market. Malta is not. On Malta, with a population that does not speak Paul's language either literally or figuratively, the engagement takes place through the formulaic exchange of goods that was expected in such situations. Even if the "Name" is never uttered, what Paul gives on the island is healing or—as Luke interprets healing elsewhere—salvation (as in, for example, Luke 6:9; 7:50; 8:50; 18:42; Acts 4:12). In Ephesus, however, there is no "engagement." Demetrius and his team understand, and rightly so, that the gospel Paul teaches threatens their livelihood, their goddess, and their city. Ephesus constitutes a forthright reminder that the gospel is not a commodity to be marketed. This is not a consumer-driven religion. Instead, it is a very real danger, for it has the power to subvert those traditions we hold most dear.

How might these three narratives assist us in thinking about clashing cultures in worship today? Athens and Malta perhaps encourage us to understand that, just as the gospel is not proclaimed in the same way in every place, worship also will reflect changing communities and circumstances. The God who "does not live in shrines made by human hands" also does not live in the shrines we constitute from our own particular worship traditions. And the riot of Ephesus stands as a warning against baptizing every local custom and adopting every practice advocated in the marketplace. These are challenges, of course, not answers to our dilemma. Yet it is curious that however often God or God's agents direct the church's witness in Acts, there are also important instances in which the church must discern God's will. The God who calls us into community empowers us and trusts us not only to worship God rightly but to discern which worship practices are handcrafted shrines and which do rightly honor the living God.[25]

NOTES

1. The name "Luke" here refers to the implied author of Luke-Acts and does not presuppose the traditional identification of Luke as a physician who traveled with Paul. All biblical quotations in this essay are taken from the NRSV unless otherwise indicated.

2. A classic and accessible exploration of the multiple contexts of Acts remains Henry J. Cadbury's *The Book of Acts in History* (London: A. & C. Black, 1955).

3. The use of the term "Christian" here is admittedly anachronistic, since Luke only reports it as a term used by those outside the community (11:26; 26:28). I adopt it as a convenience that is preferable to repeated references to "Jews or Gentiles who believed Jesus to be the Messiah."

4. The plural "cultures" is essential. We have a tendency to flatten out the diversity in those cultures, speaking of "first-century Judaism" or "the Greco-Roman world" as if each were a single entity. A casual reading of any writing of Philo alongside a text from Qumran should render the perils of such generalizations obvious.

5. This is obviously the tip of a much longer hermeneutical discussion. For a more extended introduction to method in the discussion of Lukan theology, see my "Toward a Theology of Acts: Reading and Rereading," *Interpretation* 42 (1988): 146–57.

6. It is tempting, of course, to read v. 22 as an instance of sarcasm. Since speeches often begin with a *captatio benevolentiae,* a statement favorable to the audience and designed to secure their favorable attention, this introductory comment is probably to be taken at face value (see, for example, Acts 24:10; 26:2–3).

7. Paul Schubert, "The Place of the Areopagus Speech in the Composition of Acts," in *Transitions in Biblical Scholarship,* ed. J. Coert Rylaarsdam (Chicago: University of Chicago Press, 1968), 235–61.

8. See especially Bertil Gärtner, *The Areopagus Speech and Natural Revelation* (Uppsala, Sweden: C. W. K. Gleerup, 1955), 73–143; Hans Conzelmann, "The Address of

Paul on the Areopagus," in *Studies in Luke-Acts*, ed. Leander Keck and J. Louis Martyn (Nashville: Abingdon Press, 1966), 217–30; Jerome H. Neyrey, "Acts 17, Epicureans, and Theodicy," in *Greeks, Romans, and Christians: Essays in Honor of Abraham J. Malherbe*, ed. David L. Balch, Everett Ferguson, Wayne A. Meeks (Minneapolis: Fortress Press, 1990), 118–34.

9. On boldness in Luke-Acts, see Gaventa, "To Speak Thy Word with All Boldness: Acts 4:23–36," *Faith and Mission* 3 (1986): 76–82.

10. Paul's own letters, by contrast, make no reference to these synagogue visits.

11. No such silver shrines have been located, but that may simply reflect the value of the material (i.e., the silver may have been recycled into other objects). Objects made of marble and lead have been found (*New Docs* 4 [1987]: 7–10; Rick Strelan, *Paul, Artemis, and the Jews in Ephesus, BZNW* 80 [Berlin: Walter de Gruyter, 1996], 135)

12. Richard Oster, "The Ephesian Artemis as an Opponent of Early Christianity," *Jahrbuch für Antike und Christentum* 19 (1976): 24–44; idem, "Ephesus,"*The Anchor Bible Dictionary* (New York: Doubleday & Co., 1992) 2:542–49; Lynn R. LiDonnici, "The Images of Artemis Ephesia and Greco-Roman Worship: A Reconsideration," *Harvard Theological Review* 85 (1992): 389–415; and Rick Strelan, *Paul, Artemis, and the Jews in Ephesus,* esp. pp. 41–94.

13. Pausanias, *Description of Greece*, Book IV, 31.8.

14. A revealing example is discussed by F. Sokolowski, "A New Testimony on the Cult of Artemis of Ephesus," *Harvard Theological Review* 58 (1965): 427–31.

15. See Strelan, *Paul, Artemis, and the Jews,* 143–44.

16. It is not even clear whether Alexander is a Jew who believes in Jesus. It may be that Ephesian Gentiles eyed all Jews with suspicion for their lack of commitment to Artemis.

17. The threat exists at the level of the narrative. That someone may have *perceived* Christian preaching as subversive is not the same thing as saying that Christian preaching actually made significant inroads. Probably we are to imagine a small group of believers that in no way threatened the standing of the chief deity of the city. Indeed, Artemis and her temple thrive and continue vigorous in the third century (Oster, "Ephesian Artemis as an Opponent," 29).

18. E.g., Dio Chrysostom, *Oration* 7; Lucian, *True Story* 1:28–29; 2:46; Xenophon, *An Ephesian Tale* 2, 2, 4. See the discussion and further examples in Richard Pervo, *Profit with Delight* (Philadelphia: Fortress Press, 1987), 50–57.

19. E.g., Plutarch, *On Exile* 601B; *Greek Anthology* 9:290; Heliodorus, *The Ethiopian Story* 2:20; Pliny the Elder, *Natural History* 8:85–86.

20. Pervo, *Profit with Delight,* 65.

21. See also Luke 10:19. The fact that Paul prays does tacitly acknowledge that the healings are not his own doing. On the place of this scene in the larger Lukan portrait of Paul, see F. Scott Spencer, "Paul's Odyssey in Acts: Status Struggles and Island Adventures," *Biblical Theology Bulletin* 28 (1998): 150–59.

22. Talbert takes the prayer of v. 8 as sufficient indication that Paul refuses the acclaim, but that action is remote from the earlier scene and scarcely parallels the urgency of 14:14–17 (*Reading Acts* [New York: Crossroad, 1997], 222).

23. John Bell Mathews, "Hospitality and the New Testament Church" (Ph.D. diss., Princeton Theological Seminary, 1964); A. R. Hands, *Charities and Social Aid in Greece and Rome* (Ithaca, N.Y.: Cornell University Press, 1968), 26, 30; Peter

Marshall, *Enmity in Corinth: Social Conventions in Paul's Relationship with the Corinthians* (WUNT 2.23; Tübingen: J.C.B. Mohr, 1987), 1–34.

24. In the *Iliad,* Diomedes and Glaukos, although engaged in battle with each other, immediately reconcile and become friends on recognizing that their grandfathers had been guest-friends of each other (6.119–236); see John Fitzgerald, "Friendship in the Greek World Prior to Aristotle," in *Greco-Roman Perspectives on Friendship,* ed. John T. Fitzgerald (Atlanta: Scholars Press, 1997), 13–34.

25. I am grateful to Brian Blount, Donald Juel, and Patrick Willson for their comments on an earlier draft of this essay. I also received genuine instruction from extended conversations with students in the M. Phil. in Christian Studies program at the University of Port Elizabeth in South Africa, and I appreciate the hospitality of Professors Elna Mouton and Lionel Hendricks on that occasion.

Chapter 4

Multicultural Worship

A Pauline Perspective

DONALD H. JUEL

I had always believed that the letters of Paul had power to effect change, but I was unprepared for what took place in the first course I taught at Princeton Seminary in the fall semester of 1974. The subject was Galatians and First Corinthians. At a particular point in the course we worked on 1 Corinthians 11:2–16, a discussion of head coverings for women. I suggested that perhaps one reason for the disagreement among the Corinthians was something Paul had said or done that got the Corinthians thinking about gender distinctions and clothing—something like what he writes to the Galatians in 3:26–28:

> For in Christ Jesus you are all children of God through faith.
> As many of you as were baptized into Christ have clothed yourselves with Christ.
> There is no longer Jew or Greek, there is no longer slave or free, there is no longer male and female; for all of you are one in Christ Jesus.

The suggestion struck the class as plausible. The lines are formulaic, and they are introduced as having to do with baptism. It is not unlikely, they agreed, that the baptismal ritual in Pauline congregations—in Corinth—included words and actions that had to do with these distinctions. It would help explain why there might be some pressure to experiment with social forms like the removal of head coverings for women in worship.

One member of the class was a devout Roman Catholic woman who had come to Princeton Seminary out of a sense of call to study theology. Though she knew she could not be ordained as a priest, she was sure there was some vocation for her within the church. Her encounter with Galatians left her stunned. She had never read the passage before. She had never imagined what it might mean for her as someone who had been baptized into Christ that there is "no longer male and female." By the end of the semester, she had begun exploring the possibility of becoming an Anglican priest. The next year, she withdrew from membership in the Roman Catholic Church, joined the Episcopal Church, and was eventually ordained. She later became the first ordained Episcopal woman priest to be a Navy chaplain.

At the beginning of my teaching career, such a dramatic event startled me. I had not taken seriously enough what might happen if people believed what they read in the Bible. I have come to have enormous respect for that small passage in Paul's letter to the Galatians. It has changed people's lives.

And this small passage, this baptismal formula, has potential to enable us to reimagine Christian worship. It offers a vision of a Christian community characterized by diversity and hospitality. It is noteworthy that the verses, crucial to Paul's argument, are taken from the liturgy of a Pauline church. It is not only the ideas conveyed by the words, but the experience of unity in Christ, that Paul draws on. At the beginning of the crucial third chapter in his letter to the Galatians, Paul opens his argument with a reminder of what has actually occurred in the life of the congregation.

> You foolish Galatians! Who has bewitched you? It was before your eyes that Jesus Christ was publicly exhibited as crucified!
>
> The only thing I want to learn from you is this: Did you receive the Spirit by doing the works of the law or by believing what you heard?
>
> Are you so foolish? Having started with the Spirit, are you now ending with the flesh?
>
> Did you experience so much for nothing?—if it really was for nothing.
>
> Well then, does God supply you with the Spirit and work miracles among you by your doing the works of the law, or by your believing what you heard? (Gal. 3:1–5)

Paul wrote an intense letter to his Galatian congregations because some "teachers" insisted that what the Galatian believers experienced was insufficient. They supplemented Paul's preaching with instruction about how to be true children of Abraham.[1] The particular issues that are the focus of attention include circumcision and the observance of a religious calendar—matters that have implications for and are very much related to worship practices. The most pressing issue in Paul's context was the relationship between Jews and Gentiles. On what basis were they to relate, including relations at the Lord's Supper? Could Jewish and Gentile believers in Jesus eat together without Gentiles observing Jewish law (i.e., becoming Jews)? The teachers were arguing that Gentiles were obliged to observe at least some of the law of Moses, including circumcision. Paul disagrees.

In the context of his argument, Paul tells the extended story of his dealings with the Jerusalem congregation (1:18–2:21).[2] He includes mention of Titus, whom he brought with him to a conference at Jerusalem that was to settle the status of Gentile believers in the church. Titus's presence posed a practical question to the church: Would he be compelled to be circumcised to have fellowship with the church, or would he be invited to join them at the table as he was? That he was not compelled to be circumcised Paul regarded as a major victory for Gentile freedom from law. Paul reports a subsequent confrontation with Peter in the church at Antioch when he believed Peter was observing these distinctions at meals. At issue were the social implications of Paul's gospel—a gospel that announced the dramatic end of a world characterized by the distinctions between Jew and Greek, slave and free, male and female.[3]

The Relevance of the Baptismal Formula for Worship

It is not at all difficult to imagine the relevance of the baptismal formula for our understanding of worship. What we celebrate at worship, most particularly at the Lord's Table, is our unity in Christ. Particularly in a multicultural, pluralistic setting, worship may offer the possibility not only of announcing the dawning of a new age, but of experiencing a fellowship within the body of Christ in which "there is no longer Jew or Greek, there is no longer slave or free, there is no longer male and female." References to baptismal practices in Galatians (3:26–28); 1 Corinthians (12:12–13); Colossians (3:10–11); and Ephesians (2:11–16; 4:4–6), and to the Lord's Supper in 1 Corinthians (11:17–24), presume not only the idea of a community formed from diverse members but the actual formation of such a community through the experience of worship. It is clear from Paul's letters to the church at Corinth that what occurred in worship was worth discussing (especially 1 Corinthians 11 and 12–14) because it had a considerable bearing on the shape of the community and the way people treated one another. His letter to the Galatian churches sees embedded in worship practices the truth of the gospel, which cannot be compromised.

Many Christians who participate regularly in worship seldom experience anything that seems as culturally or socially potent. Many, like the young woman in my class, have never heard the verses from Paul's letters, much less celebrated them in a service of Baptism or the Lord's Supper. That suggests Paul's letters may offer unrealized possibilities for worship as well as for the intellectual life of the church. In the remainder of this chapter, I will discuss how and under what circumstances Paul's baptismal formulation can offer promise for more effective multicultural worship.

The Formula

Paul was not the first to use these distinctions in formulaic fashion.[4] Aristotle used similar pairs to speak of happiness: to be truly happy, one must be a Greek and not a barbarian, a free man and not a slave, and a male and not a female. Some of the reasons were obvious: only free Greek males could be citizens and participate in the life of the polis. The pairs say a great deal more, however, about what distinctions are most characteristic of humans.

The Jewish community had—and has—its own version of the three-part statement. In blessings preliminary to the morning service, Jewish worshipers pray:

> Blessed art thou, O Lord our God, King of the universe, who hast not made me a heathen.
> Blessed art thou, O Lord our God, King of the universe, who hast not made me a bondman [lit, "slave"].

The men then pray:

> Blessed art thou, O Lord our God, King of the universe, who hast not made me a woman.

The women pray:

> Blessed are thou, O Lord our God, King of the universe, who hast made me according to thy will.[5]

In his notes in the prayer book, Rabbi Hertz proposes that the phrase "not made me a woman" be paraphrased: "[Blessed art thou, O Lord our God, King of the universe,] who hast set upon me the obligations of a male."[6] In some bilingual versions of the prayer book, this is in fact the translation given. While by no means literal, the paraphrase has some justification. The three benedictions are part of a larger section in which God is blessed for the gift of the Torah. The paraphrase is thus not inappropriate, since the full "burden" of the law falls on a free Jewish male. One can easily understand, however, why some comment in the prayer book is necessary. In our current cultural context, it is difficult to hear the prayers without deep suspicions about racial prejudice, classism, and male domination in the history of Western culture.

In various traditions, these distinctions are at the heart of what it means to be a human being. They serve as a shorthand for characterizing what it means to be part of a structured, ordered creation in which people are differentiated by race, class, and gender. It is hardly accidental that precisely these distinctions appear in the baptismal formula to identify the dramatic consequences of baptism into Christ—or "putting on Christ."

The background does not solve the interpretative problem. It only raises the stakes. If these distinctions most aptly characterize human society, what does it mean to say that "in Christ" these distinctions no longer apply? Paul's argument in Galatians offers some help in answering this question with regard to the distinctions between Jew and Greek. Paul argues vigorously not only that Gentiles are under no obligation to observe the law of Moses; he insists they cannot. Believers in the Galatian churches were probably shocked to learn from Paul that any male believers who undertook circumcision were "cut . . . off from Christ" (Gal. 5:2–4).

> For freedom Christ has set us free. Stand firm, therefore, and do not submit again to a yoke of slavery. (Gal 5:1)

His argument that the law is for the Galatian Gentile believers the equivalent of a "yoke of slavery" is radical. If it were not for his comments in Galatians 1:13–14 and Philippians 3:4–11 about his life in Judaism prior to his encounter with Christ, including his zeal for the law and his note that as to "righteousness under the law" he was "blameless" (Phil. 3:6), one might be tempted to agree with some commentators that Paul simply misunderstood Jewish views of the law. It should be noted that Paul does not offer a systematic exposition of his views regarding the law. His argument, for example, is not carried through consistently with regard to Jewish believers, and his comments about the law in Romans may suggest that Paul was obliged to explain himself a bit more carefully. He does not insist that Jewish believers cease in their observance. His comments in 1 Corinthians 9 may imply that Paul is even willing to observe the law when not in the company of Gentile believers (1 Cor. 9:20). Understanding Paul's radical view of the law has engaged some of the best minds in the history of the church, and learned students of Paul still disagree in their interpretations.[7] What is beyond dispute is that Paul opposed any distinction between Jew and non-Jew within the body of Christ, and he was willing to oppose even Peter, the Rock.

Paul is of less help in spelling out what it might mean that in Christ there is no longer slave or free, male and female. Some of Paul's most thoughtful interpreters in the first centuries of the church tried their hand at interpretation. The most radical—and the most interesting—were people like Marcion and Valentinus, whose views proved too dangerous. For some Gnostic groups, "Neither male and female" meant that in Christ, gender is transcended.[8] Whether the idea is that in baptism the two separated parts of an originally androgynous being are now united or, as in the Gospel of Thomas, that females "become males" like the angels, the point of these interpretations is that embodied differences among human beings are false and misleading. The truly human is disembodied—whether a divine spark or a "soul." Baptism is the occasion for the eschatological return; worship, particularly the Lord's Supper, is an experience of this essential similarity.

While such views made possible a certain flexibility with regard to social roles, freedom is purchased at the expense of embodied life. And life as we know it is embodied. There continue to be differences among us in regard to race, class, and gender in which society has considerable investments. One response has been to rein in Paul's radical views by individualizing them, implying that the abrogation of distinctions is "real" in individual minds and hearts but not in the public realm. That can hardly be the case for the distinction between "Jew and Greek," as the argument in Galatians testifies. At least in this case, Paul's interest is in the social implications of the doctrine of justification. Understanding what implications the abrogation of distinctions between "slave and free" and "male and female" have for life in society—and for Christian worship—requires an imaginative extension of Paul's own argument.

Worship and the Other

Human identity, according to the formula, is embodied in difference. One way of understanding the formula is to insist the differences no longer exist, at least not in the church, or at least not in God's vision for the church. There is no longer Jew or Greek—only "one new humanity" (Eph. 2:15). There is no longer class differentiation. And there is no essential difference between men and women.

Such arguments have been advanced in various ways, and the results are not encouraging. What often happens is the subsuming of the identity of the weaker into that of the stronger. The announcement that "there is no longer Jew or Greek" led many in the history of the church to argue that there is only one people of God, a "New Israel." The persistence of Jews who do not believe in Jesus seems to contradict such a view—and on more than a few occasions Christians, whether during the Spanish Inquisition or the Third Reich, have sought to make reality consistent by forcibly eliminating Jews. The poor have not always fared well at the hands of those who have advocated a "classless society." And the argument for the unity of male and female has been used against women, denying their particularity. There is something ominous about the last saying in the Gospel of Thomas:

> Simon Peter said to them: Let Mary go away from us, for women are not worthy of life. Jesus said: Lo, I shall lead her, so that I may make her a male, that she too may become a living spirit, resembling you males. For every woman who makes herself a male will enter the kingdom of heaven.[9]

According to this view, what we celebrate in worship, perhaps most particularly at the Lord's Table, is the possibility of a primal—and eschatological—unity that transcends our differences. What we are to *experience* is an essential similarity that will develop as we become better acquainted. The reality is that in most congregations, the "essential similarity" is defined by a particular group, and those integrated into the congregation conform in terms of class and race. Genuine difference is often perceived as a problem to be overcome, and strategies are developed to accomplish this end.[10]

Paul as an Interpreter of New Creation

Paul, however, does not argue for the complete abrogation of difference. An example is the discussion of head coverings in 1 Corinthians 11:1–16. The enormous literature generated by these few verses, including a doctoral thesis reviewing various interpretative proposals, indicates there is little chance a short chapter will provide convincing exegetical solutions to the various problems in the passage. I am interested in just one aspect of the discussion: Paul deals with something as seemingly trivial as head coverings because "neither male and female" does not mean that in Christ there is no difference between men and women. The reality into which people are baptized has social implications, since those so baptized are embodied selves.

In helping his congregation decide how to conduct worship that appropriately reflects how things are "in Christ," head coverings are important because there is a difference between male and female. However we are to imagine the eschatological state, the Corinthians are not in that state, and live not in the heavenly places (Eph. 2:6) but in the earthly world where bodies are a reality. I am not arguing that Paul's views about head coverings are appropriate; his arguments, in fact, seem quite flimsy. It may be that Paul is unprepared for more radical social consequences of his gospel. His insistence that women wear head coverings may be interpreted as capitulating to conservative social forces or as wise pastoral strategy. His arguments, in any case, insist on taking seriously the actual setting of life in the body.

The same may be said about Paul's discussion of Israel "according to the flesh" in Romans 9–11. While providing justification for the view that there is no longer Jew or Greek but only those who are heirs of Abraham "in Christ" through faith, Paul spends several chapters reflecting on what it means that the majority of his brothers and sisters "according to the flesh" have not accepted the gospel. God's promises to Israel were not made to a "spiritual" Israel but to real people who embody a way of life. While Paul can only hope that one day "all Israel will be saved," life in this world for Gentiles grafted into Israel through faith in Christ will involve relating to men who are circumcised and men and women with whom God is not yet finished who observe God's law but do not believe in Jesus.

Finally, Paul's letter to Philemon indicates that while there is no longer slave or free, he lives in a world where such differences exist and are determinative. The status of Onesimus before the law depends on the decision of his owner, Philemon. While Paul does everything but insist that Philemon take back his runaway slave—and free him to serve Paul— he must respect the reality of embodied life. Paul, Onesimus, and Philemon live in a society in which their relations are governed by realities over which they have limited control. To ignore those realities would make the gospel a fantasy and rob it of its transforming power.

That does not mean the world cannot be changed. That we exist in political and social structures surely does not imply the particular forms are somehow eternal. It does suggest, however, that the "reality" of the baptismal formula that is to be lived out in the life of the church must take account of embodied life.

The Other as Stranger

Recent decades have witnessed a dramatic shift in philosophy and hermeneutics to an appreciation of "the other." The philosopher

Emmanuel Levinas has been a significant voice in identifying the primacy of encounter with another, whose very presence lays claim on our attention.[11] Self-consciousness is more than self-awareness; it presumes face-to-face encounter with an other.

> Before we exist as an "I," we must exist face-to-face as strangers. . . .
> A moral summoning takes place within the face-to-face encounter, even before a self takes shape. That other summons me to care and be for the other.[12]

The people we encounter are "other" also in the sense that they are not just like us, even those who constitute family or intimate friends. And the public world in which we live is peopled by strangers—people who are irreducibly other. We are all embodied selves, and life in this world is essentially social and political. We are involved with others, as Jews and Greeks, rich and poor, male and female. To deny the validity of these distinctions is to remove Christian life from the realm where the neighbor exists to be appreciated and confronted. The lines in Galatians must play in a world of real people, in the church as well as in the larger society, who bear the scars and hurts of destructive social systems but depend on an order that respects the differences between "male" and "female," black, white, and hispanic; and among people who have been indelibly stamped by the class within which they have been raised.[13] Such differences are essential to what we are as embodied people. If we look forward to the redemption of our bodies, the baptismal formula cannot mean that in Christ differences are obliterated.

Viewing the "other" as "stranger" may perhaps provide a fruitful avenue of reflection. The term "stranger" has good biblical precedent and is appropriate for other reasons as well.[14] The challenge in multicultural worship is singing and praying, eating and drinking, with people who are genuinely different, in such a way as to become the body of Christ. That there are differences is obvious. It was certainly obvious to my family and me when we celebrated Reformation Day in a congregation of non-English-speaking people at the Coventry Cathedral in England. The congregation was made up largely of refugees from East Germany and Eastern Europe. They did not sing the English translations of Luther's hymns, did not participate in the worship service from the (American) *Lutheran Book of Worship*, and prayed the Lord's Prayer in their own languages. While there was something moving about celebrating our Lutheran identity in an Anglican cathedral that was rebuilt after the original was destroyed by German bombs in the Second World War, the service was itself an experience of alienation. We discovered that we were strangers in ways more profound than the worship planners had anticipated.

Our differences extend beyond matters of language. And because we really are different from one another in profound ways, there are good reasons to be wary. "Strangers" cannot always be trusted. In the midst of an enthusiastic conversation about the wonderful richness and diversity of the community where we lived, a colleague—a mother of two children— was suddenly struck by how differently she spoke to her children about people who were different, that is, "strangers." "Never accept a ride from a stranger" was drummed into them from their earliest years. "Don't even talk to strangers." Such advice is appropriate not only to children. "Don't ever look anyone in the eyes," we were advised by South African friends in anticipation of walking the streets in Capetown. A welcoming greeting could become a provocation. We ourselves are wary of strangers, and we teach our children to be wary because strangers can be dangerous.

Strangers pose a challenge not only in terms of physical violence. Encountering a stranger is genuinely unsettling. One of the great challenges of teaching is to help students discover that there are other ways than their own of imagining the world. It is remarkably difficult, because significant opinions about life's major questions are presupposed by the culture and taken to be common sense. As "common sense," they are never subjected to scrutiny. Those opinions, in turn, provide the very conditions for perceptions and judgments. Those raised in another culture— "strangers"—can raise questions that constitute a deep challenge to notions that we take to be foundational to everything we think and do.

A regular occurrence in dealing with students from certain African and Asian cultures is the discovery on an examination or research paper of words, sentences, sometimes whole paragraphs taken from a secondary source. In most cases there is no effort to conceal the "borrowing," but neither is there scrupulous crediting of sources in footnotes. Students are inevitably astonished when they are accused of plagiarism. The whole notion is foreign to them. "Ideas are not property," my African student told me. "Ideas belong to the community." He pointed out that most of his native songs and poems are anonymous, bearing no author's name. "It would never occur to us to order a book by the name of the author," he said. "Most people don't even notice who the author is." Before that exchange I had never really considered how completely our academic culture, even in a theological seminary, reflects and supports a society in which property rights are primary. Whether or not this is the best way to organize a society and an educational system is not debated, but taken for granted. My student raised an important question about a system in which the greatest academic penalties are reserved for using someone else's ideas without proper credit (plagiarism), while cooperation—in the long run, far more crucial to the success of society—is actually inhibited.

The stranger—someone who is genuinely different and sees life from another perspective—is a destabilizing force. An encounter with a stranger is decentering. One discovers that one is not necessarily the point around which life revolves and that a person's perspective is not only one among many but may be severely limited. Several of us were discussing life in small towns, noting the cultural limitations. One of my colleagues challenged us. "What do you know about life in small towns?" he asked. Most of us knew nothing, having been raised in the suburbs of major cities. He spoke rather eloquently about the heights and the depths of small-town life where he had grown up, including a few comments about grandparents who, when they left the farm, could only afford a trailer house in town. "How many of our students would feel free to speak about visiting their grandparents in the trailer park?" he asked. We began to realize not only that we knew little about the life of small towns from which many of our students came, but that our preference for life in a major city had planted in them a growing contempt for small towns so as to make them useless for most of the parishes to which they would be called.

"Neither male and female," Paul writes. I recall the first time I was paired with a female colleague in a conference focused on Christian understandings of the atonement. She began with a scathing attack on historic doctrines in the Christian tradition—interpretations, she argued, that were patriarchal, justified violence by abusive husbands and its toleration by female victims, and depicted God as little more than a child abuser, needing the death of his son in order to be merciful. My first inclination was to launch a counterattack on behalf of the tradition. It occurred to me, however, that given the constituency of the conference, an attack would only confirm everything my colleague had said—and, not insignificantly, the whole notion of a "counterattack" is couched in a metaphor appropriate to war, not conversation. What the speaker was telling us is that she did not hear gospel words as "good news." Telling her she was wrong would hardly make the words any more palatable. The more I thought about her presentation, the more impressed I was that whatever the intentions of the great thinkers in the history of the church who had constructed theories of the atonement, their actual effect on a significant proportion of the human family was and is unsalutary. Few moments have been as significant a challenge to my own theological reading of the scriptures.

The accumulation of such experiences can undermine confidence in our ability to perceive and make sense. As we come to know "strangers" better, we may discover that differences are not erased but increased. Real friendship may include a growing recognition of and respect for remarkably different ways of viewing and experiencing the world—a genuine threat for those who, according to the philosopher Richard Bernstein, suffer from the "Cartesian Anxiety," the need for a clear and distinct idea on which to build one's life.[15] That we view things from a limited and often warped perspective beyond which we cannot see without the assistance of others is deeply unsettling to some who yearn for a "foundation," while others may take the radically perspectival character of reality as permission to dismiss questions of truth, leaving themselves unaccountable to anyone, free to believe anything.

If it is true that we are very much limited to our own perspective and require the perspective of another—a stranger—to appreciate the world, God, our neighbors, and even ourselves more fully and appropriately, the promise of a body of people in which the distinctions among us as strangers do not inhibit but encourage taking seriously our differences is a great gift.

An Evangelical Conversation on Behalf of the World

Formation of and growth in the body of Christ requires conversation.[16] In the church, that conversation should be centered in the gospel. If the conversation is on behalf of the world, there will be practical matters that require deliberation and decisions. If in the body of Christ there is "no longer Jew or Greek, . . . slave or free, . . . male and female," one requirement is that everyone have equal voice in the conversation. Perhaps such a situation is not difficult to imagine if the church is viewed as a family gathered around a table—though even in such instances the dynamics of power are complex and tend to favor one family member over others. What about the church as a large body, however?

I have attended a few synodical and national church gatherings during my career, but none was more instructive than the gathering of the United Church of Christ in Hawaii at which I was asked to open each session with a Bible study. The polity of the church was congregational. In order for the larger body to make decisions, all congregations had to have an opportunity to speak. There were two highly controversial issues before the convention. One had to do with proposed reparations to Native Hawaiian churches for property seized at the end of the nineteenth century; the other had to do with a proposal that the convention affirm "the Christian family" in the face of a vote in the state legislature to legalize same-gender "marriages." The issues were complex and had received considerable attention in the public press. It was obvious that the delegates were deeply divided.

I was amazed at the character of the debate. Everyone had access to the microphone—men and women, young and old, rich and poor, Samoans, Native Hawaiians, Filipinos, Chinese, and Caucasians. The debates went on for hours—but no one came to the microphone to discover he or she had been disconnected or switched off, as regularly happens at political conventions. When at last the vote was taken, everyone had had a chance to speak. The results were as controversial as the debate, and people went home exhausted and divided.

The ritual of the convention included a brief business meeting before a final celebration of the Lord's Supper. When the group reconvened in the morning, there were apologies to the convention from one and another speaker for harsh words, and numerous requests for forgiveness. The concluding worship was a powerful experience of God's uniting grace in the face of significant differences and differences of opinion. No one left imagining that the differences would disappear: the wealthy descendants of white colonialists, the Native Hawaiians, the Samoans, the Filipinos, and the Chinese who comprised the membership of the United Church would continue to maintain their own customs and to have quite distinctive views of the world. There was little chance that many of the several hundred people would become close friends. But church members left having experienced a kind of hospitality from one another and ultimately from God that made their ongoing conversation possible.

In that context, it seemed clear to me that Paul's baptismal formula was embodied in practices that ensured equal access to the microphone, and in a recognition that what made their difficult conversations possible was a willingness to extend hospitality to those who were genuinely different in view of God's willingness to extend hospitality to them.

Multicultural Worship:
Hospitality to the Stranger

Following the proposal of Patrick Keifert in *Welcoming the Stranger*, I am suggesting that we understand the baptismal formula in Galatians in light of the metaphor Paul suggests in Romans when he speaks of "extend[ing] hospitality to strangers" (Rom. 12:13). In this view, the baptismal formula does not envision a community in which differences disappear, but one in which they do not separate. Further, I am suggesting that a primary locus for this welcoming of strangers is Christian worship, because this is a central place at which God is at work breaking down "the dividing wall, . . . the hostility" (Eph. 2:14).

While Paul's discussion in Galatians 3 is not primarily about worship, the vision of community on which he draws for his argument arises from baptismal rites. The practices presupposed ("cloth[ing] yourselves in Christ," Gal. 3:27) appear to have included baptism by immersion and the changing of clothing. Hippolytus's description of baptism from a somewhat later era may well preserve something of the actual practices in Pauline churches. The rite was not "symbolic" of changes; it marked the change itself. The persons who emerged from the baptismal water were not the same. They were members of a community that embodied different rules for living. Membership in this new group often entailed breaking ties with the old world, including family and friends.[17]

Baptismal rites were one of the ways the changes were actually effected. The Lord's Supper was likewise a powerful force in building up the body of Christ. Paul's lengthy discussion of the Corinthians' experience of the Lord's Supper (1 Cor. 11:17–34) indicates the degree to which this was the case. The problem that warrants Paul's condemnation and a warning that the Corinthians may be eating and drinking "judgment against themselves" was the lack of concern for "the body of Christ"—that is, the lack of recognition of the community whose reality was celebrated and formed at the Table. The lack of concern for the poor who had no food to contribute, the consumption of meals without concern for those absent—such things constituted a violation of the whole purpose of Communion.

Baptism and the Lord's Supper were part of God's strategy to form a community of strangers. That is still the case. In Baptism and the Lord's Supper, it is God who acts as host to a company of strangers. It is the presence of Christ that effects the sort of change Paul speaks of when he says, "It is no longer I who live, but it is Christ who lives in me." What makes it possible to welcome strangers who pose genuine threats to the way we think and the way we perceive ourselves and the world is a God who claims us and promises that "neither death, nor life, nor angels, nor rulers, nor things present, nor things to come, nor powers, nor height, nor depth, nor anything else in all creation, will be able to separate us from the love of God in Christ Jesus our Lord" (Rom. 8:38–39). Worship is crucial as a place where God acts to extend a welcome that will alone exorcise our

need to protect ourselves from the stranger. It will allow us to give ourselves "out of delight in God's gift of the stranger."[18]

Some Implications for Christian Worship

One might ask first of all why there is so little Pauline influence on
contemporary Christian liturgies. Few baptismal services speak of baptism as "dying and rising with Christ" (Ephesians 2, Romans 6, Colossians 2), and even fewer enact something that is vaguely like death and
resurrection. It may be that the early Christian experience of conversion
and the cost/gain of incorporation into Christ has been obscured in
"Christian" culture, where it is difficult to see any difference between the
mores of mainline congregations and those of the dominant culture. That
is surely changing, however. There are, even in mainline churches, adult
baptisms where the new situation of the person being baptized is dramat-
ically enacted in a way that makes the language of death and life more
than theoretically appropriate.

The same might be said about the lines from Galatians 3. What if baptism were spoken of in terms of the distinctions Paul insists are now in the
past? To put it another way, what if baptism were an enactment of that
new reality? Such a performance would require more than adding a line
to the liturgy. It would entail particular preparation for baptism and an
introduction to congregational practices that embody the new reality. At
the very least, baptismal practices in which the abrogation of distinctions
had a central place might have a dramatic impact, particularly at a time of
growing pluralism—and at a time when many congregations simply
reflect the social patterns of the larger culture.

Such an emphasis would, of course, bring certain controversies within
the churches out of the shadows and into the light. If for those who put on
Christ there is "neither male and female," the matter of women's ordination—in some congregations, even women's place on governing bodies of
the church—would have to be dealt with as something central and not
peripheral, particularly if worship is central to forming a Christian community. Dealing with the issue is by no means simple. The Corinthian
correspondence provides useful examples of pastoral reflection, which
respect the complexity of effecting change in a world where there are differences that are more than peripheral to our identity as embodied selves.
As men and women, we are not simply "the same." Precisely how we are
different and what those differences should mean for the way we live
together are questions that are ancient and fundamental to our life

together. God has done a new thing, but in precisely what that newness consists and how it is to be embodied are matters for deliberation.

Most so-called mainline churches have determined that in light of the gospel there are no good reasons for denying ordination to women and very good reasons to encourage the practice. Experiencing worship led by a woman pastor or priest is a powerful way of forming a community in which the distinction between male and female has nothing to do with qualification for the pastoral office. Churches that embrace this possibility will, of course, find themselves at odds with Rome and the Orthodox. The issue is more than trivial. It goes to the heart of understanding the gospel. What Protestant churches can ask of partners in ecumenical conversation is a reasonable response to what might be termed Pauline baptismal theology. Many believers in contemporary Christian congregations would be shocked to read what Paul wrote to the churches of Galatia.

Our freedom in Christ should give us the opportunity to discover how different we are from one another. Congregations seriously invested in mission will soon discover that those invited to share in worship do not experience the world the same way. It isn't simply that the uninitiated are lacking in something—like taste in music, one of the regular suspicions in congregations where those in charge of the music program feel threatened by those interested in evangelism. The whole "argument" of the worship service is aimed at a particular audience formed by a whole history and particular cultural forces. Recognition of differences that are more than "skin deep" may suggest that if churches aim to conduct worship in such fashion as to embody the radical newness of Paul's theology in the face of a culture that continues to separate us based on race, class, and gender, the way to move forward is not by pretending that differences do not really exist and that we are all the same. More appropriate is to respect the mystery of the other, even to the point of recognizing that we cannot imagine how others hear the stories and experience the tradition familiar to those raised in it.

> In sum, the face-to-face encounter is fraught with both danger and promise. Since the face of the stranger cannot, without remainder, be reduced to analogies of my experience, cannot be held within the horizon of my experience, it remains an open horizon; it is an encounter with the eschatological.[19]

There are, to summarize, not only historical and cultural, but theological reasons for recognizing the central role worship can play in a genuinely cross-cultural ministry. Planning and executing such worship requires a new imaginative framework within which to work. Without attention to that framework, it is certain we will operate with the unquestioned assumptions of contemporary culture. The argument of this chapter is that Paul's letters hold great promise for reimagining Christian worship. The vision offered by the baptismal formula in Galatians is best realized through a strategy formed by another of Paul's metaphors, that is, extending hospitality to strangers. Such worship will be effected not by rituals of forced intimacy, like shaking hands with the person sitting next to you, but embodying a gospel message in which God extends hospitality to all of us—in a setting in which we are all strangers and also members of the body of Christ, in which there is no longer Jew or Greek, slave or free, male and female.

NOTES

1. Lou Martyn, in his masterful commentary on Galatians (*Galatians,* Anchor Bible 33A [New York: Doubleday, 1997]), discusses the various options for reconstructing these "teachers" and their views.
2. On the function of the autobiographical section, see Charles Cousar, *The Letters of Paul* (Nashville: Abingdon Press, 1996), 43–45, and Beverly Gaventa, "Galatians 1 and 2: Autobiography as Paradigm," *Novum Testamentum* 28 (1986), 309–26.
3. Nils A. Dahl, "The Doctrine of Justification: Its Social Function and Implications," in *Studies in Paul* (Minneapolis: Augsburg Press, 1977), 95–120.
4. Martyn (pp. 378–80) discusses several proposals regarding the origin of the formula, which include a development of Stoic/Neoplatonic notions about spiritual and mental freedom from distinctions, proto-Gnostic notions about a return to a lost state of undifferentiation, and apocalyptic notions about the end of sexual differentiation at the resurrection. He does not rule out any of these possibilities.
5. Joseph H. Hertz, *The Authorised Daily Prayer Book,* rev. ed., Hebrew text, English translation, with commentary and notes (New York: Bloch, 1948), 18–21.
6. Hertz, *Prayer Book*, 20.
7. For a balanced and insightful discussion, see Steve Westerholm, *Israel's Law and the Church's Faith: Paul and His Recent Interpreters* (Grand Rapids: W.B. Eerdmans, 1988).
8. Wayne A. Meeks, "In One Body: The Unity of Humankind in Colossians and Ephesians," in *God's Christ and His People*, ed. Wayne Meeks and Jacob Jervell (Oslo: University Press, 1977), 209–21; idem, "The Image of the Androgene: Some Uses of a Symbol in Earliest Christianity," *HR* (1974), 165–208. Elaine Pagels, "Adam and Eve, Christ and the Church: A Survey of Second Century Controversies Concerning Marriage," in *The New Testament and Gnosis*, ed. A. H. B. Logan and A. J. M. Wedderburn (Edinburgh: T. & T. Clark, 1983), 146–75. In her essay, Professor Pagels indicates the complexity of views among Gnostic groups, particularly the Valentinians, who advocated marriage, and the views of some of the church fathers, like Clement and Tertullian, who barely tolerated it.

9. The translation is from K. Aland, *Synopsis Quattuor Evangeliorum* (Stuttgart: Wuettembergische Bibelanstalt, 1964), 530.

10. According to Patrick Keifert, a common way to deal with the threat of the stranger is to "project our self upon the other in an effort to wipe out his or her difference. Intimacy, through this technique of projection, can thus simply erase and destroy the other, rather than supporting that person" (Keifert, *Welcoming the Stranger* [Minneapolis: Fortress Press, 1992], 78).

11. Works of Levinas include "Beyond Intentionality," *Philosophy in France Today,* ed. Alan Montefiore (Cambridge: Cambridge University Press, 1983); *Totality and Infinity,* trans. A. Lingis (Pittsburgh: Duquesne University Press, 1969); *The Levinas Reader: Emmanuel Levinas,* ed. Sean Hand (Cambridge:Blackwell, 1989).

12. Keifert, *Welcoming the Stranger,* 77.

13. Failing to take cultural differences seriously in constructing "standardized" tests is only one indication of how difficult it is to understand the stranger and how serious the consequences are.

14. See the helpful discussion in Keifert, *Welcoming the Stranger,* chapter 5.

15. Richard Bernstein, *Beyond Objectivism and Relativism: Science, Hermeneutics, and Praxis* (Philadelphia: University of Pennsylvania Press, 1983).

16. The title above is an image taken from Keifert, *Welcoming the Stranger,* 76.

17. Paul's discussion of marriage and divorce in 1 Corinthians 7:12–16 presumes such a situation, as does the story of the man born blind in John 9.

18. Keifert, *Welcoming the Stranger,* 79.

19. Ibid.

PART 2

Theological Foundations
for Multicultural Worship

Chapter 5

Diversity and Power

Cracking the Code

RICHARD K. FENN

The Church Has Lost Its Monopoly over the Sacred

*W*hen an institution or social system is in trouble, its last line of defense is often to tinker with its rituals. Certainly the Soviet Union, for years before its demise, was experimenting with liturgies that would incorporate individuals into the working class or bury them as members of the wider Socialist community. I am not saying that liturgical reform is the last resort of ecclesiastical scoundrels, but only that desperation over a society's or an institution's ability to survive inevitably shows up in concern over the vitality and inclusiveness of its rituals. In the United States, for instance, burning the flag is part of a ritual of protest and rebellion. To outlaw such a deviant rite is a sure sign that the nation is unsure of its own authority. *When a country is worried about its rituals, it is also anxious about its capacity to stand the test of time.*

The same could well be said of the church. It is no accident that the church's interest in adding diversity to its liturgies comes at a time when women have been creating their own rituals. Women know what it means to be incorporated and subsumed within a larger social entity, that is, within a generic humanity defined as "man." They know what it means to be treated liturgically as a minority, emblematic of a part of the social universe rather than of the whole. Colonized as part of a larger social universe, any category of people becomes a case of a larger, more general form of humanity. Once any group or community accepts the invitation to express its identity in a larger liturgical context, it is acknowledging that it is merely an interesting deviation from some hypothetical norm.

It is also no accident that the church's renewed interest in making its liturgies more open to diversity comes at a time when liturgical experiment is flourishing under auspices that do not recognize the authority of the church itself or the authority of the larger society. No wonder the church is worried about the diversity of its rituals; its very survival is at stake. In many prisons African Americans have their own services, often Islamic, and these rites allow them the spiritual freedom of regarding themselves as prisoners rather than inmates. These deviant liturgies stand as a rebuke not only to the church but to the legitimacy of the nation and its institutions. African Americans know liturgies when they see them, especially those rites that begin with the burning of a cross and end with the burning of an African American. *Indeed, the present call for the church to allow for more diversity within the liturgy is itself a sign of the church's own estrangement from local communities and from particular ethnic groups.*

Certainly churches have lost their monopoly on identifying, defining, producing, and interpreting the sacred. By the sacred I simply mean whatever a group or community considers to be essential to its identity. The sacred may consist of cherished memories, of hopes for the future, of times and places that are approached with veneration and celebrated with enthusiasm. It may be enshrined in temples or reenacted on special days of remembrance and thanksgiving. *Most forms of the sacred, however, now flourish outside the church and are not easily collected within the framework of any single institution's liturgies.*

Thus it has become increasingly evident that the sacred is taking on new, unauthorized, and widely diverse forms. The sacred has become more widely dispersed, more widely diffused, and therefore harder to concentrate under professional auspices. The sacred is thus less easily identified and more accessible: more variable, contingent, ambiguous, temporary, and negotiable. Is this turn of events surprising? Actually, given the history of this nation it is more surprising that there are not more liturgies of rebellion and protest by groups and communities that refuse to be incorporated and subsumed in the liturgies of the majority community under the rubric of diversity.

The more the church seriously entertains the project of providing for more diversity in the liturgies, then, the more necessary it is to ask why the church is doing so at this time. Is the institution of the church estranged from local communities? Is the clerical leadership of the church in need of providing various services in order to legitimate its position of authority? Is the church faced with competition from indigenous or local forms of community life that have escaped its control? Is the church competing for membership with other institutions that seem to have a more intimate and vital connection with some aspects of the community?

The Church: No Friend of Diversity

It has long been the obligation of the nobility to provide bread and circuses for the people. Thus the church's interest in allowing for more diversity in its services smacks of a certain noblesse oblige. Indeed, the practice of liturgy has its origin in the Greco-Roman world, where the notable families of a region periodically provided feasts or entertainments for the people, or various other forms of relief and welfare. Donations to local temples, relief from taxes, and the provision of protection were the means by which noble families created popular support for themselves. *The liturgy was thus a form of social control; it gave legitimacy to the ruling families and provided services to the people.*

Rulers, of course, have a vested interest in controlling diverse expressions of the sacred. Take, for instance, the celebration of ethnic and regional identities under Communist auspices in Beijing. Under Mao Tsetung, rituals celebrating the diversity of the Chinese people were offered by the Party as a means of consolidating its control over the nation. To remind ethnic or regional groups that they must preserve their identity within the framework of the nation-state reinforces the legitimacy of the party in power. However, as divergent centers of loyalty and allegiance are brought within the sphere of the nation-state, they lose some of their distinctiveness and their independence. No longer do unique groups with long memories and particular histories define and perpetuate themselves with rituals under their sole ownership and control. Once they become wards of the state, these distinctive ethnic or regional groups exist under the protection of the party in power. They are part of a covenanted nation: so long as they are good, they can count on the state for support and protection. For the church to permit more diversity within its rituals, then, could well be a sign that a new, implicit covenant is being offered to subordinate groups and communities.

Indeed, the church does have a long and similar history of allowing diversity for the sake of maintaining its control. As the church expanded throughout Europe after the fall of Rome, it enjoyed the patronage of aristocratic families and regional warlords. These families and chiefs had an overriding interest in pacifying their serfs and keeping order within their domains. The church proved itself a particularly useful institution in subduing local leaders and in incorporating diverse communities within the larger society. To be sure, the church often allowed local languages and devotions to find a place within the liturgy. In the long run, however, these expressions of local culture were gradually replaced by a liturgy that was increasingly uniform over large stretches of territory.

Any group or community should therefore be careful before accepting the church's offer to allow it to celebrate its identity within the church's context. Even many of the ecclesiastical base communities of the church in Central and Latin America have lacked enough autonomy to define themselves liturgically. While the church may tolerate festival celebrations of ethnicity or of local traditions, the liturgy itself has remained under the ownership and the control of the clergy.

Thus the church has a questionable record in allowing diversity within its domain. During its European expansion, local pieties, to the extent that they survived outside the church, slowly became deviant and anomalous. To the extent that communities or groups based on ethnicity or gender retained the capacity to organize, they were regarded as potentially dangerous and heretical. The fate of witches is a case in point.

Diversity *among* Rituals

In contemporary American society many traditional rituals have become increasingly empty and lifeless. Other rites, however, have begun to take their place. Generated at times by the clergy, but more often than not by groups and communities without clerical authorization or the expertise of liturgical commissions, these new rites have helped people to break with a past of servitude and humiliation or to mobilize mass support for new political and social obligations. The keys of the kingdom are still in the hands of the people, regardless of the state of liturgical reform.

One result of this resurgence of popular liturgical formation is the remarkable diversity among rites. Indeed, many contemporary rites define the sacred in ways that have little or nothing to do with church buildings and clerical authority. Some of these new rites celebrate the hopes and sufferings of particular ethnic communities, for example, Kwanza, Hanukkah, and Thanksgiving Day. Others define boundaries between generations, genders, and forms of sexuality such as the anthems and dances of the lesbian and gay community. Still other rites express more fluid and temporary forms of social solidarity based on economic or political interests or on affinities for celebrities or for other centers of popular culture.

The church, of course, has a vested interest in collecting these manifestations of the sacred in liturgies. While its rituals may reflect various kinds of diversity in the population, once framed in the liturgy these alternative centers of loyalty and devotion can be celebrated only under the church's auspices. To frame local pieties, various communal identities, and the devotees of charismatic leaders within the authoritative and conventional forms of the sacred is one traditional task of religion.

An Initial Conclusion

I have been making three points: the first, about the larger society's use of ritual in colonizing local ethnic or regional groups; the second, about the church's record in aiding and abetting that colonization for its own purposes; the third, about liturgical experimentation as a sign of the larger society's apparent uncertainty about its own ability to transcend the passage of time. Together, they suggest that any discussion of the composition of rituals will expose a struggle for social control.

The good news is that many groups already know that ritual is a source of symbolic power. Any attempt to develop an inclusive liturgy therefore can, and I believe should, stimulate various forms of cultural resistance. Most groups would be well advised, I am arguing, to see the movement to achieve diversity within the liturgy as an attempt to incorporate and neutralize smaller, distinct, and diverse groups within a larger institution or community. Certainly national rites such as the Fourth of July or Memorial Day are visibly an attempt by the larger society to subsume other loyalties within a framework of national allegiance and devotion.

In societies like the United States, however, it will be very difficult to colonize the personal, communal, ethnic, or regional sources of identification and loyalty within the larger framework of religious institutions or of the nation itself. What used to be embedded in taken-for-granted images is now open for discussion. Ethnic groups themselves are alert to the struggle for power that is implicit in various forms of culture; note the intensification of "identity politics." The machinery of ritual clanks more audibly when its techniques for including some and excluding others are clearly the result of decisions made by activists, specialists, and bureaucrats.

Ritual as the Attempt
to Transcend the Passage of Time

To put it all too simply, rituals give people what seems to be a chance to participate in a social order that transcends time. In fact, their participation subjects them to a social system, to particular elites, and to an invasive and demanding form of social authority. In the *Alternative Service Book* of the Church of England, one rite had a number of optional words and gestures in its first thirteen lines, but only two were required. One was "kneel," the other was "stand." For rituals to accomplish their magic, however, the participants have to be relatively unwitting, naive about the intentions of those who offer them "inclusion" in ritual, and easily deluded about their own capacity to control their social destiny. What works with peasants and the illiterate may not work quite as easily with those who have learned the hard way to distrust liturgical commissions or the central committees of national political parties. Of course, not even literacy and disillusionment are enough to prevent people from being duped into compliance by rites that give legitimacy to the very authorities that limit and define one's own place in the scheme of things. That is because rituals, when they have the power to capture the means of self-recognition, do so in ways that impress themselves on the psyche at relatively deep levels of the self.

There is more good news. Attempts to revise rituals are often not only self-defeating, because they create resistance, but they are also often transparently political. I once made a study of the way the Anglican Church introduced revisions to the liturgy in what came to be known as the *Alternative Service Book*. The minutes of the Standing Liturgical Commission of the Church of England revealed the Commission's distrust of democratic procedures and their preference for official or expert opinion. Furthermore, significant changes to major texts were often made by vote rather than a more open and fluid consensus. The minutes of the Commission also revealed the church's anxiety about losing constituents; the church itself was worried about running out of time. No wonder, then, that its alternative liturgies were *transparently experimental, temporary, and therefore secular.* Indeed, many of the changes in liturgical forms over the last thirty years have reflected just this combination of institutional anxiety, visible struggles for power, and self-conscious temporizing.

This is not to say that liturgies are properly devoid of any reference to power or to the passage of time. As Paul Binski has shown in his recent study of death in medieval art and literature, the development of the "transi" tomb accomplished both.[1] On the one hand, a tomb displayed the social body of, say, a particular prelate, ornate in its full regalia. On the other hand, the transi tomb displayed the effigy of a rotting and largely naked corpse. The passage of time was thus fully displayed, although it was superseded and transcended by the effigy of the prelate in his vestments. What earlier tombs had concealed of the human body's subjection to the forces of nature, to the inevitability of decay, and to the passage of time, these later tombs displayed. Both the passage of time, then, and the attempt to convey power through the use of imagery were fully apparent in these tombs.

It is the role of any ritual, of course, to display and overcome the contradiction between social institutions and the passage of time: to synthesize the transcendent with the ordinary, the social with the natural, the general with the particular, the eternal with the temporal, the necessary, and inevitable with the optional and expendable. Often, therefore, it is the individual, the local, the ethnic group, or the particular community that seems to belong to the world of the temporal and the expendable. For them to be included is thus an act of grace by those who are custodians of the given, the necessary, and the inevitable. In revising the liturgy, not everything is put on the table for discussion, not everything is up for grabs. The traditional framework remains, and the diverse groups are (graciously) incorporated within it. It is the given social order that appears to be timeless, not the inferior groups within it or the individual. These are temporary, optional, and subject to the forces of time and nature. Therefore to incorporate ethnic forms of prayer, gesture, music, dance, and imagery into a more uniform and permanent liturgy is to accomplish what the "transi" tombs themselves sought to impose through impressive sculpture and imagery. The timeless order remains above, below reside the remains of the particular community.

Rituals as a Way
of Recovering Lost Parts of the Self

Earlier I suggested that rituals have a way of impressing themselves on the individual at fairly deep levels of the psyche; that is why not even a good education gives one immunity to the power of a rite. One can easily be led to accept the inclusion of one's particular community, therefore, in a rite that subsumes and incorporates it into a larger society, where it can at best only be an object of minority affection and loyalty. The power of ritual to engage the psyche depends on the ability of the rite to present to the individual aspects of the self from which the individual is more or less estranged. The most obvious example of this alchemy is in the transformation of violence. In the liturgy, one can celebrate the death of a prophet and remember in loving detail the torments that preceded the prophet's death on the cross while deploring the event, distancing oneself from its perpetrators, and committing oneself to a way of life that could never issue in such harm to anyone else. To be sure, one confesses a certain measure of guilt, and even acknowledges that in some fashion the prophet's death was "for us." However, participation in the rite provides a structure for vicariously experiencing both the acting-out of lethal cruelty and various forms of self-mortification by which one pays for the satisfactions of imaginary violence. To put it another way, the violence in such a rite allows us to treat as alien and strange aspects of ourselves with which it would be somewhat painful to become more familiar.

The origin of diversity in rituals is precisely in this form of self-alienation. The elements of human nature, the motives that cannot pass social inspection, the dreams of glory that are too grandiose for ordinary consumption, and the buried longings for satisfaction, triumph, recompense, and revenge can all be disguised in very diverse symbols, stories, events, and symbolic gestures. If these more bizarre, grotesque, tragic, or mythic aspects of liturgy are removed, there will be no point in filling the symbolic vacuum with a potpourri of ethnic or cultural signs and symbols, songs, and stories. None of us will be able to recognize our own depths, and thus our common humanity, in a sanitized liturgy of good feeling and common sense. Instead of finding in other societies various recollections of the demonic aspects of human nature, one is expected to find in other societies particular variations of the expressive and the admirable.

If we experience something uncanny or mysterious in a liturgy, it is because we are indeed facing something that is part of our own psyche, while treating it as unfamiliar. Nonetheless even in disguise the self comes through and demands at least a tacit recognition. It is in this act of recognition that one's soul is strengthened. Just as ancient Greeks stared into the face of death, so did medieval Christians encounter their own mortality in the macabre sculptures of shrines and sepulchers. In that encounter, they recognized their own mortality and their own being-in-time. It is an encounter designed to elicit an awareness of one's being before it is too late.

Rituals thus allow participants to imagine that they are crossing psychological boundaries. To cross such a boundary is to break a psychological taboo, as, for example, the one against violence. That is why rituals evoke a sense of sin and require moments of confession and expiation. Presenting themselves as the cure for sin, such rites are in fact a major source of the original infection. To put it another way: rituals create the very sense of transgression for which they offer the symbolic remedy. What is "other" in such a ritual, then, is a part of one's common humanity: a violent part or a part that is mortally afraid of death.

The original "double" was just such a source of uncanny and alienated self-recognition. The double stood for the self that, ideally speaking, would be eternal, a self that could stand the test of time. As such, the double is easily identified with heroes and effigies or found in sacred imagery and icons. On closer inspection, however, the double is clearly mortal, like Dorian Gray, and its image shows progressively the signs of inevitable and disgusting mortality.[2] The "other" is thus one's own mortal self, at first disguised, and then rediscovered after the fatal identification of the self with the other has once been made.

Of course, there are other parts of the self to which rites give indirect recognition and partial access. In the book to which I referred earlier, Paul Binski describes the enthusiasm and the ecstasies surrounding veneration of relics of saints or of Jesus himself during the Middle Ages. These occasions would find individuals often imitating the sounds of animals: barking and yowling and growling like a local bestiary. One does not have to be Sigmund Freud to interpret these sounds as expressions of animal spirits that had long been suppressed or repressed by individuals in an effort to conform to social standards of civility.

Indeed, in rituals parts of the self return that have long been repressed. Binski speaks, as does Freud, of presences in the liturgy that are "revenants."[3] By this term he and Freud both mean aspects of the self that have been lost, split off from consciousness through repression, and recovered only in the disguises offered by dreams and rituals. For Freud, these are ghosts: images of others who have died or who have been eliminated psychologically by the dreamer, who is still bound to them by ties of unsatisfied anger and affection.

Proponents of diversity in ritual are thus offering a similar but highly edited and neutralized experience of the self in the disguise of the other. Precisely because of their cultural diversity, these eclectic rites will be less able to personify the violent, animalistic, and mortal aspects of the self in an "other" that is nonetheless uncannily familiar. In a traditional rite, I am suggesting, these alienated aspects of the self become reappropriated as part of the individual's self-understanding. In a liturgy that has contrived to embody carefully selected items of cultural diversity, one may find a range of cultural alternatives, none of which might confront the self with the bestial or the mortal aspects of selfhood in a form with which the individual can identify. The other ceases to be a panhuman self that incorporates one's own mortality and comes to be represented by a variety of cultural expressions, each of which offers a species of alternative vitality.

Rituals as a Means
of Limiting Human Potential

There is within the human, of course, a repertoire of possibilities: magical thinking; obsessive efforts to control the uncontrollable; passions that threaten to disrupt both the psyche and the community; animal spirits that resist the process of socialization; aspects of the psyche that refuse to recognize the passage of time or to adopt adult roles; and so on. Within any community or society, furthermore, there is also a vast array of possibilities that must be understood and, if possible, encompassed: the rivalry between genders and generations, threats and opportunities posed by outside influences, by neighbors, and by nature itself. Social systems are also perennially threatened by the loss of collective memory, which would devastate the society's arts, crafts, economy, politics, family life, and self-understanding. It is therefore the function of any ritual to reduce the vast array of human possibilities to a range that can be understood and perhaps controlled.

Every society does indeed need a "reality-principle": an agreement on what is possible and on what is permitted. The reality-principle, as any reader of Sigmund Freud knows, imposes obligations, requires sacrifice, and sets limits on the range of desire that can be satisfied. Thus the reality-principle always breeds a certain discontent that has to be assuaged or suppressed. Now, it has traditionally been the function of rituals to provide a definition of the reality-principle and to impress it on the individual's psyche. When rituals succeed in this function, the reality-principle itself is assumed to be part of the nature of things, is taken for granted, and becomes the object of serious devotion.

Rituals thus define certain possibilities as mysterious, unknowable, and beyond the pale of legitimate satisfaction. The custodians of the reality-principle, whether they be priests or philosophers, psychiatrists or politicians, have the authority to set limits not only on what one can legitimately expect to understand and control but on the satisfactions that life can legitimately be expected to offer. Those who design and perform rites in which certain amounts of diversity are included and permitted are also setting limits on the amount of diversity, satisfaction, and personal authority that is permissible or desirable. Be careful, then, in choosing who will own and control any project to design more inclusive liturgies or to embody diversity in the rites of the church.

To put it another way: the reality-principle is a principle of selection. Any attempt, therefore, to set limits on the range of legitimate social interaction or of personal exploration and satisfaction is an exercise in reducing possibilities and uncertainty to manageable proportions. What is acceptable sexuality? How and when will the young become adults? How will the older generation give up authority to the younger? How will the environment be known and pacified? Which outside influences will be permitted and which excluded? How will unwanted influences within the community or society be removed? How will old virtues and institutions be maintained or, when necessary, restored? There will always be certain choices that have to be made. It is, therefore, crucial to know who will make those choices and the principle of selection by which these choices will be made.

In a relatively stable and highly stratified society, many may be called, but few will be chosen, to become leaders or spouses, defenders and guardians, priests and other agents of purification. In a society, however, whose boundaries are relatively open, and where the range of possibilities for legitimate social interaction and personal satisfaction are the constant subject of public discourse, the reality-principle itself will not be clear or consistent. Indeed, the reality-principle will be increasingly contested and ambiguous, subject to discussion and rethinking, to negotiation and revision.

It would be easy to imagine that, in a relatively open and rapidly changing society, rites based on a principle of inclusiveness will be relatively diverse and liberating in many ways. These rites might adopt the songs and prayers of many different groups. They might permit dancing or other forms of bodily expression rather than require people to sit still over long periods of time. For instance, the young in nations as tradition-bound as Iran and Japan have found expressive liberation in American pop music. Certainly the discovery of new freedoms may indeed have an effect on the demands placed by the young on the elders for jobs and mobility, sexual satisfaction, and political power. Similarly, battles over whether women and gays can be ordained, or over the use of folk or ethnic prayers and music in the churches, or on the inclusion of dance or electronic media in worship all suggest that by opening the range of liturgical interaction one can also increase the degrees of personal and communal freedom in major institutions and the larger society.

That increased openness and fluidity, however, does not necessarily bring with it a decrease in repression and unnecessary suffering. People will still have to work for low pay at useless and stultifying jobs. The electorate will still have to vote for politicians whose choices have already been limited by the source of their campaign funds. Sexual satisfaction will still have to be found in conventionally acceptable channels. Infants will die unnecessarily from poverty enforced by the stroke of a bureaucratic pen. Major institutions like schools and churches will still try to convince the young that they have to earn the right to be respected. Each generation will still be told that it has to accept a lifetime of probation, testing, and self-improvement. Those who seek the credentials of respectability and competence will continue to seek further accreditation, licensing, and professionalization, while others seek to prove themselves in the marketplace of public opinion. Interest rates will still drive some people into bankruptcy, divorce, depression, and suicide. Those who can steal public money through legal channels will continue to enrich themselves, while making it impossible for millions to receive adequate housing or medical care or education. The churches will still seek to attract as much interest, energy, money, talent, and attention as they can in an effort to develop themselves rather than the communities around them. I am therefore less than optimistic that these liturgical freedoms will provide access to a wider range of opportunity, satisfaction, or legitimate authority.

It is important to know in advance, then, who will decide how much and what sorts of diversity to permit in the liturgy. It is one thing to allow gays and women into positions of leadership within the churches or to enrich the liturgy with ethnic and communal dance, song, prayer, and speech. It is quite another to allow liturgical expression to those who would take from the clergy their apparent monopoly over the word and sacraments. Would the arbiters of diversity welcome a laity that demands the right to perform baptism, celebrate the Lord's Supper, pronounce the absolution of sins, and ordain to the ministry on their own terms and not under the conditions carefully stipulated by various liturgical commissions or committees? Suppose that the laity really did believe that the Lord's gift of the keys of the kingdom gave them the right to bind and loose, forgive and condemn, here and now on this earth, with the full authority of the gospel and the conviction that what they bind or loose on earth is loosed or bound forever in heaven as well? Secular juries nullify the accusations of the prosecution or the instructions of a judge. Cannot two or three gathered together in the name of the gospel offset and overturn the councils of the church?

If the laity were ever to take seriously their possession of the keys of the kingdom, we would not have to write books about diversity in the liturgy. Prisoners at Sing Sing have pronounced the absolution of sins for Presbyterians who have come to them for forgiveness, forgiveness for having operated and benefited from the same social system that drastically reduced the prisoners' own chances for a lifetime of love and work. Blighted lives and premature deaths are evil. They call out for condemnation and renewal. Can we ever expect liturgical diversity with any strength, integrity, authenticity, and depth until and unless the laity take the liturgy into their own hands? This is not to suggest that the clergy seek to "empower" the laity by giving them more chances to participate in, or even construct, liturgies. On the contrary, there is a hidden notion in the use of that word: that the clergy are entitled to own and control liturgies. In this view, the clergy are sharing their own authority by delegating to the laity some liturgical tasks.

I am suggesting that, as I understand the gospel, the authority to baptize and to forgive and to celebrate the Eucharist was not given to a clerical elite but to the people of God. It was only later that the clergy were able to expropriate these powers from the laity and to concentrate them in their own hands. That is one reason why the liturgies of confession and absolution at Sing Sing are so important. This is what happens when two or three or twenty or thirty of the faithful gather together in the name of Jesus. They discover their own spiritual authority and their right to put the past behind them in order that the future may begin. Otherwise the kingdom never comes.

The need for liturgical change to bridge the growing gap between Euro-American and African American peoples was dramatized during the 1960s by leaders of a movement for reparations. One young man interrupted a eucharistic liturgy, took the chalice of wine, and poured its contents out on the chancel floor with a reminder that it represented the blood of his people. Before there can be any reconciliation along racial divides there will necessarily be many more liturgies of repentance and forgiveness of the kind born in Sing Sing. To go on with liturgical business as usual when vast numbers of Euro-Americans have yet to honor the dead of the African American community makes a mockery of the communion of the saints and of the eucharistic community. There will need to be services of repentance and thanksgiving, where the sacrifices of past generations of all races are honored, before the future can begin. Those services will inevitably require Euro-Americans to honor the fathers and mothers of African Americans, their sacrifices, and their sacrifice at the hands of a majority community that burned crosses before burning their victims alive.

There are indeed liturgies to consecrate the memory of those who have died in the Holocaust, and many Gentiles have participated in the services to honor the Jewish victims of that ethnic cleansing. Since roughly six million Gentiles also died in the Holocaust as victims of the Reich, it is necessary also to enshrine their memory in appropriate liturgies, if only as a reminder that each generation must fight fascism in its own time, even when that fascism bears the name "Christian." There may come a day, furthermore, when Jews accept an invitation to honor in solemn liturgy the sacrifices of the Gentile victims of the Nazis.

It may well be that the most pressing task facing the churches is to allow new, rebellious, radical, and reconciling rites room to breathe, to grow, even to flourish. Rather than liturgies that represent diversity, we need diverse liturgies, and in creating them the clergy do indeed have a role. There are far more transitions in life now than can be represented by those that are solemnized in most prayer books. Some clergy, like Barbara Fillette, have enriched their congregations with liturgies that solemnize a wide range of difficult transitions in life: divorce, moving away, retiring, and the death of a child, to name only a few. There are indeed liturgies for the consecration and burial of a stillborn child, thanks to a woman, a member of the clergy, who saw the need and vowed never again to let a mother suffer alone through the death of an unbaptized fetus or infant.

Rather than diversity within liturgies, there must first be diversity among liturgies. That is because the sacred has long ago escaped from its institutional confinement and from the control of the clergy. Various aspects of life are now being recognized as sacred: moments of critical passage, loss, change, endearment, commitment, and renewal that do not fit neatly into the passages sanctified by the churches.

Many clergy are indeed sensitive to the needs of their congregations for witnesses who can share with them the most painful passages in life, but the laity need not wait for the clergy to give them the authority to construct their own rituals. Note that women have not waited for clerical permission to design their own rites. They have produced rituals that bind them to the community of women throughout the world and in solidarity with women of past generations and centuries who have carried humanity on their backs and have suffered varying degrees of exclusion for their pains. Those seeking liberation from the Iron Curtain joined hands all across Europe without requiring authorization from a liturgical commission. Where the church fails to see the sacred in its own times and places, God raises up even from the stones in the street new sons and daughters of Abraham. They march on Washington, make promises, and return to their communities sanctified for a future that is indeed a break from the past.

NOTES

1. Paul Binski, *Medieval Death* (Ithaca, N.Y.: Cornell University Press, 1999).
2. Ibid., 137.
3. Ibid., 139ff.

Chapter 6

The Linguistic Inculturation of the Gospel

The Word of God in the Words of the People

PETER J. PARIS

*M*usic, song, prayer, and preaching are the quintessential elements in African American liturgies. They express and are united by a distinct rhythm, which invariably manifests a unity of reason and feeling, motion and imagination, moral character and spiritual devotion.

All this is undergirded by the understanding that the Christian gospel for the most part assumes the cultural forms of those who embrace it. In African American worship we see evidenced what missiologist Lamin Sanneh has described as the art of translation, through which the gospel has undergone a process of inculturation and transformation of meaning.[1] Sanneh claims that a part of the uniqueness of the Christian message relates to its translatability into the various vernacular languages of the world. He also maintains that when Christian missionaries used translation as a primary instrument of evangelism, they unwittingly provided indigenous African peoples with some basic tools with which to effect their own liberation from colonial domination. In other words, the very act of translation by indigenous peoples implies an affirmation of indigenous cultures which, in turn, can stimulate the development of cultural pride, critical self-consciousness, cross-cultural dialogue, and cultural reciprocity. Once the message is translated into the mother tongue of the indigenous peoples, the latter receive a tool of immense interpretative and psychological advantage.

Rather than viewing the Christian missionary movement as being solely the religious arm of Western colonialism, Sanneh writes: "By their root conviction that the gospel is transmissible in the mother tongue, I suggest that missionaries opened the way for the local idiom to gain the ascendancy over assertions of foreign superiority."[2] Yet Sanneh also makes it very clear that he is fully aware of the complicity of Christian missions with colonialism. He certainly is not attempting to render them blameless. Rather, he seeks to look at his subject matter from the perspective of the recipients, namely, the indigenous African peoples, and to do so by attending to the "internal forces that activated as part and parcel of promoting mother tongue literacy."[3]

In my judgment, Sanneh's thesis about translation can be extended to include the experience of African Americans in slavery and, especially, the way they succeeded in inculturating Christianity into their own linguistic idiom, thereby making it their own. Let me hasten to add, however, that as the translation of the Christian message into the African vernacular of indigenous Africans constituted a veritable theological change of meaning from its Western to its African adherents, a similar change occurred among the African slaves who eventually converted to Christianity.

Elsewhere,[4] I have argued that the African slaves in the United States gradually discerned a resource in the Bible that enabled them to declare a contradiction between the biblical understanding of humanity and the institution of chattel slavery. This enabled them to reconstruct the traditional Christian understanding of humanity and, in so doing, to plant the seed for an alternative form of theological thought that became the basis for the abolitionist spirit. Not surprisingly, the slaves rapidly embraced this new form of Christianity and eventually made it foundational for their understanding of God and especially of God's relation to them. Gradually they were able to syncretize their Christian and African understandings of a caring and loving deity. That process marked the origins of the black church.

Both traditional African religion and the Christianity of their slaveholders had led them to see the cause of their enslavement as internal in themselves, that is, either as divine punishment for wrongdoing or as the destiny they had received before birth. Both explanations implied a fatalistic orientation to life, in which the only appropriate response would be some form of adaptation to subservience as normative practice. Their nascent Christian understanding taught them to locate the primary cause of their bondage neither in themselves nor in God, but in the deliberate actions of their captors. More importantly, they could now use the religion of their slave owners as a weapon against them. Gradually African peoples throughout the diaspora and subsequently on the African continent came to understand the Christian gospel as integrally related to their enduring struggle for freedom, equality, and dignity.

Although enslaved Africans gradually appropriated the formal features of their slaveholders' Christianity with respect to ritual practices, language, and symbols, they soon invested each of them with new meanings. In doing so, they quickly seized on the method of double entendre, which was evidenced most clearly in the so-called "Negro spirituals," the primary repository of African American theological thought. For example, the distinguished African American theologian and preacher Howard Thurman vividly described the way in which the slaves used heaven not only as an eschatological symbol, but also as a concealed normative principle of social criticism. Reflecting on the master's talk about heaven, the slave was puzzled as to how slave and slave owner would inhabit that eternal abode. Thus he reasoned:

> "There must be two separate heavens—no, this could not be true, because there is only one God. God cannot be divided in this way. I have it! I am having my hell now—when I die I shall have my heaven. The master is having his heaven now; when he dies he will have his hell."
>
> The next day, chopping cotton beneath the torrid skies, the slave said to his mate—
> "I got shoes,
> You got shoes
> All God's children got shoes,
> When I get to Heaven
> We're going to put on our shoes
> An' shout all over God's heaven
> Heaven! Heaven!"
> Then looking up to the big house where the master lived, he said,
> "But everybody talking about Heaven
> Ain't going there."[5]

As with many of the spirituals, the above is a song of protest that is clearly concealed in its linguistic format of double entendre. Now, we need to keep in mind that slaveholding Christianity did, in fact, posit the practice of racial segregation in heaven. Thus the refrain, "shout all over God's heaven" subtly acknowledges that there is no segregation there whatsoever. Other renditions of the song (one with which I grew up) substitute the verb *walk* for *shout* in order to make the point all the more clear. Similarly, in addition to "I got shoes" (a commodity that slaves did not have) other verses are "I got a robe" and "I got a crown." Such images vividly contrast with the condition of the slaves, who had no such possessions. In fact, the contextual understanding of the terms implies that such possessions pertain to royalty. Thus the slave argued accordingly: If God is sovereign and all human beings are God's children, then it should follow that all humans are heirs of sovereignty and, hence, should rightly wear shoes, robes, and crowns. Again, it is easy to see the subtlety of the protest, which was on the one hand hidden from the slaveholder but on the other hand clearly evident to the slaves themselves.

James Cone, the progenitor of black theology, argues that enslaved Africans viewed the kingdom of God as partially breaking into history in the life and ministry of Jesus of Nazareth. Since its eschatological mission is to overthrow all heteronomous powers, the slaves viewed the kingdom as a revolutionary force demanding disobedience to every power and authority that would hinder its reign. That included the condition of slavery first and foremost. Thus Cone writes:

> Heaven then did not mean passivity but revolution against the present order. Against overwhelming odds, black people fought the structures of slavery and affirmed their membership in a "city whose builder and maker was God."[6]

Cone claims further that in the spirituals the image of heaven helped liberate the slave's mind from the existing values of the slaveholding society. Some viewed heaven as synonymous with the escape route to the North and Canada. Others equated heaven with the triumphal vision of crushing their oppressors by armed rebellion. Still others viewed heaven in spiritual terms, namely, as another world . . . "not made with hands."

> It [heaven] was a black life-style, a movement and a beat to the rhythm of freedom in the souls and bodies of black slaves. It was a hum, a moan, and a hope for freedom. Blacks were able, through song, to transcend the enslavement of the present and to live as if the future had already come.[7]

Both for African slaves and their foreparents on the continent, songs, music, dance, and rhythm played significant roles in every dimension of their daily life, including work, worship, and play. In fact, songs and music were arranged for times of celebration and times of sorrow. It is important to note, moreover, that Africans both on the continent and in the diaspora made no radical distinction between the so-called sacred and secular worlds. Rather, everything was sacred. Thus the spirituals were not relegated to a particular place and time, but could be sung anytime and anywhere. Like all their songs, the function of the spirituals was, on the one hand, to preserve traditional values pertaining to communal solidarity, and, on the other hand, to enable the people to transcend the adversities of life. These were supported and reinforced by the call-and-response structure of the songs and music which the slaves brought with them from Africa and preserved on these shores. Lawrence Levine describes it well:

> The overriding antiphonal structure of the spirituals—the call and response pattern which Negroes brought with them from Africa and which was reinforced in America by the practice of lining out hymns—placed the individual in continual dialogue with his community, allowing him at one and the same time to preserve his voice as a distinct entity and to blend it with those of his fellows.[8]

Thus the spirituals clearly reveal that though the slave system destroyed many of the beliefs and practices that African slaves brought with them from Africa, it was never able to obliterate totally traditional African values and especially the importance of community as the paramount virtue in every African society.

W.E.B. Du Bois and others called the spirituals "sorrow songs," because they often dealt with the tragic elements of life. While that is partly true, it does not characterize them as a whole. For certain, African slaves sang about trouble and pain, but even the most sorrowful songs contain a note of triumph. For example, the deep sadness attending the song "Sometimes I Feel like a Motherless Child" gives way to the spirit of victory in the stanza that begins, "Sometimes I feel like an eagle in the air . . ./Fly, fly, fly." As a matter of fact, the spirituals are replete with feelings of confidence and are totally void of despair. Again, hear the words of Levine:

> For all their inevitable sadness, slave songs were characterized more by a feeling of confidence than of despair. There was confidence that contemporary power relationships were not immutable: "Did not old Pharaoh get lost, get lost, get lost . . . get lost in the Red Sea?"; confidence in the possibilities of instantaneous change: "Jesus make de dumb to speak . . . Jesus make de cripple walk . . . Jesus give de blind his sight . . . Jesus do most anything"; confidence in the rewards of persistence: "Keep on inching along like a poor inchworm, /Jesus will come by'nd bye"; confidence that nothing could stand in the way of the justice they would receive: "You kin hinder me here, but you can't do it dah," "O no man, no man, no man can hinder me"; confidence in the prospects of the future: "We'll walk de golden streets / Of de New Jerusalem."[9]

Though the slaves did receive some lessons from white preachers that they affirmed, by and large they preferred their own preachers. This was due in large part to the way they had translated Christianity into their own vernacular. No white person could proclaim the gospel in the linguistic idiom of African slaves. Thus the gospel remained distant to them whenever it was expounded in the language and style of white preachers. Since it was necessary for Africans to feel their religion, only those who shared their experience in slavery could inspire them to feel the Christian spirit. In brief, preachers had to feel it before they could make their listeners feel it. The same was true both then and now with singing the songs of the slaves. Thus, Levine cites the diary of Ella Storrs Christian in Alabama, who wrote in her diary that African slaves did not like singing in the church of their master, where whites sang from books. Rather, they much preferred their own meetings, where they made up their own words and tunes. Thus she reported the words of a slave named Nancy Williams:

> "Dat ole white preachin' wasn't nothin," Nancy Williams observed. "Ole white preachers used to talk wid dey tongues widdout saying nothin' but Jesus told us slaves to talk wid our hearts." "White folks can't pray right to de black man's God," Henrietta Perry agreed. "Cain't nobody do it for you. You got to call on God yourself when de spirit tell you."[10]

James Weldon Johnson, one of the earliest scholarly commentators on the spirituals, claimed that "the capacity to feel these songs while singing them is more important than any amount of mere artistic technique."[11] The spirituals need to be sung by those who can feel them, and that, in turn, causes their listeners to feel them as well. In contrast to others who thought otherwise, Johnson rightly discerned in the songs an element of triumph that is blended with the misery and sorrow on which they reflect. The power of feeling in that blend empowers the hearts of singers and listeners alike. In the following well-known spiritual, we can see the pathos in the first three lines of each stanza. Yet, the last line of the refrain sets forth the hopeful note of triumph: "Glory, hallelujah!"

> Nobody knows de trouble I see
> Nobody knows but Jesus;
> Nobody knows de trouble I see,
> Glory, hallelujah!
>
> Sometimes I'm up, sometimes I'm down,
> Oh, yes, Lord.
> Sometimes I'm almos' to de groun',
> Oh, yes, Lord.
>
> Although you see me goin' long so,
> Oh, yes, Lord;

> I have my trials here below,
> Oh, yes, Lord.
>
> Oh! Nobody knows de trouble I see,
> Nobody knows but Jesus;
> Nobody knows de trouble I see,
> Glory, hallelujah!

Another spiritual that speaks a word of hope to the experience of sorrow is the following:

> O Mary, don't you weep, don't you moan,
> O Mary, don't you weep, don't you moan,
> Pharaoh's army got drowned,
> O Mary, don't you weep.

Though the spirituals spoke about the particularity of suffering, struggle, and striving, they also addressed the universal experience of mortality, as seen in the tragic nature of human life. Inevitable struggles with good and evil, pain and suffering, death and dying comprise the warp and woof of human life, a truth that was verified continually by the daily experiences of the slaves; a truth that the slaves did not deny but confronted boldly and directly.[12]

In keeping with their African traditions, certain rituals attending the experiences of dying and death were necessary in order to effect a safe, victorious transition from this life to the realm of the ancestral spirits, in which the deceased would assume heightened responsibilities as spiritual protectors of their mortal families. The prominence of such metaphors in the spirituals as "taking wings," "cleaving to the air," and "flying" signaled that inevitable spiritual journey which all souls must take, which, when it occurred in old age, indicated a good death that merited a festive celebration. Note the depth of African realism and spiritual triumph embedded in the following slave song:

> O sinner, sinner, you better pray,
> Death's gwine-ter lay his cold icy hands on me,
> Or yo' soul will get los' at de judgment day,
> Death's gwine-ter lay his cold icy hands on me.
>
> Some o' dese mornings bright an' fair,
> Death's gwine-ter lay his cold icy hands on me,
> I'll take-a my wings an' cleave de air,
> Death's gwine-ter lay his cold icy hands on me.

Cryin', O Lord! Cryin', O my Lord,
Cryin', O Lord!
Death's gwine-ter lay his cold icy hands on me.

Throughout the African continent and the diaspora, funeral rituals have always been elaborate festivals in which the entire extended family and the larger community of friends and acquaintances were and are expected to participate. The solemnity and dignity of the occasion was thought traditionally to usher the soul into the realm of ancestral immortality. In the Christian context, the ancestral realm has been replaced by an eternal heaven.

Whether in story or song, African Americans have always loved those biblical persons who were clearly identified with their social context. Paramount among these were Moses leading his people across the Red Sea, little boy David humbling Goliath, Daniel in the lion's den, blind Samson bringing down the mansions of his conquerors, Noah and his ark, Jonah and the whale, Jesus being tormented and crucified, and Paul and Silas in prison. All these stories became the subjects of their spiritual songs, which, in turn, became the repository for the theological thought of the enslaved Africans in America.

Since enslavement implied virtually no liberty whatsoever, the African slaves used their capacity for singing as a weapon of transcendence over their miserable condition. In keeping with the function of song and music in Africa, illiterate African slaves preserved their communal story of joy and sorrow through the medium of song and music. Thus Miles Mark Fisher has written: "The first extended collection of slave songs was advertised as historical documents from the Negro people. . . . Negro spirituals are best understood in harmony with this historical interpretation."[13]

Fisher gives numerous examples of how the enslaved Africans kept their group consciousness concealed from their masters. As in their native Africa, they at first summoned one another together by means of a drum or a horn. Fisher writes that when that form of communication was discovered and outlawed, they found apt substitutes for the drum and horn in their spiritual songs:

After the Colony of Virginia took the lead in 1676 in prohibiting the assemblage of Negroes by drum beat, a non-Christian slave there might have sung this spiritual for a gathering of his fellows:

Let us (ah) praise Gawd togedder on our (mah) knees.
Let us (ah) praise Gawd togedder on our (mah) knees.

> Let us (ah) praise Gawd togedder on our (mah) knees.
> When Ah falls on mah knees
> Wid mah face to de risin' sun;
> Oh, Lord, hab mercy on me.[14]

Fisher claims that the above song does not itself relate to Holy Communion, which does not require a devotee to face to the east. In the eighteenth-century, however, it was used to convene secret meetings.

The spirituals were replete with ambiguous content, which both praised God and spoke of the present situation of the African slaves. In fact, any aspect of communal desire and longing might be woven into a spiritual. Thus their love for Africa is revealed in many songs like this one:

> I am huntin' for a city (home), to stay awhile,
> I am huntin' for a city (home), to stay awhile,
> I am huntin' for a city (home), to stay awhile,
> O Believer (Po Sinner) got a home at las'.

Similarly, enslaved Africans had infinite patience and sang ambiguously about their longings for manumission either by the hands of their owners or by the coming of Jesus. Thus,

> O Brothers, don't get weary,
> O Brothers, don't get weary,
> O Brothers, don't get weary,
> (Us) We're waiting for the Lord

was inextricably connected with their longing for freedom. (Even the term "Lord" often had double meanings, referring sometimes to the master and sometimes to God, often to both, not caring especially which one might become the cause of their deliverance. Many of their songs of patience revealed their own patience in waiting for the time of deliverance.

Yet the songs of deliverance and trust in the rise of a new Moses were prominent parts of their repertoire. The plea to Moses not to get lost but to come over and deliver them because they are the children of God reveals this idea rather clearly:

> Come along, Moses, don't get lost, don't get lost,
> Come along, Moses, don't get lost, don't get lost,
> Come along, Moses, don't get lost,
> We are (Us be) the people (or children) of God.
>
> He sits in Heaven and He answers prayer,
> He sits in Heaven and He answers prayer,

He sits in Heaven and He answers prayer,
We are (Us be) the people (or children) of God.

Stretch out your rod and come across,
Stretch out your rod and come across,
Stretch out your rod and come across,
We are (Us be) the people (or children) of God. [15]

Fisher also draws attention to the following freedom medley in order to depict its ambiguity, by glorifying Jesus on the one hand and calling for a secret meeting down by the riverside on the other hand.

King Jesus lit de candle by de waterside,
To see de little chillun when dey truly baptize,
Honor! Honor! Unto de dying Lamb.

Oh, run along chillun, an be baptize
Might pretty meeting by de waterside.
Honor! Honor! Unto de dying Lamb.

I prayed all day, I prayed all night
My head got sprinkled wid de midnight dew,
Honor! Honor! Unto de dying Lamb.

Some have suggested that the words "Honor! Honor!" probably reveal a bit of antebellum lore creeping into the spirituals as warning to those who bestow an inordinate measure of praise on Abraham Lincoln and the Civil War instead of giving priority in their praise to Jesus, the dying Lamb.

Clearly, many spirituals were composed to celebrate and commemorate the so-called Colonization Movement to Liberia in the 1820s. In fact, the colonization movement reached its zenith in the year 1825, when the movement was endorsed by many state legislatures and Christian denominations. Though all African slaves wanted to go to Africa, most of them knew that only a few would be selected. Thus, they prayed that they might be among the chosen. Many of the songs pertaining to the "Ole Ship of Zion" reflect this movement. The song "Git on board little chillun, /Git on board little chillun, /Git on board little chillun, /Dere's room for plenty a-more" is such a spiritual. The African slaves also imagined themselves hearing the church bell ringing in Africa and themselves following the road that led to their ancestral homeland. It was natural for them to equate Africa with heaven, the Promised Land, Canaan, Zion, paradise, and new Jerusalem, to mention only a few places. Interestingly, in the following spiritual Jesus is depicted as sitting along the waterside, supposedly waiting for the ship to take him to Africa also.

> Heaven bell aring, I know de road,
> Heaven bell aring, I know de road.
> Heaven bell aring, I know de road,
> Jesus sittin' on de waterside.
>
> Do come along (across), do let us go,
> Do come along (across), do let us go,
> Do come along (across), do let us go,
> Jesus sittin' on de waterside.[16]

Enslaved Africans thought of the ship to Africa as destined for the Promised Land with Jesus as its captain. Everyone wanted to be on board.

> Don't you see that ship a-sailin',
> (See that ship) a-sailin', a-sailin'.
> Don't you see that ship a-sailin',
> Gwine over to the Promised Land.
>
> *Chorus*
> I asked my Lord, shall I ever be the one,
> (I asked my Lord) shall I ever be the one,
> To go sailin', sailin', sailin', sailin',
> Gwine over to the Promised Land.
>
> She sails like she is heavy loaded,
> She sails like she is heavy loaded,
> Don't you see that ship a-sailin',
> Gwine over to the Promised Land.
>
> King Jesus is the Captain,
> King Jesus is the Captain,
> Don't you see that ship a-sailin',
> Gwine over to the Promised Land.
>
> The Holy Ghost is the pilot,
> The Holy Ghost is the pilot,
> Don't you see that ship a-sailin',
> Gwine over to the Promised Land. [17]

Obviously, enslaved Africans in America viewed their return to Africa as the ultimate liberation from slavery and the conditions of misery: the misery of working in the falling rain, burning sun, stormy weather, and always under the merciless whip of the drivers. Thus, they sang:

> Dere's no rain to wet you.
> *O yes, I want to go home,*
> *Want to go home.*
>
> Dere's no sun to burn you,
> O yes, etc. [repeat after each line]
>
> Dere's no hard trials.
>
> Dere's no whips a-crackin'.
>
> Dere's no stormy weather.
>
> No more slavery in de kingdom (heaven).
>
> No evildoers in de kingdom.
>
> All is gladness in de kingdom.[18]

Another beloved spiritual, "Swing Low, Sweet Chariot," naively viewed by its heirs as a celebration of an otherworldly heaven, actually celebrates the historical possibility of returning home to Africa. Fisher contends that the chariot might have been a synonym for a lift lowered from the deck of the ship to the passenger at water's edge, and the band of angels coming to carry the singer was probably a metaphor for the ship's crew. Once again, the double entendre is very creative:

> *Chorus*:
> Swing low, sweet chariot,
> Comin' for to carry me home,
> Swing low, sweet chariot,
> Comin' for to carry me home.
>
> I looked over Jordan, an' what did I see,
> Comin' for to carry me home,
> A band of angels comin' after me,
> Comin' for to carry me home.
>
> If you get-a dere befo' I do,
> Comin' for to carry me home,
> Tell all my friends I'm comin' too,
> Comin' for to carry me home.

Certainly, one of the most beloved of all the thousands of "Negro spirituals" is "Steal Away."

> Steal away, steal away,
> Steal away to Jesus.
> Steal away, steal away home,
> I hain't got long to stay here.
>
> My Lord, He calls me,
> He calls me by the thunder,
> The trumpet sounds within-a my soul,
> I hain't got long to stay here.
>
> Green trees a-bending,
> Po' sinner stands a-trembling,
> The trumpet sounds within-a my soul,
> I hain't got long to stay here.

Fisher argues most persuasively that Nat Turner was the author of this song. Such a claim is an invariable shock to all who hear it for the first time, for two reasons: (a) Nat Turner led the largest of all slave revolts in the United States; (b) in the twentieth century, "Steal Away" has become one of America's favorite spirituals learned and sung by countless numbers of children at summer camps and elsewhere. Not infrequently that spiritual has been sung as a finale by such prominent African American classical singers as Paul Robeson, Marian Anderson, Leontyne Price, and Jessye Norman, to mention only a few.

Clearly the numerous African American spirituals expressed the painful living experiences of human bondage. Contrary to the misunderstandings of many, they were not fleeting forays into otherworldly escapism. Rather, they were communal forms of communication, transcendence, and empowerment that nurtured and made possible the integration of aesthetics, musical composition, literary creativity, folk art, spiritual hope, moral virtues, sociopolitical protest, theological understanding, and the full range of human expression, with reason and emotion always united.

In brief, African slaves expressed their basic values more clearly in the spirituals than anywhere else. Thus, their endurance should not be surprising. While other types of slave songs also depicted African forms of transcendence over adversity, the spirituals revealed their trust in God as the primary source of their empowerment. In those songs they sang about their faith in a God who they unquestionably believed was concerned about their well-being; hence, they were confident that God would protect them from the evil of slavery and eventually enable them to gain their freedom. Accordingly, they believed and sang confidently, "Gawd will take care ob me. /Walkin t'ru many ob dangers, Gawd will take care ob me."[19]

Beyond Song and Music

Since freedom of speech was disallowed during slavery, and since African singing was pleasing to the ears of most slaveholders, their songs became the principal medium for expressing their deepest feelings, hopes, and strivings. But they also prayed and preached and rendered testimonies to one another in similar rhythmic styles that have endured up to the present day. In fact their style marks this uniqueness. Few books of prayers in our day contain more imaginative uses of the vernacular, whereby the ordinary things of everyday life are transformed into sacred meanings. Note the following:

Almighty! And all wise God our heavenly Father! 'tis once more and again that a few of your beloved children are gathered together to call upon your holy name. We bow at your foot-stool, Master, to thank you for our spared lives. We thank you that we were able to get up this morning clothed in our right mind. For Master, since we met here, many have been snatched out of the land of living and hurled into eternity. But through your goodness and mercy we have been spared to assemble ourselves here once more to call upon a Captain who has never lost a battle. Oh, throw round us your strong arms of protection. Bind us together in love and union. Build us up where we are torn down and strengthen us where we are weak. Oh, Lord! Oh, Lord! Take the lead of our minds, place them on heaven and heavenly divine things. Oh, God, our Captain and King! Search our hearts and if you find anything there contrary to your divine will just move it from us Master, as far as the east is from the west. Now Lord, you know our hearts, you know our heart's desire. You know our down-setting and you know our up-rising. Lord you know all about us because you made us. Lord! Lord! One more kind favor I ask of you. Remember the man that is to stand in the gateway and proclaim your Holy Word. Oh, stand by him. Strengthen him where he is weak and build him up where he is torn down. Oh, let him down into the deep treasures of your word.
And now, Oh, Lord; when this your humble servant is done down here in this low land of sorrow; done sitting down and getting up; done being called everything but a child of God; oh, when I am done, done, done, and this old world can afford me a home no longer, right soon in

the morning, Lord, right soon in the morning, meet me down at the River of Jordan, bid the waters to be still, tuck my little soul away in that snow-white chariot, and bear it away over yonder in the third heaven where every day will be a Sunday and my sorrows of this old world will have an end, is my prayer for Christ my redeemer's sake and amen and thank God.[20]

No one can attend traditional African American worship services in our day and not observe the structure and hear most of the phrases of the above prayer often intoned in cadences very similar to those uttered by countless generations of church leaders, both lay and clergy. Both the structure and content of the following traditional prayer is similar to the one above. It was reported by the renowned African American anthropologist Zora Neale Hurston in her collection of folklore.

> You have been with me from the earliest rocking of my cradle
>   up until this present moment.
> You know our hearts, our Father,
> And all de range of our deceitful minds,
> And if you find anything like sin lurking
> In and around our hearts,
> Ah ast you, My Father, and my Wonder-workin' God
> To pluck it out
> And cast it into de sea of Fuhgitfulness
> Where it will never rise to harm us in dis world
> Nor condemn us in de judgment.
> You heard me when Ah laid at hell's dark door
> With no weapon in my hand
> And no God in my heart,
> And cried for three long days and nights.
> You heard me, Lawd,
> And stooped so low
> And snatched me from the hell
> Of eternal death and damnation.
> You cut loose my stammerin' tongue;
> You established my feet on de rock of salvation
> And yo' voice was heard in rumblin' judgment.
> I thank Thee that my last night's sleepin' couch
> Was not my coolin' board
> And my cover
> Was not my windin' sheet.
> Speak to de sinner-man and bless' im.
> Touch all those

Who have been down to de doors of degradation.
Ketch de man dat's layin' in danger of consumin' fire;
And Lawd,
When Ah kin pray no mo';
When Ah done drunk down de last cup of sorrow
Look on me, yo' weak servant who feels de least of all;
'Point my soul a restin' place
Where Ah kin set down and praise yo' name forever
Is my prayer for Jesus sake
Amen and thank God.[21]

Like most of the folk traditions of African Americans, not only were the prayers and songs passed on from one generation to the next, but their sermons were also preached over and over again. In fact, in various places, preachers would often preach their so-called "successful" sermons annually and countless people flocked to hear them year after year. The historian and poet James Weldon Johnson speaks about sermons he heard in his boyhood that were passed on with very slight modification from preacher to preacher and from locality to locality.

Such sermons were "The Valley of Dry Bones," which was based on the vision of the prophet in the thirty-seventh chapter of Ezekiel; the "Train Sermon," in which both God and the devil were pictured as running trains, one loaded with saints, which pulled up in heaven, and the other with sinners, which dumped its load in hell; the "Heavenly March," which gave in detail the journey of the faithful from earth, on up through the pearly gates to the great white throne. Then there was a stereotyped sermon which had no definite subject, and which was quite generally preached: it began with the creation, went on to the fall of humanity, rambled through the trials and tribulations of the Hebrew children, came down to the redemption of Christ, and ended with the judgment day and a warning and an exhortation to sinners. Thousands of people, white and black, flocked to the church of John Jasper in Richmond, Virginia, to hear him preach his famous sermon proving that the earth is flat and the sun does move. John Jasper's sermon was imitated and adapted by many lesser preachers.[22]

Though not written in traditional African American dialect, yet true to the form and content of African American preaching, James Weldon Johnson provided a compelling depiction of that phenomenon in his classic book, *God's Trombones: Seven Negro Sermons in Verse.* No other rendition of African American preaching has captured more poignantly the rhythm, beauty, movement, imaginative license, and lyrical prose than Johnson's *Trombones.* That small collection of poems, dramatized by countless professional and amateur performers, invariably captivates the hearts of African American audiences who are easily transported back in their memories to those local contexts where they once heard similar performances on a weekly basis. In fact, most African Americans are amazed by the evocative power this art form continues to have for them. Undoubtedly, its enduring significance is due in large part to its paradigmatic function in assessing African American rhetorical excellence, the marks of which are clearly discernible in the speeches and sermons of its greatest exemplars, some of the most notable of whom are Martin Luther King, Jr., Kelly Miller Smith, Sr., Joseph H. Jackson, William Holmes Borders, Samuel DeWitt Procter, Susan Johnson Cooke, Jesse Jackson, Gardner C. Taylor, James Forbes, Prathia Hall, Jeremiah Wright, and Charles Adams, to mention only a few. A further mark all these rhetoricians have in common is their extraordinary grasp of the biblical source material and their capacity to synthesize its authority with their own imaginative powers, with the final result being the persuasive communication of the gospel in the vernacular.

Johnson's *Trombones* also sets forth the clearest possible portrayal of the similarity between preaching and praying in the black church tradition. Both exhibit a distinct, rhythmic cadence, coupled with metaphorical imagery drawn from everyday experiences mingled with biblical insights. The aim of both is to bring comfort to the sorrowful, uplift to the weary, encouragement to the disappointed, faith to the despairing, courage to the weak, repentance to self-destructive sinners who either ignore or betray God's way of life. In addition to this pastoral mission, both praying and preaching have a prophetic aim, namely, to condemn every form of racism, both in thought and in practice. Often this is done implicitly, if not explicitly. In either case, African liturgical practices have often been the means by which the Christian gospel has been liberated from the controlling clutches of racism. In their own tongues, African American preachers and laypersons have been the bearers of a renewed faith: a faith that has been their only source of hope and courage, love and justice, freedom and equality. As a consequence, that faith which they had received from their conquerors, and which they reformed by the miracle of God's grace, has constituted the grounds for all their pastoral and prophetic utterances. From the latter, we have inherited one basic truth, namely, that Christian theology and Christian ethics imply each other: that the truth of God implies the good of all human beings and the whole of creation; that the Word of God continuously undergoes linguistic translation into the words of the people.

NOTES

1. See Lamin Sanneh, *Translating the Message: The Missionary Impact on Culture* (Maryknoll, NY: Orbis Books, 1996).
2. Lamin Sanneh, *The Jakhanke: The History of an Islamic Clerical People of the Senegambia* (London: International African Institute, 1979), 19.
3. Ibid., 19.
4. See Peter J. Paris, *The Spirituality of African Peoples: The Search for a Common Moral Discourse* (Minneapolis: Fortress Press, 1995).
5. Howard Thurman, *Deep River: Reflections on the Religious Insights of Certain of the Negro Spirituals* (New York: Harper & Brothers, 1955), 43–44.
6. James H. Cone, *The Spirituals and the Blues* (New York: Seabury Press, 1972), 95.
7. Ibid.
8. Lawrence W. Levine, *Black Culture and Black Consciousness: Afro-American Folk Thought from Slavery to Freedom* (Oxford University Press, 1977), 33.
9. Ibid., 40–41.
10. Ibid., 44.
11. James Weldon Johnson and J. Rosamond Johnson, *The Books of American Negro Spirituals* (New York: A Da Capo Press, 1989), chap. 3.
12. For an excellent analysis of the ubiquity of death in the everyday experience of African American slaves, see Margaret Washington Creel, *A Peculiar People: Slave Religion and Community Culture among the Gullahs* (New York: New York University Press, 1988), 308ff.
13. Miles Mark Fisher, *Negro Slave Songs in the United States* (New York: Citadel Press, 1963), 26.
14. Ibid., 29.
15. Ibid., 54.
16. Ibid., 60.
17. Ibid., 61.
18. Ibid., 121.
19. Creel, *A Peculiar Book*, 352.
20. Langston Hughes and Arna Bontemps, eds., *Book of Negro Folklore* (New York: Dodd, Mead & Co., 1958), 256–57. The editors, Hughes and Bontemps, stated that this prayer was offered by a deacon during a camp meeting held in South Nashville, Tennessee, in the summer of 1928. It was reproduced as accurately as possible from the notes taken during the occasion.
21. In Zora Neale Hurston, *Mules and Men* (New York: Harper & Row, 1990), 25–26.
22. James Weldon Johnson, *God's Trombones: Seven Negro Sermons in Verse* (New York: Viking Press, 1927), 1–2.

Chapter 7

Worship on the Edge

Liminality and the Korean American Context

SANG HYUN LEE

*W*hen I worship at Korean American churches, I often find myself having two strong feelings that appear to be at odds with each other. On the one hand, I feel at home. Everyone is Korean, and I don't stick out. We sing familiar hymns in Korean that I used to sing as a young boy back at home. I don't have to wonder what anybody may think about the presence of an Asian person in their midst. I am not a stranger anymore, but "one of us" for a change.

At the same time, I sense an uneasiness in me. I notice that everything about the worship experience is so traditionally Korean. Not in the prayers, sermons, or anywhere else do I find any aspect of Korean immigrants' actual life in America significantly reflected or addressed. Invariably pastoral prayers will mention the president and other leaders of the Republic of Korea, but one waits in vain for any intercession for Bill Clinton, who is the president of the country of which most of these congregants are now citizens and where their children are now growing up. I feel uneasy about this hyper-Korean atmosphere at Korean American worship services because I worry that such worship might be functioning, at least in part, as an hour of escape from reality rather than as a time of being empowered to face up to that reality.

Korean Americans, whether of the first generation or of later generations, live very much in an in-between world—straddling socio-cultural worlds of both Korea and America. They are not in Korea anymore, nor do they feel that they really belong to mainstream America. They are in between these two worlds and, therefore, existing on the edges of both. They live in ambivalence, and often find that their self-identity has become ambiguous. Yet where in Korean worship services is this ambivalence of their in-between existence reflected or addressed? On the other hand, why should Korean American worship services pay any attention to their in-betweenness at all?

In this chapter I want to address these questions and related issues that are often discussed by Korean American Christians: To what extent is it desirable that Korean American worship services try to celebrate the Korean cultural heritage, as some believe that they should? What are the first-generation Korean American churches to think of the emergence of independent second-generation churches? How can Korean and Caucasian American joint services be more meaningful for the participants than they usually appear to be? In other words, what is the essential requirement for "successful" cross- and multicultural worship?

Before addressing these questions, however, the more fundamental matter of "in-betweenness" and how it can and does function in Korean American communities must be addressed. For some time I have been intrigued by the fact that Korean Americans' experience of in-betweenness and being on the edge in American society has something in common with the in-between experience that some scholars believe is an essential dimension of worship. Worship, these scholars suggest, is a ritual process that can be truly communal and transforming only when the participants are led to experience a structural ambiguity or openness by being liberated for a moment from social roles, status, and hierarchy.[1]

The way in-betweenness links worship and the Asian American experience is what I want to pursue in this chapter. My hunch is that worship, as conceived by the theory I just mentioned, can be a sacred time when Korean Americans can safely experience and address their in-between predicament. This exploration should also have some implications for how worship and in-between experiences are related for people of any and all races and backgrounds.

I will first discuss the Korean Americans' experience of in-betweenness and their usual responses to it and then outline the theory of worship as an "in-between" ritual process. I will conclude by drawing out implications for some of the issues in Korean American and cross- or multicultural worship.

The Korean American Context: Marginality as Coerced Liminality

Korean Americans' experience of in-betweenness does not exist in isolation, but rather in the context of the racist realities of American society.

Korean Americans, like other nonwhite peoples, are not just "in-between," but are coerced to remain there by the barriers (nowadays quite subtle but real as ever) erected by certain social structures and attitudes of the dominant center in U.S. culture. So the in-betweenness of Korean Americans is a coerced in-betweenness. To refer to this twin situation of nonwhite persons being in between and being coerced to remain there, the literature in social sciences has used the concept of "marginality" or "marginalization."[2] The marginality of Korean Americans is, in other words, a predicament of "coerced in-betweenness" or "being coerced to remain on the edge."

Yet "in-betweenness," as anthropologist Victor Turner argues, can also be a creative state in which there is great potential for transformative change. In his well-known studies of change processes,[3] Turner says that all social and individual changes involve three stages: separation, liminality, and aggregation. A change involves leaving something or someplace behind, being in transition or "in between," and then finally, arriving at or achieving a new state of affairs. The middle, in-between or "liminal" (from the Latin word *limen* meaning "threshold") stage, is usually an ambivalent time, but this stage, according to Turner, is what makes all creative change possible. Turner emphasizes the antistructural nature of liminality. That is, in liminality one has left behind the "culturally defined encumbrances of role, status, reputation, class, caste, sex or other structural niche." Liminality is "structural ambiguity" in which the usual hierarchy and status in society are momentarily suspended. In liminality, persons are freed up temporarily from all that binds them in society. [4]

It is liminality that also engenders a genuine sense of community among persons. *Communitas*, to use Turner's term for community, is the egalitarian relationship among persons in which people "confront one another not as role players but as 'human totals,' integral beings who recognizantly share the same humanity."[5] Released for a moment from social structure, persons in liminality can relate to each other simply and fully as human beings and experience an intense quality of human communion usually impossible in structured society.

It is in such moments of liminal communitas, Turner points out, that persons can be free enough to reflect on their lives or society, envision new ideas and ways of doing things, and dream new dreams. Powerful rituals latent with ultimate meanings, new or old insights, and alternative ways of interpreting reality can have their powerful impact on persons in liminal communitas.[6]

Korean Americans can be thought of as liminal persons. Their reference groups (the peoples they consider they are a part of) are inevitably double: Korean and American. They often find themselves feeling ambivalent.[7] But Turner's work suggests that this ambivalence also has a liminal character and can therefore be profoundly creative—that is, conducive to communitas and transformation. But is this actually the case for Korean Americans?

My own observation is that Korean Americans' liminality usually does not lead to creative consequences. For one thing, their human predilection to avoid open-endedness and ambiguity makes them reluctant to face up to their liminality. The "traditionalist" Korean Americans (usually the first generation) try to avoid an explicit awareness of liminality by clinging unrealistically to their Korean past. They are often more "Korean" in their outlook and action than Koreans in Korea, because the Korea they left years ago has not stood still but has been rapidly changing. The "assimilationists" (often some of the second- or later-generation persons), on the other hand, may try to forget their Korean side and believe that they are "white." These are extreme tendencies, which may be found in varying degrees in individual instances.[8]

The escapism one finds in Korean Americans is, however, not merely due to their very human tendency to avoid ambiguity. As mentioned earlier, Korean Americans' liminality is not temporary, as it would be in the case of white European immigrants, but is made seemingly permanent by the hegemony of the dominant center. To be liminal, for Korean Americans as well as for other nonwhite groups, is a dehumanizing and oppressive experience. Thus there is increased reason for Korean Americans to try to run away from liminal awareness. In their escapist tendencies, Korean Americans are just as much victims as they are actors.

Worship as Liminality

It is in light of these realities that the question arises: What can and should be the nature and meaning of Christian worship, given the context of Korean Americans? In order to deal with this question, I want to first ask what it is that happens at worship. Here again we run into the ideas of liminality and communitas. Building on Victor Turner's writings, scholars in recent years have developed the concept that worship itself is a transforming ritual involving liminality and communitas.[9]

According to Turner's theory, worship is a time of liminality—that is, an experience of being freed up from social structures (such as hierarchy, status, and role-playing) and placed in an in-between state. Liminality is "antistructure" in the sense that the usual social conventions are momentarily suspended. And worship as a liminal experience is a "time out of time," when what does not ordinarily happen in society has the potential to happen. Liminality can also evoke communitas—a "communion of equal individuals."[10] And it is in this liminal communitas that the ritual acts of worship can have profound impact on the worshipers.

The worshipers' experience of liminal communitas functions as the "containment," to borrow Robert L. Moore's term,[11] in which they feel safe to bring to the surface their hidden anxieties and fears, examine the meaning of their individual and social existence, and envision new ways of thinking and living. Liminal communitas, according to Turner, is society's "subjunctive mood, where suppositions, desires, hypotheses, possibilities, and so forth all become legitimate."[12] In liminal communitas, the worshipers are free and open to consider alternative ways of social order. The worshipers can experience a profound transformation, and, as J. Randall Nichols puts it, are "able to carry the fruits of that transformation back into the world of structure, perchance to work toward its reformation."[13] In short, when worship is an experience of liminal communitas, ritual acts and words can change individual lives as well as the world in which worshipers lead their daily lives.

Implications for Worship in the Korean American Context

When we connect together the above notions of the Korean American context and the liminal nature of Christian worship, what can we say about some of the issues surrounding Korean American worship?

The first issue has to do with the relation between worship and Korean Americans' existential predicament. The link between them is liminality. This means, for one thing, that Korean American Christians bring to worship their daily experiences of liminality and, therefore, can be, at least in principle more receptive and open to the liminality of worship itself. But, as we saw earlier, Korean American Christians have a difficult time facing up to their liminal predicament. They bring to worship suppressed liminality.

It is at this juncture, however, that the power of the worship ritual itself to engender liminality plays its crucial role. In the liminal communitas that is evoked by the worship ritual, in other words, Korean Americans can feel safe enough to become explicitly aware of their existential liminality and to address it by reflecting on alternative responses to it that are more meaningful than their usual escapist strategies. The biblical accounts of the wilderness and its meaning in the lives of Abraham, Moses, Ruth, Esther, and Jesus himself can help evoke in Korean American worshipers' minds their own wilderness of liminality and alternative ways of understanding its meaning. The ways God used liminal and marginalized persons for God's own purposes, especially God's becoming incarnate as Jesus the Galilean, can lead Korean American worshipers to new insights about the purposefulness of their own life as strangers "on the edge."

In short, what Korean American Christians often try to avoid in worship (namely, an awareness of liminality) is precisely what is needed in worship. The note of grace even in this anthropological discussion of worship is that Christian worship can both enable Korean American worshipers to become aware of their own existential situation and help them see the meaning in it.

2   The second issue has to do with the demand in Korean American churches for a greater presence in worship of Korean cultural values and practices. This demand is made for a variety of reasons. Some are deeply concerned that the younger generations are so thoroughly Americanized that they may completely lose any sense of self-identity as Koreans. Others point out that Koreans in the United States are marginalized by the dominant group for their Koreanness and that therefore the churches must affirm precisely the dignity of their Koreanness. Still others maintain that Christian faith in a God who became incarnate into a particular culture and society calls for the enculturation or indigenization of the gospel and of Christian worship. We must overcome, it is argued, the over-Westernization of Christian worship and introduce into it Korean cultural forms and expressions.[14]

For all these reasons, many Korean American churches have Korean language schools, to teach their youth the Korean language. A small number of churches use rice cakes—rather than bread—in their Communion services. Korean holidays, such as *chu-suk* (the harvest festival in the fall) and the lunar New Year, are celebrated as part of the life of the church. There is also a growing use of hymns and anthems written and composed by Koreans.

From the perspective of the interpretative frameworks we are considering in this essay, there is both merit and danger in this cultural mandate. Korean Americans are, on the one hand, indeed marginalized for their Koreanness, and thus the Christian affirmation of them as human beings with dignity would have to involve a positive lifting up of their Korean heritage in the life of the church, including worship. However, Korean culture also involves a strong emphasis on social and economic hierarchy, occupational and other kinds of status, and patriarchy. In the name of preserving Koreanness, these cultural structures are brought into the worship of many (but certainly not all) Korean American churches. Yet hierarchy, status, and role-playing are precisely what have to be left behind if worship is to be an experience of Christian liminal communitas.

For example, during the Eucharist—potentially the most liminal communitas–generating ritual in Christian worship—many Korean American churches allow only the elders (usually only male) with white gloves to have the privilege of serving the elements to the seated members of the congregation. Only the elders handle the white sheet covering the eucharistic elements. Elders and the minister serve one another as other members passively watch. In this way, even the Eucharist may end up reinforcing the dehumanizing aspects of Korean culture, instead of evoking life-changing liminality and egalitarian communitas.

Certainly I am not arguing against the existence of elders and other offices in the church. I am saying, rather, that elders and other officers are often deployed in worship services in such a way that their hierarchical superiority and status achievement of an ecclesiastical sort are paraded and reinforced. In this regard, the practice of having some members of the congregation hold the elements at the front of the sanctuary with all others coming up in single files to take the elements themselves might have a considerable merit. Forming a circle around the Communion table (or circles around tables for larger congregations) also may be conducive to liminality and communitas.[15]

Turner makes a distinction between ritual and ceremony. Christian worship with liminality and communitas can be a transforming ritual that motivates participants to try to reform the existing social order. But worship that is not freed from social status and hierarchy can degenerate into mere ceremony that only reinforces the existing culture and social structure.[16] In short, Korean American churches do need to affirm their Korean heritage, for all the reasons mentioned earlier. However, Korean culture (or any culture, for that matter) should not be affirmed in such a way that all the existing elements in that culture are unthinkingly reinforced.

The third issue about worship much talked about in Korean American churches has to do with the differences between the worship styles of the first and second generations. First-generation Korean American churches have become acutely aware of the ministry needs of their highly Americanized English-speaking second generation. Many Korean American churches have instituted English-speaking worship services to occur alongside the first-generation worship in Korean. Some second-generation Korean Americans have organized their own English-speaking congregations completely independent from first-generation churches.

This latter development (which some have called "the silent exodus") worries many first-generation Korean Americans, for two reasons. The worship style of those independent Korean American churches (with their use of gospel songs rather than hymns from the hymnal, for example) appears too "informal" and not "proper" in the eyes of the first-generation. And some first-generation churches feel that their youth's independence is a "betrayal" of their ethnic loyalties and cultural heritage.[17]

This is indeed a complex issue, with many angles to it. Here we simply ask what light our conceptions of worship and of the Korean American context might shed on the matter. The second generation often do not find the English services at their parents' churches satisfying, and one of the reasons for this could be that those services are not effective in evoking liminality and communitas for the second generation. When English services are held as a part of the first-generation churches' programs, English is spoken, but the order, music, and all other aspects of worship are usually exact copies of first-generation worship. It is possible that the traditionally Korean worship style of the first generation is not conducive to liminality and communitas for the second generation.

The second-generation Korean American Christians typically spend a lot of time before and during worship singing gospel songs. If these songs engender liminality and communitas for the second generation, then these songs should be used, assuming that they have no theological problems in content. The order of worship, the way things are said, and the body language—especially of the worship leaders—can all be factors that may or may not evoke a sacred and transforming experience for the second generation of Korean Americans, just as for the first.

So the second-generation Korean Americans' desire to have their own kind of worship and even to establish their own independent congregations does not have to be viewed as a betrayal either of their ethnic and family loyalties or of the proper way that Christians should do things—again assuming that the acts and words in their worship ritual are fundamentally Christian in content. The indispensable need for liminality and communitas in worship constitutes at least one legitimate reason for the second generation's own churches and ministry.

4   The fourth and final issue has to do with multi- or cross-cultural worship. Korean American congregations, especially those that share facili-
ties with white American congregations, are occasionally invited by their
host churches to a joint worship service. Such invitations are usually
taken as a friendly gesture by Korean American church people. But
according to my limited experience, Korean Americans' attendance at
such white American host churches' worship is usually very poor, and I
have rarely heard Korean American church members speak of their cross-
cultural worship experiences as moving or in any way memorable.

Why are such very well intended cross-cultural worship services so
often found wanting? Of course, there is the language barrier problem and
some cultural gaps as well, as everyone says. I suspect, however, that the
problem goes deeper. Our conception of worship as liminality would
imply that if truly cross- or multicultural worship is to occur, the people
of both cultural backgrounds should be led by their joint worship to an
experience of being freed up from their own cultural structures as well as
from their status in the society as a whole. White American church members and Korean Americans must be thrown into a wilderness together if
a sense of communitas is to occur. Multi- or cross-cultural worship, in
other words, requires leaving home, a pilgrimage.

But the dynamics of Asian Americans' marginalization by the white
dominant center would require something more. White Americans and
Korean Americans occupy quite different social and cultural status in
American society, with white Americans occupying a higher rung in the
hierarchy than Korean Americans. Sociologically and culturally, white
Americans are at the center while Korean Americans are marginal and
peripheral. If this is the case, then white Americans would have to give up
more, be freed up more, than Korean Americans if they are to experience
genuine liminality and communitas. Turner, as far as I know, does not
speak about this kind of issue. His theory would seem to imply, however,
that the culturally and socially privileged would have more status to leave
behind than the culturally and socially disfranchised.

To be more concrete, if Korean Americans and white Americans are to
have joint worship, it may be better if white Americans leave their comfortable and beautiful sanctuaries and "come down," so to speak, to where
their Korean American counterparts meet for worship. Whether the worship is in English or Korean, the leadership in the service could consist of
more Korean Americans than white Americans. Instead of having the
Korean American church be represented only by their choir (as is often
the case), the sermon could be preached by the Korean American pastor,

even if he or she has to be simultaneously translated into English. In other words, if liminality or the state of being freed up from status and hierarchy is going to happen for Korean Americans and white Americans gathered together for worship, white Americans have in fact more status to give up and must give up more. To put the matter in more general terms, I am saying that when we discuss multicultural worship or any other kind of multiculturalism, we must keep in mind the different social positions that white Americans and minority peoples hold in the United States.

I once witnessed an extreme case of a lone white American person participating in Communion service at a national meeting of Korean American pastors and their spouses. Here was a top white American leader of the Presbyterian Church (U.S.A.) at an all-Korean Presbyterian gathering. Let us call him Dr. Smith. I noticed that at the beginning of the meeting, Dr. Smith appeared understandably quite isolated as he awkwardly walked by groups of Koreans talking to each other in Korean. Few seemed to know who this white person was, and he seemed somewhat at a loss as to how to act in this kind of situation.

At the opening worship of the conference there was a Communion service, and I noticed Dr. Smith receiving the elements of the Eucharist sitting with about five hundred Korean clergy and their spouses. There he was, a white American of a high status all by himself partaking in the Lord's Supper with Korean Americans. I know that he did not understand a single Korean word throughout the service. But he was probably a man of sufficient grace not to take offense at this situation. He probably was also sensitive enough to know that all these Koreans who at this worship service made up the majority had suffered much alienation in American society. At the same time, he must have known the tunes of the hymns sung in Korean and also the meaning of much of what was going on. Though in Korean, the worship still was for him a Christian ritual. This was nevertheless a highly unusual situation for a white Anglo person. For about an hour, much of Dr. Smith's social, cultural, and ecclesiastical status was in suspension. He was in communion with five hundred Korean American persons who were now equal with him in Christ. And in and through this liminal communitas, the symbols of the Eucharist could exercise their efficacious power.

After the Communion service, I accidentally passed by Dr. Smith talking enthusiastically with several Korean American pastors. I could not hear exactly what he was talking to them about. But I did not have to hear what he was saying to know that his demeanor had completely changed. He did not appear awkward interacting with Korean Americans. He was at ease with himself and with his Korean American fellow pastors. They were no longer strangers to one another. Perhaps this experience also made Dr. Smith want, more than ever, to make a change in the existing social order.

But such an act of letting oneself be freed even for a few minutes from status and role-playing is difficult for any group of human beings. The nonwhite minority persons are under heavy pressure to keep their liminal experiences suppressed inside them. This suppressed liminal energy manifests itself through an unrealistic clinging to the comfort zones of ethnic enclaves or an excessive desire to assimilate to white America. Turner himself noted that when a socially marginalized group experiences communitas with the people of the group's social or ethnic category, its members can easily turn inward with an exclusive attachment to their own kind of people, and thus paradoxically go against the "drive to inclusivity" inherent in communitas.[18]

What I have discussed in this chapter, however, makes one thing clear: Liminality and communitas are among the important ordinary means of grace that the sovereign God uses to redeem the fallen creation.

NOTES

1. See notes 9–14 below.
2. H. F. Dickie-Clark, *The Marginal Situation: A Sociological Study of a Coloured Group* (London: Routledge & Kegan Paul, 1966); Won Moo Hurh and Kwang Chung Kim, *Korean Immigrants in America: A Structural Analysis of Ethnic Confinement and Adhesive Adaptation* (Rutherford, N.J.: Fairleigh Dickinson University Press, 1984); Sang Hyun Lee, "Pilgrimage and Home in the Wilderness of Marginality: Symbols and Context in Asian American Theology," *The Princeton Seminary Bulletin*, n.s., 16, no. 1 (1995): 49–64.
3. Victor Turner, *Ritual Process: Structure and Anti-Structure* (New York: Aldine Publishing Co., 1969).
4. Victor Turner, *From Ritual to Theatre: The Seriousness of Human Play* (New York: Performance Art Journal Publications, 1982), 48.
5. Victor Turner, *Dramas, Fields, and Metaphors: Symbolic Action in Human Society* (Ithaca, N.Y.: Cornell University Press, 1974), 269.
6. See Tom Driver, *The Magic of Ritual: Our Need for Liberating Rites That Transform Our Lives and Our Communities* (San Francisco: Harper San Francisco, 1991), 152ff.
7. Hurh and Kim, *Korean Immigrants in America*, 73–169.
8. Everett V. Stonequist, *The Marginal Man: A Study in Personality and Culture Conflict* (New York: Russell & Russell, 1937).
9. J. Randall Nichols, "Worship as Anti-Structure: The Contribution of Victor Turner," *Theology Today* 41, no. 4 (1987): 401–9. (I want to express my indebtedness to my colleague Randall Nichols for a helpful conversation on Victor Turner and worship.)

See also Victor Turner, "Passages, Margins, and Poverty: Religious Symbols of Communitas," *Worship* 46 (1972): 390–412, 482–94; Timothy L. Carson, *Liminal Reality and Transformational Power* (New York: University Press of America, 1997); Bobby C. Alexander, *Victor Turner Revisited: Ritual as Social Change* (Atlanta, Ga.: Scholars Press, 1991).

10. Turner, *Ritual Process*, 174.

11. Robert L. Moore, "Ministry, Sacred Space, and Theological Education: The Legacy of Victor Turner," *The Chicago Theological Seminary Register* 75, no.3 (1985): 1–10.

12. Turner, *Ritual Process*, vii.

13. Nichols, "Worship as Anti-Structure," 405.

14. Greer Anne Wenh-in Ng, "The Asian North American Community at Worship: Issues of Indigenization and Contextualization," in *People on the Way: Asian North Americans Discovering Christ, Culture, and Community*, ed. David Ng (Valley Forge, Pa.: Judson Press,1996), 147–75. For a description of worship in the Korean tradition, see Paul Junggap Huh, "The Making of a Book of Cross-Cultural Worship: Resources for Korean-American Churches" (Ph.D. diss., Drew University, 1999).

15. Similar suggestions are made by Driver, *The Magic of Ritual*, 195.

16. Turner, *Ritual Process*, 174.

17. For a good discussion of the issues facing ministry with the Korean American second generation, see Sukhwan Oh, *The Ministry of 2nd Generation in 21st Century: Korean Americans, Arise and Take the Land!* (Bellflower, Calif.: Christian Han-Mi Association, 1999).

18. Turner, *From Ritual to Theatre*, 51.

Chapter 8

Polyrhythm in Worship

Caribbean Keys to an Effective Word of God

MARK TAYLOR

> Only rhythm gives the word its effective fullness; it is the
> word of God, that is, the rhythmic word, that created the
> world.[1]
>
> *Léopold Sédar Senghor*

With these words, the African statesman, poet, and philosopher
Léopold Senghor (b. 1906), prompts theological reflection: What is
the Word of God in its "effective fullness?" Is the Word of God having grandeur and extent a "fullness"? How can it be at work, pow-
erfully, in the world as "effective"?

Senghor points us toward "the rhythmic word" as a response to
such questions. Similarly, I argue here that Christians at worship, in
theory and practice, need to embrace rhythm (especially
polyrhythm) in order to know and live their Word of God in Jesus
Christ in *its* effective fullness. Christians in worship will be helped
in this if they embrace a particular mode of worship, one that is
informed by Caribbean cultures and peoples in diaspora, who know
that polyrhythmic practice is a source not just of entertainment, but
of life itself, of life thriving under some of the worst powers of colo-
nialization and repression.

Making this argument will require three moves that define
the three sections of this chapter. First, I highlight the relationship of worship with an understanding of the church in its always-
dialectical engagement with the world. Second, it is important
to understand "worship" in a broad sense, as the interaction of
four spheres of meaningful practice in one "matrix of adoration."
This prepares us to see, third, the importance of the Word as related
not only to "Spirit," but to Spirit as alive in the kind of communal

performance and polyrhythmic celebration practiced in many Caribbean settings.

Worship and the World-engaging Church

Worship shares in one of the most fundamental tensions of Christian ecclesial existence. This tension is the experience of the church's having boundaries and identity, but always shifting, always being redefined. This is a function of the church's opening itself to others, to new peoples, to new ways. This is properly called a *dialectical* relation, because interacting with the world is not a simple two-step process: first build identity, then reach out. No, instead, the having of identity and the reaching out are more intricately involved than that. The very "centering" process of church life consists in the way it embraces and navigates its shifting boundaries and identities in the world.

In a sense all organizations and communities that undergo growth experience this kind of dialectic. In Christian communities, though, this dialectic is rooted in the witness of Jesus Christ, a figure whose presence was marked by a radically inclusive love for others. I use the qualifier "radically" to mean inclusive love that gives strategic priority to subordinated peoples. Radically inclusive love is another way of speaking of God's "nonexclusive, preferential option"[2] for subordinated peoples.

"Subordinated peoples" are those whose otherness is taken in such a way as to produce discriminatory practices that treat them as less than human or as nonhuman, and hence subject to repression. This repression may be evident in occasional, blatant actions ("hate crimes") or in routinized, institutionalized patterns of oppression. Women, diverse communities of color, the poor, the disabled, the sexually different, the aged have all been subject to such suffering.

Jesus, whom we worship as the Christ, as God incarnate in history, is one who catalyzed gatherings of rejected others. A Christian community that lives most fully into the distinctive way of its Christ, then, into the radically inclusive love exhibited and embodied by Jesus, will be one whose communal life (its very identity and boundaries) is always undergoing a kind of communal death (the shifting and redefining).

Indeed, Jesus' own witness, his practice of radically inclusive love, so angered and violated repressive religious and political powers that his practice took him to death. The church may celebrate a risen Lord, but it is the life of one who died *this* way, amid the practice of a love that engages, and enrages, the powers of the day.

Worshiping peoples who forget their connection to an ecclesial practice of living and dying for others, for those who need justice and love, are subject to frequent critique in the scriptures. There is the famous rebuke of Amos: "I take no delight in your solemn assemblies" (Amos 5:21). Jesus reinforced this prophetic critique of pious worship: "But woe to you Pharisees! For you tithe mint and rue and every herb, and neglect justice and the love of God (Luke 11:42, RSV). These texts, and many more, are examples of a long line of biblical critique excoriating worship that retreats from moral action into ritual correctness.

Worship and the Matrix of Adoration

A "worship service" on a given Sunday, then, needs to be seen theologically as a world-engaging act.

I will here use the term "adoration" to break the hold on our minds of the term worship, which often is limited to performances occurring in collective church gatherings. The broader set of significations for the term adoration was eloquently elaborated in the liturgical theology of Russian Orthodox theologian Alexander Schmemann. His well-known phrase *homo adorans* ("human as adorer [of God]") reminds us that worship is intrinsic to our full humanity, and is part of the many spheres of living.[3]

Four spheres of meaningful action are crucial to recall in the matrix of adoration. None of these is reducible to another one, but all overlap and intersect with one another in worship of the God of Jesus Christ (see figure). Where the spheres unite is the vibrant heart of Christian *homo adorans* in the world.

I have selected each of these four spheres of meaningful action because it (1) is mandated by the theological nature of the church of Jesus, which I sketched in the previous section, (2) was a defining feature of the early growth of the Jesus movement and the early Christian church, and (3) remains important as we read today's "signs of the times."

Collective Celebration

The first sphere of meaningful action is that of *collective performance and celebration* in local communities. In this sphere the people of God meet together locally, face-to-face. This may occur in a traditional church building or in the "storefront church" that houses a new Pentecostal community. It may thrive in the "base ecclesial community" that so stunningly gave rise to liberation theology in the 1960s and 1970s and still exists

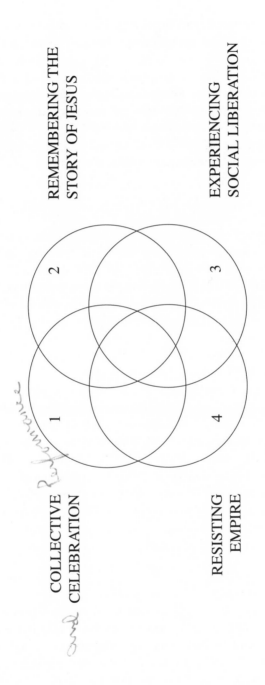

REMEMBERING THE
STORY OF JESUS

EXPERIENCING
SOCIAL LIBERATION

2

3

1

4

COLLECTIVE
CELEBRATION

RESISTING
EMPIRE

Performance

and

throughout Latin American Christianity. It was exemplified in the gatherings of "the brush harbor" to which many a slave could steal away for collective worship.

This local face-to-face contact, wherever it occurs, is a crucial sphere in the matrix of adoration. Whether individuals enter this local space for personal ecstasy, for some common talk and comfort, or for reading and hearing the key scriptures, sermons, and doctrines of the church, the significant point is that this is a "coming together," a being-with-and-for-others, or (just as important) a becoming-of-self-in-relation-to-others. Here we find a crucial expression of the sociality that is intrinsic to the gospel. The gospel of Jesus' radically inclusive love means little if locally we are not being challenged to live, work, and celebrate alongside the other, especially among and as subordinated peoples.

Drawing on the philosophy of Jewish thinker Emmanuel Levinas, Edward Farley has reminded us that ecclesial existence is a "community of the face." To encounter the face of the other and not just the abstract "other" is to see "the species being," the common, one humanity. To see the face is also, however, to confront the "unsubstitutable distinctiveness of each being."[4]

The "community of the face" in Christianity, with members physically present to one another, practicing radically inclusive love, may be especially important in today's age of globalization, powered as it is by volatile market economies. Populations of the poor are readily subjugated to new levels of poverty by processes in which they have little or no voice, no presence, no face.[5] Christian worshiping communities, cultivating and foregrounding the face and faces of the poor in their local settings, are a crucial resource for fighting the devastation done by increasingly abstract markets. Christians who are present to one another in worship, especially gathered in solidarity with subordinated others, help keep these faces from being lost.

Remembering the Story of Jesus

A second sphere of meaningful action is that of *remembering the story of Jesus*. This may occur through reading scripture, sermons proclaiming Jesus Christ, and doctrinal teachings. I refer to it as a distinctive sphere of adoration, however, because this remembering does not belong only to the sphere of Christians' collective celebrations. It is often appropriate in some manner to remember the story of Jesus in other sites of human adoration of God: the social movement, the hospital, the home—in short, wherever Christians engage the world.

Remembrance does not simply remind the community of the strange identity it derives from Jesus' incarnation of radically inclusive love. That is essential. The simple actions of remembrance also themselves strengthen the existence of Christian witness *as* a communal reality and power. Remembrance through story is a powerful reinforcement of communal life.

Historian Sheldon Wolin has argued that communities that lose touch with the rhythms generated from the past and its stories are communities that often come apart in the present. In fact, he suggests that the current decimation of communal life at local levels, leaving only a global "megastate," often goes hand in hand with a "collective amnesia," a forgetting of the past.[6]

Thus remembrance of Jesus is crucial not only because we remember Jesus, but also because we experience the power of remembrance. Such remembrance has been viewed as a near theological virtue ever since the time of St. Augustine's *Confessions*. The embrace of the past, indeed, our very ability to embrace the past in one horizon that includes the present and the future in continuity, or oneness, is made possible by a divine presence that is beyond, yet holds, all times. The One whose moving presence is within us and who inhabits all times makes possible *our* engaging of all times.[7] The important human and sociological function of remembrance, then, is rooted in the presence of God.

Experiencing Social Liberation

A third sphere of meaningful action in the matrix of adoration is *the experiencing of social liberation*. Radically inclusive love entails entering one another's worlds and experiencing new freedoms from whatever grinds us down, whatever oppresses a suffering humanity and a groaning creation. There are no quick victories over oppression here. There is, however, the experience of God at work in history, of our being gifted for and given to a moral striving for the disfranchised of the earth. For the Christian this moral striving is no mere spin-off from faith in God; it is intrinsic to our reverence for God.

Christians worship the God of Jesus Christ for a reason, we might say—a sense that there is something liberating, something salvific at hand. Christians may lift voice or hands, tongues of oratory or of glossolalia; they may use words, clapping hands, stomping feet, or quiet prayer, but all are intrinsically yoked to experiences of social liberation, whether anticipated, partially known, or realized.

Research into both the early Jesus movement and the successful rise of the early Christian church suggests just how important was this experience of social liberation. Neither the early Jesus movement nor later Christian movements were "revolutionary and proletarian," but they were full of revolutionary and political assumptions and potential.

In the words of historian Richard A. Horsley, Jesus and those around him seemed to believe that God had already inaugurated a political revolution, even though it was still embryonic.

[I]n the confidence that it [the political revolution] was underway, it was [their] calling to proceed with the *social revolution* thus made possible by God's rule, to begin the transformation of social relations in anticipation of the completion of the political revolution.[8]

Sociologist Rodney Stark portrays early Christianity as one of "the most successful revitalization movements in history." It had a unique capacity, he writes, to foreground central doctrines that "prompted sustained and attractive, liberating, and effective social relations and organizations." [9] Especially under conditions of devastating epidemics, urban disorder, and widespread poverty, early Christians distinguished themselves for putting in place, as part of their witness and worship, care for the poor.

It was an ethic of liberating care that had to be tested under severe conditions. During devastating epidemics, early Christians nursed the sick and organized themselves around the giving of this care. Though many Christians died in this process, their work actually increased survival rates in some communities.[10] Christian efforts, spontaneous and organized, had given rise to "a miniature welfare state in an empire which for the most part lacked social services."[11] Even the "apostate" emperor Julian reluctantly noted it.

I think that when the poor happened to be neglected and overlooked by the [pagan] priests, the impious Galileans observed this and devoted themselves to benevolence. The impious Galileans support not only their poor, but ours as well, everyone can see that our people lack aid from us.[12]

As many Christians lost their lives in this process of care for victims of epidemics, they were remembered, celebrated, prayed for—in other words, their actions (remembered and anticipated) were crucial to the worship experience. Although they were referred to as "impious Galileans," this moral action actually was the enacting of a worship that was their true piety and distinguishing mark as followers of the Galilean Jesus.

Resistance to Empire

The final sphere of meaningful practice to highlight in the matrix of adoration is *resistance to empire*. From the very beginning and throughout the church's history, Christians have often found that their lives as *homo adorans* entail resistance to empire. We already have a hint of this in Emperor Julian's critique of Christians. By "empire," I mean the exercise of power over aggregate nations and peoples, maintained by regular acts of force and exploitation.

As Rodney Stark puts it, "The early church was a cult movement in the context of empire."[13] For many the word "cult" has a negative connotation, a system of brainwashing, violation, extremism. I am using it in the more general and positive sense of an intense worshiping community, which finds itself surrounded by other systems and institutions that have a more official, and often threatening, status.

I am arguing that both in its beginnings and now, Christian ecclesial life, especially if enlivened by the radically inclusive Jesus, is such an intense worshiping community. What makes it "intense" is not simply its devout worship life, but the worship of the God of Jesus Christ under the conditions of a need to resist imperial power. To be sure, Christianity has often made common cause with imperialism, but this is a betrayal of its calling and essence. Ched Myers has shown how the Markan narrative, for example, gains its full richness when we acknowledge the fact that the setting of Mark's Gospel is "the *locus imperium*."[14] Many others have shown how the community that celebrated Jesus as Lord was routinely brought into conflict and resistance with the sovereigns of this world. The "paschal joy," at the heart of Christian worship, is joy that "passes through *the conflict with the great ones of this world* and through the cross in order to enter into life."[15]

When we think of empires to resist, we may think of Pax Romana, the ordered "peace" enforced by Rome in the first centuries. Perhaps we recall the more recent Pax Britannica, that ordered "peace" worked by British colonialism to produce an empire on which "the sun never sets." But there is now a special need to worship with a sense of U.S. empire, or of Pax Americana. Today the leaders of the United States assume the right to seek and implement unrivaled power. In a Pentagon document released to the public in 1992, officials made this quite clear: "Our first objective is to prevent the re-emergence of a new rival," especially from among "advanced industrial nations."[16]

Although U.S. military actions are usually justified by claims of doing justice, fighting tyrants, or protecting democracy, a U.S. imperialist intention is often clear. The recent bombing of Yugoslavia without even first attempting to secure United Nations approval displays just how free the U.S. assumes it is to act on its own, even when lives are to be lost or displaced through war. Just a few more lines from the Pentagon's document cement the point:

> [T]he U.S. should be postured to act independently when collective action cannot be orchestrated . . . [T]he world order is ultimately backed by the U.S. . . . We must maintain the mechanism for deterring potential competitors *from even aspiring to* a larger regional or global role.[17]

To my knowledge this policy statement has never been denied by members of the Clinton administration, nor have any distanced themselves from it. In fact, Clinton's administrators, among them U.S. Trade Representative Mickey Kantor, refer to the twenty-first century as the "New American Century."[18] When a pharmaceutical plant in the Sudan was destroyed by a U.S. bombing mission (for dubious reasons), the mission, with imperial pretension, was dubbed "Operation Infinite Reach."[19]

Meanwhile, a kind of de facto imperium grows within the United States, amid its rituals and rhetoric of democracy. Although more wealth circulates within U.S. borders than in any other nation, the U.S. has more people below the poverty level than any other industrialized nation.[20] Even during the economic boom years of the late 1990s, the U.S. maintains the most rapid growth of wage inequality in the Western world.[21] The United States has the smallest middle class percentagewise among "developed" nations,[22] and scholars continue to show that with mergers an ever-smaller number of corporate owners of capital control ever-larger segments of economic power. According to one study of corporate power, the U.S. business elite is one of the smallest ever in the history of state powers.[23]

The *locus imperium*, then, is a reality for U.S. Christians at worship even now. How then shall we worship the God of Jesus Christ today?

"Word and Spirit" in a Caribbean Mode

The Caribbean has a distinctive history and cultural presence that gifts it for responding ably and fully to the "matrix of adoration." In Caribbean worship and performance, the mother continent of Africa has creatively forged itself anew on the anvil of Caribbean slavery and repression, thus yielding a life of doxological action in the Americas.

The Caribbean Meta-archipelago

A preliminary word is in order about the significance of the Caribbean. Antonio Benítez-Rojo reminds us that the Caribbean is not just an archipelago of small islands to the south of the U.S. It is an astonishingly dispersed cultural presence. This is so much so that he speaks of it as a "meta-archipelago."

> [A]s a meta-archipelago it has the virtue of having neither boundary nor center. Thus the Caribbean flows outward past the limits of its own sea with a vengeance, and . . . may be found on the outskirts of Bombay, near the low and murmuring shores of Gambia, in a Cantonese tavern of circa 1850, at a Balinese temple, in an old Bristol pub, in a commercial warehouse in Bordeaux at the time of Colbert, in a windmill beside the Zuider Zee, at a café in a barrio of Manhattan, in the existential *saudade* of an old Portuguese lyric.[24]

We are speaking, then, of no island tourist site; we are speaking of a worldwide phenomenon that can convey new insights to a global and ecumenical church.

Caribbean diaspora cultures, however, are not only significant for having forged this pervasive global presence. Caribbean diaspora peoples also carry the burden of a people long suffering political repression and colonization. Benítez-Rojo yet again eloquently summarizes what the Caribbean has had to bear:

> Let's be realistic: the Atlantic is the Atlantic (with all its port cities) because it was once engendered by the copulation of Europe—that insatiable solar bull—with the Caribbean archipelago; the Atlantic is today the Atlantic (the navel of capitalism) because Europe, in its mercantilist laboratory, conceived the project of inseminating the Caribbean womb with the blood of Africa; the Atlantic is today the Atlantic (NATO, World Bank, New York Stock Exchange, European Economic Community, etc.) because it was the painfully delivered child of the Caribbean, whose vagina was stretched between continental clamps, between the *encomienda* of Indians and the slaveholding plantations, between the servitude of the coolies and the discrimination toward the *criollo*, between commercial monopoly and piracy, between the runaway settlement and the governor's palace; all Europe pulling on the forceps to help at the birth of the Atlantic.[25]

Caribbean diaspora peoples, then, also carry the pain of systematically subordinated others. Caribbean bodies have been torn asunder to birth the worlds that are privileged in this age of "globalization," with its transnational market powered by Wall Street and by U.S. military might.

Yet these peoples persist, thrive, celebrate. Caribbean thought and practice can enable us to rethink worship theologically, as well as to experience it more vitally in Christian community. One important way to see this is to rethink the relation of "Word and Spirit" as it has been stressed in Protestant theology.

"Word and Spirit" in Communities of Rhythm and Repetition

John Calvin, one of the theological and ecclesial forerunners of Protestant culture, gave the terms "Word" and "Spirit" a special prominence in his *Institutes of the Christian Religion* (1536). In the midst of Reformed Protestantism's word-oriented worship and theology (in which preaching is profoundly important, often as well as creedal statement and doctrines), Calvin insisted on holding Word together with Spirit.

His expositions on "Word and Spirit" occur mainly in discussions of scriptural authority, but also occur throughout the *Institutes*.[26] In general, how we understand these terms and their relation will be reflected in understanding worship. How we strike the relation between Word (text, sermon, creed, formula) and Spirit (illumination, ecstasy, mystical sense, etc.) will say much about how we practice communion with God.

Calvin sometimes seems to exhibit a preference for the Word. His most significant summaries of the relation, however, stress that Word and Spirit are joined in a "mutual bond"[27]: "the Word fails to find acceptance" in people's hearts without the "testimony of the Spirit." Moreover, within the mutual relation of Word and Spirit, there is a dynamic interplay between them. Calvin also stressed that the Spirit, which makes the Word effective, was an unlimited power. It is Spirit "transfusing into all things" a vitality that could be characterized variously by Calvin as energy, essence, life, and movement.[28] The fusion of Word and Spirit yields a lively, powerful locus of spirituality and revelation.

What is problematic about Calvin's mutual bond of Word and Spirit is that by Spirit he usually refers to a kind of "inward testimony." This gives the impression that Spirit is action going on only inside an individual, between God and the inner life of the believer.

A perspective more biblical than Calvin's would keep the experience of Spirit more closely related to notions of "the love of Christ" and "the body of Christ."[29] This situates Spirit fully in the dynamism at work *in community,* shaped and infused by the radically inclusive love of God. The Spirit of God in Christ is not primarily an individual, inner reality; it is that, but more distinctively it is a living together in "liberating dominion."[30] It exists not just *in* individuals, but in the power of God enlivening communal bonding for love and justice.

Caribbean worship and spiritual practice carries this sense of the communal. Drawing on a profoundly African sensibility,[31] Caribbean worship, like most of its cultures' performances, is intensely communal. Theologian Kortright Davis notes that the success or failure of Caribbean performance depends on whether it creates a high level of interplay between performers and audience. Without that collective participation, the performance is "not sweet."[32] Similarly, ethnomusicologist Kenneth Bilby writes that the criterion of collective participation functions as an "aesthetic canon."[33]

This emphasis on the communal nature of celebration, if brought to an understanding of "Word and Spirit," intensifies the Word-Spirit relation and drives it on to effective fullness. The crucial development is the emergence of "repetition." In *community,* both Word and Spirit are "replayed." This replaying occurs as Word and Spirit move among the different members in any one celebratory event, each member repeating Word and Spirit in slightly different ways. In addition, each subsequent performance (of a worship celebration, a reading, a story, a sermon) is also an occasion for this replaying. As Word is replayed in spiritual community, inflected with ever-new themes and variations, however slight, its journey becomes a journey of repetition, and so it more and more becomes rhythm word.

Especially in communities struggling with oppressive power, the rhythm born of repetition can actually create security, identity, and continuity.[34] In the long-oppressed Caribbean, the powers of repetition and rhythm are embraced as a mode of resistance to colonizers' legacy of violence. The area's polymorphism is evident in its polymusicality and its supersyncretistic belief systems. Word and Spirit, in polymorphic abundance, create an aesthetic for resisting the violence of empire, a violence that often moves to more "binary rhythms." The Caribbean mode surrounds the binary with a greater rhythmic complexity (a polyrhythmic one), and overwhelms it, so to speak, for the guarding of aesthetic pleasure, vitality, and life. [35]

The Word-Spirit relation, then, is "saved" in the Caribbean mode from its tendencies to create or support mere binary thinking. Often Word and

Spirit are presented in mere binary relation, with Word seen as something traveling in a linear mode from one place or person to another, then meeting Spirit for lively action or "sealing" as an end result.

Unfortunately this binary understanding dovetails with, expresses, and often reinforces, the kinds of "white rhythms" that musicologists often describe as characterizing Western culture, the "rhythms of steps marching, or running, of territorializing . . . of conquest and colonization, of the assembly-line of technological knowledge, of computers and positivist ideologies."[36] The Caribbean mode takes the binariness of "Word and Spirit" and intensifies it through communal performance— heats it up, as it were, to the point that it is transcended in rhythmic repetition that creates polymorphic complexities that defy mere binary rhythms. Can it also defy, however, the colonizing and imperialist powers that use the binary rhythms? Polymorphic complexity by itself cannot do so. The Caribbean mode has another effect on the Word-Spirit relation, which helps generate effective resistance to oppressive political power.

"Word and Spirit" in Polyrhythmic, Embodied Praise

A Caribbean mode of worship drives Word and Spirit into not just any context of polymorphic communal rhythm, but one where Word and Spirit unite in the movement of *bodies*, often in dance. Here, Word and Spirit interplay in community in such a way as to approach the necessity of becoming physical. Word and Spirit, without losing their power to convey transcendence and mystery, each in its own way becomes incarnate in a mode of physicality. Word does not remain text, whether spoken, heard, or read. Spirit does not remain sheer energy or elusive presence, either as internal mystical sense or more external universal force.

Word, when enlivened by communal Spirit, tends to find its roots in its deepest origins, that is, in the shaping of breath by the human body in a landed space. Here are the in-and-out movements of breath, shaped by the contractions and shifts of throat, lips, and larynx. Word takes on its rhythmic, organic physicality. Word puts on, we might say, its deepest powers, those of breath and movement. It is a short step from the repeated movements of breath to the movement of bodies, as breath and muscle also interplay in dance.

From the other side, Spirit, while moving toward Word in community, never really becomes Word. Certainly it doesn't become text. It does, however, become a kind of language, a language of the body and of bodies moving in concert. Spirit, in its enlivening of bodies, can become communicative action. Its signs are not written codes, but the coded figures of gestures and movements carried by the body.

Word and Spirit, then, are synthesized and transcended not only in polymorphic communal rhythms, but now also, more specifically, in the complexity of *the body's polyrhythmic actions.* Kortright Davis stresses, therefore, that for Caribbean churches, "the crucial and pivotal locus of that God-experience is the human body."[37] Quoting African theologian of the early church Tertullian, he affirms that "the flesh is the central point of our salvation." The apostle Paul's words in 1 Corinthians 6:20b summarize Caribbean doxology and spiritual practice: "Therefore glorify God in your body."

This synthesis of Word and Spirit in polyrhythmic embodied praise, in the Caribbean mode, makes two key contributions to the "matrix of adoration."

First, it suffuses *all* the spheres in the matrix with a sense of the material creation, the energy and power of nature. Through bodies' movement in praise, worship is opened up to the natural world. Collective gathering, remembrance, liberation, and resistance are not only social and political events of spirit; they are also part of the natural creation. Worship lives in relation to body, land, wind, trees—all in interaction. Classical Western spiritualities are prone to see this turn to material nature as a move away from Spirit. In fact, for Caribbean spirituality, as for many indigenous peoples, materiality is the locus of that which is beyond. This explains why Senghor could say about "black rhythm" in another context, "It is the most perceptible and the least material thing."[38]

Second, polyrhythm's embodied praise is especially important because it greatly facilitates Christian "adoration of God" in the two spheres of the matrix of adoration (experiencing social liberation and resisting empire) that often go unrelated to much Christian worship.

The polyrhythmic motion of the body is a necessary strategy for *homo adorans*, for those who face, as Caribbean peoples have, what oppressing and regimenting empires do to bodies. The oppressed body will lose yet again if it tries to deploy imperial power's own binary rhythms and marches. Direct frontal assaults against larger powers will usually mean certain loss for weaker forces. Oppressed peoples need a more complex rhythm of movement, one that absorbs direct attack, reworks it, deals with it, survives, and even thrives in the face of it. With a repertoire that includes polyrhythm, so available to the "Peoples of the Sea," one resists greater powers by dodging, shifting, being able to change beats, moving on and off a binary beat, encircling the binary with new meters, new beats—beats that "break" differently and maybe even break down the power seeking to drive one down.

There is, indeed, sheer and simple aesthetic delight to be found in polyrhythmic dance, praise, walk, and talk. Here, however, I want to affirm the polyrhythmic intensification of Word and Spirit as having a utilitarian function in a liberating practice of resistance for oppressed bodies, minds, and spirits. Polyrhythmic practice and embodied praise are crucial for effecting social liberation and resistance to empire.

Benítez-Rojo claims ordinary walk in the Caribbean is affected by cultural tendencies to embrace polyrhythmic performance. Indeed, this can be seen in the walk of African American urban youth in the United States, in "the cool pose" that moves as if it has to dodge, shift, stay ever alert to taking space or avoiding certain spaces.[39] The cool pose is matched by a musical aesthetic, rap music, where a heavy drumbeat, and lightning fast staccato lyrics, are often made further complex by other beats, "breaks," and "noise." Rap is a polyrhythmic resistance to the force of racist empire which these youth instinctively feel all around them, as they travel through what PEN/Faulkner award–winner John Edgar Wideman called today's "second Middle Passage" for black families in the U.S.[40]

Rap, an aesthetic with its musical roots in a synergy between the Bronx and the Caribbean,[41] serves as a mode for forging liberation and resistance for black youth and for many other urban and suburban groups living at the margins of urban America. Embodied polyrhythmic motion in all its forms can be viewed as nonviolent, effective word, a Rhythm Word, necessary for absorbing and resisting the overwhelming powers that drive us down.

Conclusion: Toward a "Polyrhythmic Sensibility" in Christian Worship

Certainly more is involved here than embracing rap music in Christian worship. That is important, and, in fact, is already occurring in some church and Christian groups. But rap can be escapist, commercial, misogynist, and worse. In this it is not unlike all music that can be put to banal or destructive ends. In the context of a matrix of Christian adoration, though, the polyrhythms of rap can release their special power to enable critique and survival of oppression. If we are going to sustain worship that releases a practice of social liberation and resistance to empire, we need this youth music of resistance in our churches.

Embracing rap music in worship, however, is only one way to embrace rhythm (especially polyrhythm) in worship. If we are going to embrace rhythm in a way that opens up to "effective fullness" of the Word, to recall Senghor's phrase, then Christian worship must embrace a whole set of practices and orientations that make up a "polyrhythmic sensibility."

By "sensibility" I do not mean only a general awareness, but quite precisely an "ability to use the senses." There is often a kind of aesthetic austerity, especially in European and North American Protestant churches, which could benefit from a greater "sense-ability," a polyrhythmic one. The need for this in the Reformed traditions especially has been noted by some Reformed thinkers themselves.[42] Of what does a polyrhythmic sensibility consist?

1. As its first trait, a polyrhythmic sensibility in the churches honors the drum. Honoring the drum will often mean bringing the drum back into those worship settings from which it has been excluded. Many a Christian community still uses the drum. I have met it in the Latina/o liturgies of a Roman Catholic church in urban America, in indigenous Protestant and Catholic services in Mexico and Central America, in Jamaican churches in Brooklyn, and in suburban Pentecostal churches in the United States. Too often, though, the drum is exiled from Christian worship, perhaps spurned as "pagan," as it was by some missionaries in the religious colonization of Latin America, Asia, and Africa. My Lutheran ancestors in Norway and Sweden excluded from their Christian worship the stirring drum of the indigenous Saami peoples of Scandinavia (name preferred by them to Lapps, short for Laplanders, thought to be derogatory). If we are ever to discover the fully effective Word where Spirit enlivens a Rhythm Word, then we need to begin with the drum's reentry into our places of worship.

To exclude the drum from worship as "pagan," is not only ethnocentric vis-à-vis drumming cultures; it might also be seen (from the perspective of this article, at least) as a kind of "blasphemy against the Spirit," against the kind of Spirit that makes Word come alive in the gathered community of Christ, which needs the Rhythm Word to catalyze the whole matrix of adoration, from gathering to remembering, to liberating, to resisting.

2. A polyrhythmic sensibility also allows the drum's rhythms to pervade the whole gathering of the community in worship. We do not honor the drum and rhythm by simply having a rhythm show, or a drumming time at the beginning of worship, or by featuring them in some "musical

moment." No, the rhythm that is creative is a pervasive *communal* force. Hence, it should pace the entire worship of the gathered community. The rhythms and polyrhythms should come throughout the service, creating a context within which Word and Spirit meet and enliven each other.

What would this look like liturgically? I do not suggest that the drums and heavy musical rhythms be going constantly throughout worship. I do suggest, however, that musical rhythms be intentionally nurtured for framing worship, for marking transitions, focusing meditation, as well as for lifting people to celebratory moments. For example, instead of having a worship leader announcing and giving out instructions ("Now let us sing Hymn No. . . . ," "Please stand and . . . ," "Turn to your bulletin and . . . ," and so on), the drum can be used to artfully signal these transitions and move people more naturally and spontaneously. The point is to honor the drum's power to speak and guide the gathered Christians, awaiting the Rhythm Word of a remembered Jesus who brings social liberation, a life of flourishing in resistance to empire.

3. Polyrhythmic sensibility nurtures the flourishing of a diversity of rhythms. The "poly" in polyrhythmic refers not just to those kinds of rhythm that are well known for their complexity (say, "Caribbean" ones), but also involves embracing many different kinds of rhythms, even the less complex ones.

Thus a polyrhythmic sensibility will welcome and seek out not only the rhythms of ska, salsa, reggae, and rock, but also of the organ, folk guitar, and country fiddle. Recall that even the most binary of rhythmic styles has its place in a polyrhythmic sensibility. It is just that the binary finds its place, is protected from its dichotomizing and territorializing ways, and so flowers within that teeming, polymorphic milieu where Word and Spirit are enlivened in ever-new combinations.

In the United States this diversity of rhythms will have to be not only "welcomed and sought after," but also planned for. Especially now, given the present interaction of ethnicity and church, rhythms and musics tend to be isolated from one another along ethnic lines as well as along those of musical preference. Different churches develop musical and rhythmic tastes that represent one or only a few styles. If churches really are serious about bringing African or indigenous drums into worship when they have not had them before, if they wish to fold in the blues with spirituals and gospel music, or mix reggae and rap with traditional hymns, or insert the folk guitar and country fiddle where they have not been heard before—all this will take planning. People do not easily open themselves up to a diversity of musical and rhythmic tastes, especially in church worship. Worshipers of God accommodate themselves to musical tastes with great care, and most churchgoers (however broad may be their *personal* tastes in music and rhythm) have a narrow range of criteria about what music is "sacred" and should be found in church.

There is much at stake here for building congregations reflective of the full diversity of God's peoples. Congregations with only one or a few types of rhythmic music will also tend to lack cultural diversity. A polyrhythmic sensibility's drive to embrace a manifold of rhythmic styles is a way to celebrate the full multicultural wholeness of creation.

4. Finally, a polyrhythmic sensibility thrives when people give their bodies to the rhythm. There are many ways to do this—clapping hands, stomping feet, nodding the head, swaying, dancing, processing into, during, and after, worship ceremonies. For those worship traditions which cultivate little or no body movement in worship, a polyrhythmic sensibility would bring about the movement of bodies. A body that is still and in repose can certainly be a contemplative worshiping body, but it is harder to participate in the full matrix of adoration as I have defined it, where worship means not only gathering together with the faithful and remembering Jesus, but also experiencing a social liberation and resisting empire. Worshipers who stand still within the lines of straight pew rows are not rehearsing themselves well for a Christian practice of liberation and resistance, which often requires "pushing the edges" and "crossing the lines" that oppressive powers like to set.

Those churches where bodily movement to rhythms *is* alive in worship will be valuable for teaching the whole church about the importance of an embodied, polyrhythmic sensibility in worship. Embodied praise and "dancing in the aisles" (may we have more of it when the spirit moves us!) do not in themselves translate, however, into ecclesial practices of social liberation and resistance to empire, which are essential to the full matrix of Christian adoration. In that matrix, a polyrhythmic sensibility is not complete if only our church aisles and fellowship halls ring with Christians' embodied praise. That praise also has to move out of church buildings, as Christians' radically inclusive love always moves into the world. Yes, dance in the aisles, but also be ready to be dancing in the streets.

Regarding bodily movement among Christians, then, a polyrhythmic sensibility strikes a continuity between action in church and action in "the streets," that is to say, in the world. The mix of song, body movements in church, and marching in the streets (and into jails) that characterized the civil rights movements of the 1950s and 1960s will always live as a powerful example of Christian worshipers at their best.

This example can be heard and seen today—here and there among those who bridge sanctuary and street for social liberation and resistance to empire. You can see them with their folk guitars (Pete Seeger and others), singing with those Christians marching against the U.S. School of the Americas, where torture and counterinsurgency have been taught and where Latin American military officers violating human rights have been honored.[43]

You can hear such worshipers among the Christians in the Haitian community who have marched (with dancing and singing) from Brooklyn into Manhattan of New York City to protest patterns of police brutality. You can catch them in the downtown streets, where Christians sing and march in front of the posh hotels to protest the international financiers who refuse to forgive the debt of poor, third-world nations. You can see such worshipers along the walls of our penitentiaries intoning with music, songs, candles, and bodies their opposition to executing the two people per week that the United States has been averaging in 1999. You can see them accompanied by both African drums and pastors' words, singing in the Philadelphia cold for the death row inmate, journalist Mumia Abu-Jamal. You can hear them among the marchers of the landless and homeless who took their cries for justice to the United Nations in October of 1999 with hymns, chants, and rhythms marking each step of their journey.

These and other Christian worshipers on the move display a polyrhythmic sensibility, and so help embody the full matrix of Christian adoration. The churches of the future, open to the "effective fullness" of the Word, must learn to welcome the "Rhythm Word" that is unfolding in their witness.

NOTES

1. Cited from Janhainz Jahn, *Muntu: Las culturas neoafricanas* (Mexico D.F.: Fondo de Cultural Económica, 1978), 277. This and other insights from Senghor can be enlightening, even if some of his arguments around his notion of *Négritude* are "essentialist" and thus problematic. For a critique of Senghor on this matter, see Tsenay Serequeberhan, *The Hermeneutics of African Philosophy: Horizon and Discourse* (New York: Routledge & Kegan Paul, 1994), 42–46.
2. G. Gutiérrez, *Gustavo Gutiérrez: Essential Writings*, ed. James B. Nickoloff (Maryknoll, N.Y.: Orbis Books, 1996), 78–148.
3. Alexander Schmemann, *For the Life of the World: Sacraments and Orthodoxy* (Crestwood, N.Y.: St. Vladimir's Seminary Press, 1973), 118.
4. Edward Farley, *Good and Evil: Interpreting a Human Condition* (Minneapolis: Fortress Press, 1990), 37–42.
5. Ralph Nader and Lori Wallach, "GATT, NAFTA, and the Subversion of the Democratic Process," in *The Case against the Global Economy: And for a Turn toward the*

Local, ed. Jerry Mander and Edward Goldsmith (San Francisco: Sierra Club Books, 1996), 92–107.

6. Sheldon S. Wolin, "Injustice and Collective Memory," in *The Presence of the Past* (Baltimore: Johns Hopkins University Press, 1989), 32–46.

7. *The Confessions of St. Augustine* 11.14.287 (New York: E.P. Dutton, 1951).

8. Richard A. Horsley, *Jesus and the Spiral of Violence* (Minneapolis: Fortress Press, 1993), 114.

9. Rodney Stark, *The Rise of Christianity: A Sociologist Reconsiders History* (Princeton, N.J.: Princeton University Press, 1996), 211.

10. Ibid., 82–83.

11. Paul Johnson, *A History of Christianity* (New York: Atheneum Publishers, 1976), 75.

12. Stark, p. 84.

13. Stark, *The Rise of Christianity,* 45.

14. Ched Myers, *Binding the Strong Man: A Political Reading of Mark's Story of Jesus* (Maryknoll, N.Y.: Orbis Books, 1988), 5–6.

15. Gutiérrez, *Gustavo Gutiérrez,* 290 (emphasis mine).

16. "The Defense Planning Guide." Cited in the *New York Times,* March 8, 1992.

17. Ibid.

18. Peter Gowan, *The Global Gamble: Washington's Faustian Bid for World Dominance* (London and New York: Verso, 1999), 77.

19. James Risen, "To Bomb Sudan Plant, or Not: A Year Later, Debates Rankle," *New York Times,* October 27, 1999.

20. Richard Jolly et al. *Human Development Report 1998* (New York: Oxford University Press, 1998), 2–15.

21. William Julius Wilson, *The Bridge over the Racial Divide: Rising Inequality and Coalition Politics* (Berkeley: The University of California Press, 1999), 27.

22. Keith Bradisher, "Widest Gap in Incomes? Research Points to the U.S.," *New York Times,* October 27, 1995.

23. John Bodley, "The American Industrial State," in *Cultural Anthropology: Tribes, States, and the Global System* (Mountainview, Calif.: Mayfield, 1997), 347–49.

24. Antonio Benítez-Rojo, *The Repeating Island: The Caribbean and the Postmodern Perspective,* 2nd ed. (Durham, N.C.: Duke University Press, 1996), 4.

25. Ibid., 5.

26. John Calvin, *Institutes,* II.v.5; I.ix.3.

27. Ibid., I.ix.3.

28. Ibid., I.xiii.14.

29. Herman Ridderbos, *Paul: An Outline of His Theology* (Grand Rapids: Wm. B. Eerdmans Publishing Co., 1975), 221.

30. Ibid., 222.

31. John Miller Chernoff, *African Rhythm and African Sensibility: Aesthetics and Social Action in African Musical Idioms* (Chicago: University of Chicago Press, 1979).

32. Kortright Davis, *Emancipation Still Comin': Explorations in Caribbean Emancipatory Theology* (Maryknoll, N.Y.: Orbis Books, 1990), 43.

33. Cited in Davis, *Emancipation,* 43.

34. James A. Snead, "On Repetition in Black Culture," *Black American Literature Forum* 15, no. 4 (1981): 146–54.

35. Benítez-Rojo, *The Repeating Island,* 16–17, 21, 36.
36. Benítez-Rojo, *The Repeating Island,* 27.
37. Davis, *Emancipation,* 108.
38. Cited in Chernoff, *African Rhythm,* 22.
39. Richard Majors and Janet Mancini Billson, *Cool Pose: The Dilemmas of Black Manhood in America* (New York: Simon & Schuster, 1992), 3–5.
40. John Edgar Wideman, *Fatheralong: A Meditation on Fathers and Sons, Race and Society* (New York: Vintage Books, 1994), xxii.
41. Tricia Rose, *Black Noise: Rap Music and Black Culture in Contemporary America* (Hanover, N.H.: Wesleyan University Press, 1994), 189 n.4, 199 n.31.
42. Nicholas Wolterstorff, "Justice and Worship: The Tragedy of Liturgy in Protestantism," in *Until Justice & Peace Embrace* (Grand Rapids: Wm. B. Eerdmans Publishing Co., 1983) 146–61.
43. Jack Nelson-Pallmeyer, *School of Assassins* (Maryknoll, N.Y.: Orbis Books, 1997).

PART 3

Toward Multicultural
Worship Today

Chapter 9

Moshing for Jesus

Adolescence as a Cultural Context for Worship

KENDA CREASY DEAN

Worshiping God is fun and all.
The only thing that makes people think it's boring is
church.

Brendan Dean, age 11

*T*he concert is hard rock all the way. "No rap music lovers here,"
notes journalist Patricia Hersch, observing the Reston, Virginia,
Community Center event. The youth pushing their way in—partially
shaved heads, lots of Megadeath T-shirts and earrings (on boys and
girls)—look like the least likely species on the planet to show up in
worship. They have come to the "Jam the Man" concert for the roar
of the music, the surging beat, the indistinguishable lyrics, the time
with their friends. But, most of all, they have come together to mosh:

> Joan and her friends. . . . stand happily at the perimeter of the
> dance floor grooving to the music. Joan is sizing up the scene,
> watching especially to see how the girls are faring. Her petite
> friend Carol is a monster on the floor, her arms like propellers,
> her footwork like a boxer's. Sweaty, dirty, bloody and bruised,
> she keeps "dancing." She is jerked out momentarily when a cut on
> her nose bleeds onto her shirt, then is back in the middle a few
> moments later, a Mickey Mouse Band-Aid on her wound. One
> boy leaves with what appears to be a broken nose. Boys and girls,
> faces frozen in furious grimaces, circle about, shoving, jabbing,
> hurling themselves against one another, their hair damp and mat-
> ted. In this rolling sea of flesh, occasionally someone gets pushed
> to the floor and stomped on. Alert fellow dancers or one of the
> brave wide-eyed adult chaperones . . . will dart in and scoop up
> the victim. One very preppie honor student . . . looks like she
> wandered into the wrong dance. But looks are deceiving. She

goes in and within moments her sleeve is torn as she whips around slamming into people until she disappears, having slipped and fallen. She emerges from underfoot tearfully, with the help of a chaperone. Her friends rush to comfort her, and a few minutes later she goes back into the fray. . . . When the music stops the vicious looks fade, the kids put happy faces back on, and everyone hugs.[1]

The Pit—the "mosh pit" to the uninitiated, the floor space bordering center stage at any rock concert—contains one of millennial adolescents' weirdest rituals. "Like the era it reflects," Hersch observes, "[moshing] has no synchronicity, no steps, just action, sensation, and physicality."[2] Rock diva Alanis Morissette recently stopped a concert midsong to advise overly enthusiastic fans in the pit: "Instead of hitting each other, jump up and down, like this."[3] Unspoken rules of touch don't apply here. Boundaries—psychological and physical—fade away. In the adrenaline rush, endorphins surge and stress dissolves.

Moshing fails to register even the slightest comprehension among those of us born on the far end of the 1960s. In the 1990s, however, teenagers turn to moshing for many of the same reasons adults attend worship: the chance "to be close to people"; for an intense if temporary bond to others who subscribe to the same practices; for the promise of being moved ("It's a rush, literally," one of my students explained); for the transporting experience of being part of something bigger than they are.[4] Youth who mosh do not deny that pain accompanies it—on the contrary, hard contact is intentional—but they insist that getting hurt is beside the point. One student told me, "The point is that you're not in control. Moshing gives you a safe place to get primal." Another noted: "Even if you get hurt, at least you feel like something *happened*."

Something happened. Compare that to the overwhelming adolescent critique of Sunday morning in American mainline congregations, namely, that *nothing* happens. Church, as it turns out, is about the last place we expect anything to "happen," including the presence of God. George Barna's research reveals that more than a third (34 percent) of churchgoing adults say they have "never" experienced God's presence in worship.[5] In 1962, cognitive psychologists David and Sally Elkind asked young adolescents where they were most likely to experience God. The most common response was "in a church or synagogue."[6] By 1999, however, only one in seven adolescents believed that participating in a church, synagogue, or other religious group was necessary to being "religious." [7]

American adolescents (like many adults) go to church to feel moved, to feel changed, to feel God, to feel *something*. Theologically, of course, this is a misguided instinct. Worship is for the benefit of God, not primarily for the benefit of teenagers. After all, hunger for visceral personal experience also causes adolescents to drive too fast, to have sex too early, to go to *Star Wars* movies. Faith gets confused with feeling all the time. As George Lucas told Bill Moyers in a recent *Time* interview, Luke Skywalker, the *Star Wars* protagonist, must learn "not to rely on pure logic, not to rely on the computers, but to rely on faith. That is what that 'Use the Force' is, a leap of faith. There are mysteries and powers larger than we are, and you have to trust your feelings in order to access them."[8]

If Christian worship is construed as "meaningful human action oriented toward the divine, celebrated communally and in public,"[9] then "feeling" has little to do with it. Modern Christians have tended to interpret "meaning" in terms of rational discourse. Despite the fact that humans also construct meaning intuitively and emotionally, and communicate this meaning through story, symbol, and ritual as well as by discursive means, for most of the twentieth century mainline Protestant worship has aimed for rational eloquence, punctuating it with a few well-placed, lyrically sensible hymns. As a result, by the late twentieth century, mainline Protestant youth seeking self-transcendence, ecstatic release, and direct access to the sacred overwhelmingly—left. Viscerally, moshing just made more sense.

Affect Matters

When worship addresses the cultural context of adolescence, feelings matter. This is a generation in touch with its sensitive side. Churches can no longer acknowledge the affective needs of adolescents only on "Youth Sunday." According to one estimate, the U.S. teen population will rise in the next decade from 29 to 36 million. "In other words," observed *Rolling Stone* (no stranger to teen marketing), "resistance is futile. Teenagers are driving our culture—and they won't be giving the keys back anytime soon."[10]

Embracing affect in worship has little to do—very little—with naked emotionalism. Let me be clear: I am not making a case for turning worship into an emotional mosh pit of whirling sensation. Nor am I advocating tearful televangelism or even "celebration services," narrowly defined. Contemporary youth recognize emotional manipulation even when they play into it; this, after all, is the first generation raised on cable TV and omnipresent advertising, where emotional excess has made them wary consumers of advertising even while making them lavish consumers of everything else.[11] Affect simply acknowledges the subjective side of God's gift of faith, the "religious affections," variously named, important in the theology of Martin Luther, Jonathan Edwards, John and Charles Wesley, and others for whom religious experience (despite charges to the contrary) had less to do with outward "enthusiasm" than with an inward conviction of love toward God and neighbor.[12]

Postmodern adolescents raised in a global culture want to experience their religion. To them, worship is a verb. "To worship" is to invoke God's immediacy—God's awesome "nowness" in which divine presence is subjectively apprehended. Although worship's primary purpose is doxological, worshiping also marks us objectively as people to whom something subjective has *happened*: the inward conviction of faith, the subjective knowledge that Christ loves us enough to die for us. In the practices of worship, Jesus reveals his mystery as often as his message, and invites us—by playful, ecstatic, and sacramental means—into the passionate love of God.

By emphasizing God's immediacy, contemporary adolescents call the mainline church to reclaim subjective aspects of faith undervalued by modernity. Practices of play, ecstasy, and sacrament acknowledge the subjective experience of God alongside more discursive forms of prayer, praise, and proclamation. Adolescent worship cannot be reduced to the "Jesus is my buddy" theology often ascribed to youth ministry (which ignores the fact that God's immediacy comes in majesty and mystery as often as in interpersonal identification). For youth, traditional elements of worship—the order of service, the presence of scripture, prayer, proclamation, musical intercession, and so on—serve as scaffolding for existential experience, sacred "dots" to be connected by leaps of faith invited by God's playfulness, affection, and grace.

The God Who "Happens": Adolescents' Hunger for Immediacy

For three centuries American youth have tried to rescue mainstream Christianity from intellectual aridity through the divine immediacy available in nondiscursive practices of worship. The First and Second Great Awakenings, the Pentecostal turn of the twentieth century, the charismatic renewal of the 1960s—all of these began as youth movements, primarily guided by and aimed at young people whose futures seemed uncertain in light of swift cultural change.[13] Some historians claim that religious renewal is the predictable companion of cultural upheaval, as religious institutions become vehicles through which culture reinvents its master narratives. Not surprisingly, then, the seismic cultural shifts accompanying global postmodernity have yielded intense interest in adolescent "spirituality."[14]

Contemporary youth worship movements can be viewed as direct descendants of these renewal movements. The Christian rock concert, the Christian "Woodstock" experience (e.g., "Creation," "TomFest," "Agape," and "Ichthus" festivals), and the "youth worship" movement (teen services that either evolve into separate intergenerational congregations or function as generationally specific congregations within a larger body) have been linked to the eighteenth-century camp meetings as well as to the revivals of the Second Great Awakening.[15] Contemporary forms of adolescent worship, like their forebears, tend to be dismissed by parent congregations, only to be embraced a generation later as "mainstream" expressions of faith. Choruses banished from traditional worship as "camp songs" in 1970, for instance, have gained legitimacy as "worship music," as "contemporary" services in the 1990s became willing to baptize rock and roll in the sanctuary.[16] A case in point: A few weeks ago our congregation's contemporary praise band planned to teach a chorus of Micah 6:8, a song I learned at a youth conference years ago. When it was omitted from the service, I asked why. "It wasn't appropriate," our pastor told me. "That's really a camp song." My husband and I found it hilarious to open the bulletin for the traditional service that same morning and see "Pass It On" (now in the *United Methodist Hymnal*) listed as the closing "hymn."

Like all worship, worship in an adolescent context must operate within the culture's primary idioms. The idiom of adolescents shaped by global postmodernity is immediacy. Today, fifty years after "the adolescent society" was first observed by sociologists, youth culture and popular culture in the United States have become virtually synonymous. Postmodernity increasingly views adolescence as a life*style* rather than a life *stage*, a choice available to adults as well as to youth. In a universalized youth culture, everyone, from toddlers to middle-aged adults, wants to be a teenager, forcing youth to turn to "alternative" cultures for self-definition.

Compounding the problem of self-definition for teenagers is global consumerism, which calls every imaginable boundary into question. With worldwide commercial, communication, and transportation systems eradicating a need for "place," issues of location become insignificant. Teenagers wear jeans made abroad, eat dim sum with Diet Coke, chat on-line with friends whom they have never met, drive to noncustodial parents' homes on weekends. For adolescents raised in a global culture, mobility and placelessness are ways of life, with jarring effects on religion. Adolescents shun the symbolic territoriality of denominations and institutional religion in favor of "portable" spiritual practices.[17] Contemporary youth, whom sociologist Wade Clark Roof describes as a generation of "questers," view life as a spiritual journey that may or may not lead somewhere. Locale is unimportant, but the journey matters enormously.[18]

Without physical geography to mark their pilgrimages, adolescents use emotional terrain as a source of spiritual landmarks. Adolescents employ distance as a primary metaphor for understanding God, but translate it into an emotion (I "feel" *close* to God). Claiming a near and intimate God—a God you can feel *close* to—risks conflating the Other with the self ("God is me": meaning, "We are *really* close"). This, of course, is the appeal of many New Age movements: becoming God ourselves suggests our ultimate emotional identification with God.

Immediacy, as it turns out, is not just an issue of popular culture. The word "now" appears in scripture 190 times, and it is usually ascribed to God. The word "wait" appears in scripture 74 times, and it is usually ascribed to a man or a woman. God acts now; human beings wait—but not very well. The lack of immediacy in much mainline worship has alienated countless young people, for whom emotional terrain is primary. For youth raised in global postmodernity, God does not merely exist; God "happens." Truth is an event.[19] Even more than the personalized gospel common to much evangelical spirituality, the acid test of meaningful worship for adolescents is objective evidence of inward "contact" between human and divine. Whether invoked through ancient liturgies (recast, for instance, in contemplative prayer or Taizé chants), through Christian youth "raves" that address youth's appetite for electronic stimulation, or through a traditional Eucharist, worship praises the God who "happens," and who chooses to be "God with us" in perceptible but subjective ways.

How to Worship like a Teenager

Worship in the cultural context of adolescence calls for alternative metaphors besides time and distance to describe the religious affections. The God of Jesus Christ cannot be reduced to the categories of global postmodernity. Christians worship a God of paradoxes: in Jesus Christ, God is at once near and far, now and forever, immanent and transcendent, revealed and hidden, active and still, dead and resurrected. The rituals of adolescence—like Christian worship throughout the centuries—dramatize paradox rather than give in to reductionist interpretations. Adolescence is at once exhilarating and painful; hence, rituals like moshing. To omit either the thrill or the anguish would make the ritual untrue. Dramatization is immediate; by practicing the paradoxical love of God, we not only communicate the meaning of the Christ-event more faithfully, we somehow gain access to it. Practices of worship invite God to "happen" to us again and again. They bring every divine paradox into full view by reenacting the life, death, and resurrection of Jesus Christ in imperfect, partial, but authentic ways.

Practicing Transcendence: Worshiping the Playful God

Liturgy means "the work of the people." Unfortunately, we have interpreted this work as the opposite of play. Most of us learned early on that playing in worship is off-limits (as is playing on Sundays generally, in some strict Christian sects). Besides distracting the folks in the pew behind us, playing risks trivializing what we have come to celebrate in worship in the first place: the life, death, and resurrection of Jesus Christ, undertaken on our behalf. Church nurseries—a telling development in twentieth-century liturgical life—were conceived so playing children could be extracted from worship until they reached the age of reason. Once they could apprehend the significance of the Christ event, they became "old enough" to know *not* to play in church, and were permitted to "worship."

The irony, of course, is that worship constitutes one of the oldest forms of play known to human society. Human beings have always engaged in "sacred games" that dramatize the values of their cultic communities.[20] Play points to a larger reality, a "true order" of things intuited but not fully grasped intellectually.[21] Children practice relationships and enact their culture's role expectations by playing house, school, doctor. Americans love football in part because it dramatizes basic (if flawed) assumptions about competitive American culture: success belongs, not to stature or birthright, but to practice, strategy, a willingness to tackle your opponents, and, above all, the ability to get up and keep going after they have tackled you.

The act of playing has a "back and forth" quality to it; it is always relational, always involves an "other"—an imaginative object, a playmate, a conversation partner, a community. Play's reward comes from the deep satisfaction of losing ourselves in the play, the moment of self-abandonment in which the reality we glimpse but cannot grasp somehow grasps us. In this surrender, "something happens" indeed: the self is re-created, infused with intrinsic worth and meaning as we give ourselves over to an Other—an Other that has already given itself over to us.

When youth call us to worship playfully, they remind us that worship makes "hard contact" with God's transcendence in acts of real participation in the life, death, and resurrection of Jesus Christ. In worship, God condescends to play with us, accepting our participation as we are, but at the same time engages us in a larger vision of who we could be. The developmental task of identity formation requires transcendence: we all choose our gods during adolescence—our "ideologies," as developmental psychologist Erik H. Erikson called them, systems of meaning by which the world makes sense.[22] After several false tries, we soon discover that not just any ideology will do; the object of our conversion matters. Only a transcendent God, one who sheds light on our selves from a point beyond the self, can both affirm who we are and invite us into something more.

Adolescents insist on playful worship—worship that is interactive, relational, self-forgetting, and which invites our participation in an expanded vision of reality. Playful worship is not synonymous with trivial, lighthearted, or even exciting worship; youth have their fill of frivolity elsewhere, and the church neither can nor should out-entertain the entertainment industry. What congregations can do, and what true worship does do, is invite youth's full participation instead of their passive assent in the practices of worship. The relational nature of play is critical to adolescents, whose developing sense of self requires the confirmation of others. The existential surrender associated with play engenders the kind of authenticity that adolescents prize, for when we play, our defenses melt. The active give-and-take, relational nature of play is inherent in prayer, praise, proclamation, sacrifice, sacrament, almsgiving—vehicles God "hot-wires" to enter our world again and again as the life, death, and resurrection of Jesus Christ reverberate in the "now."

Practicing Self-Abandonment: Worshiping the Ecstatic God

Closely related to practices of play are practices of ecstasy. If God uses practices of play to condescend to us and "meet us where we are," God employs practices of ecstasy to transport us into a state of being in which we glimpse ourselves and others, however briefly, as new creations in

Jesus Christ. True ecstatic ritual seeks an altered state of consciousness, in which the worshiper experiences something extraordinary, something different, something to be identified with the divine reality.[23] These experiences are short-lived, but profoundly liberating. Practices of ecstasy issue in a range of affective experiences, from a pleasant sense of release to trances and glossolalia. They free us to fall into the embrace of the Divine Lover, whose ecstatic love for us overflows into all creation.

Like cautious parents overseeing their child's first serious crush, mainline Protestants historically have viewed ecstatic worship askance. Ecstatic ritual, according to anthropological research, "is often practiced by the lowly and the oppressed for whom participation produces a temporary respite from the pressures of life. People whose lives are given little structure because they have been denied participation in well-defined, socially acknowledged roles seem to be especially prone to experiences of trance and possession."[24] Given the marginalized role youth assume in American culture, their interest in ecstatic ritual is hardly surprising.

But adolescents are drawn to ecstatic experience for developmental reasons as well as sociological ones. In his theory of adolescent identity formation, Erikson observed what he called the adolescent craving for "locomotion."[25] Locomotion is both a physical and an existential need of adolescents, whose primary criterion for excellence is "Did it move me?" Adolescents evaluate every experience according to the heights and the depths, the ecstasy or the anguish, it inspires. With the onset of formal operational thought, or the newfound cognitive capacity for abstract thinking, adolescents can think reflectively, express themselves extravagantly, and experience both wonder and dread in new, expansive ways. Teenagers look for a "high," quite simply, because for the first time they are cognitively capable of it.[26]

Theoretically, at least, worship offers a form of locomotion. Worship "moves" us, physically and existentially, toward the awesome nearness of God as well as to a profound sense of belonging to a larger whole: the body of Christ. Practicing abandonment means relinquishing control to God, who transports us into a new reality. In many traditions, expressive worship provides catharsis for worshipers in the same way mosh pits offer adolescents a safe space to "get primal." In some Pentecostal churches—where membership among the young is on the rise—practices of self-abandonment include glossolalia, being "slain in the Spirit," and "quaking" (a form of dance permitted because feet do not leave the floor). On the other end of the liturgical spectrum, young adults converting to Eastern Orthodoxy (also increasing in numbers) report a similar appreciation for ecstatic ritual, facilitated by a liturgy that assaults the senses with visual, aural, aromatic, gustatory, and tactile experience, making worship almost trancelike.

By far the most common form of ecstatic ritual among adolescents (and probably the most valued) is music. Whether worshiping through music involves singing, dancing, or even moshing (yes, Christian concerts have mosh pits too), adolescents insist that worshiping involve opportunities to lose themselves in song. The "universal language" of music is often cited as a boundary-breaking medium, another example of the borderless nature of global culture. The explosion of the Christian contemporary music industry since the 1970s suggests an important place for explicitly religious music, but since music is a purely subjective medium, lyrics often play a secondary role to a song's beat, tone, or "texture" in determining a song's sacred significance for teenagers. As a result, youth frequently find secular music as worshipful as Christian music, ancient chants as moving as hip-hop, as they seek a language of praise that transcends verbal discourse.

Practicing Passion: Worshiping the Suffering God

Despite our truncated use of the term to describe the trials of Jesus during Holy Week, passion does not validate divine suffering, but rather underscores divine love—a love so profound it willingly suffers on behalf of the beloved. Nobody wants to be passionately in love more than a teenager. "The single desire that dominated my search for delight," Augustine wrote of his own adolescence, "was simply to love and be loved."[27] The sign of true love, as any diehard *Titanic* fan will tell you, is love that is worth dying for. For adolescents, the authenticity of Jesus is told on the cross. He suffered for his beloved; ergo, his love was true.

Erikson called this search for "fidelity"—the strength of having something "to die for"—the most passionate striving of adolescence. In general, mainline Christianity (like mainstream American culture) expects fidelity of young people, but only reluctantly challenges them with investments worthy of the "little deaths" of self-denial. At the same time, we ignore the fact that contemporary youth are intimately acquainted with suffering. Widespread cultural denial of lifestyle-inflicted wounds caused by poverty, divorce, violence, and hopelessness only magnifies their senselessness. The deluge of data dumped on adolescents by the information age has analyzed their pain but not eradicated it. Technology has enabled them to process information quickly, but has failed to offer hope. At root, suffering is a mystery. But unlike most adults, who tend to view mystery as a source of fear, contemporary adolescents view mystery as a source of possibility. "The truth is out there," proclaims Fox TV's *The X-Files,* an affirmation of faith celebrated by millions of youthful viewers every week. Mystery—despite its undeniable discomfort—is good.

The suffering God is a mystery. Despite the advice of church growth experts to remove crosses from sanctuaries ("seekers" might be offended), the cross stands at the center of adolescent worship, which addresses a quintessential "seeker" crowd. The cross is not rational. The suffering of Jesus cannot be made logical, domesticated, or explained away. It is a mystery—and because it is a mystery, it contains the seeds of hope and redemption. As "Generation X" theologian Tom Beaudoin observes, images of a suffering Jesus have a personal meaning for this generation that these images don't have for their elders.[28]

The passion of Christ, a doctrine much overlooked by twentieth-century mainline Christianity, stands to be reclaimed for worship with adolescents in global postmodernity. While mainstream theologies since Scholasticism have favored the rational methods acceptable to the modern university, passion never lost its subjective foothold in the practices of popular piety or popular culture. Even today, a quick read through the lyrics of mainline Protestant hymnals reveals enough "blood" theology and passionate verbiage to make most of us look twice. At the same time, atonement imagery figures prominently in popular music, video channels, and movies. The point is not that adolescents want to suffer; the point is that they want desperately to love something worthy of suffering, and to be so loved.

Like all philosophical reactions, the "postmodern" swing back toward the gut overshoots its mark, leaving in its wake New Age theologies, angel lore, and a deification of personal experience that no careful reading of Christian theology can fully sanction. On the other hand, as Walter Brueggemann has demonstrated, the Biblical tradition "consistently claims that the impossibilities of *passion* will eventually prevail over the more disciplined *perspective* [of reason]." [29] Christians have thus always approached passion with two minds. On the one hand, passion is linked with "natural" impulses that place us in conflict with God and other human beings and therefore must be curbed. At the same time, passion is an attribute of God, whose love is capable of both boundless delight and unspeakable suffering, and therefore provides our own human experience with a means for self-transcendence.[30]

Worship that hopes to address the cultural context of adolescence must take into account the immediacy of the cross as a sign of God's fidelity and passion for us. Rather than recoiling from divine mystery, adolescents embrace it, especially in sacramental acts that embody the mystery of Jesus' suffering love. Sacraments invoke God's immediacy in mysterious, direct, and brazen ways. In the experience of the Eucharist, for example, "the distance between the human and the divine disappears."[31] God's unfailing promise to meet us in sacramental practice transforms these ordinary means of grace into extraordinary vessels of hope, offering the immediate possibility of divine-human contact. In these sacramental practices adolescents receive the grace necessary for the otherwise impossible task of fidelity, the strength of love that is "to die for."

Moshing to Zion

It is too simple to reduce worship in the cultural context of adolescence to marketing. What will appeal to the youth? How will we get them to come? What should we avoid so they won't leave once they get here? Hundreds of resources are produced each year to answer such questions, all of them obsolete within a week. Frankly, media-saturated, information-overloaded, advertising-savvy adolescents don't really care what we do to attract them, or how we do it. They care that, when they worship, God is present, and that something "happens" because God is there.

Experiencing God's immediacy, therefore, is crucial for adolescent worship, regardless of the form worship takes. Despite impressive statistics suggesting otherwise, God's presence during worship—even bad worship—is never in question. Our ability to perceive God's presence, however, is seriously in question. Adolescent worship is no mere tip of the hat toward "the church of tomorrow." Adolescent worship offers the mainline church a chance to tune up our divine perceptual skills, clean our God-lenses, sharpen our spiritual hearing, in order to apprehend the God who is with us in spite of ourselves. After several centuries of estrangement, reacquainting ourselves with "religious affections" in worship represents an important beginning. Practices of play, ecstasy, and sacrament represent God-initiated forms of divine-human encounter, but they also guarantee that "something happens" during worship: we apprehend God's immediacy—if not at the altar, then in the mosh pit, where the subjective experiences of transcendence, abandonment, and mystery are the name of the game.

NOTES

1. Patricia Hersch, *A Tribe Apart: A Journey into the Heart of American Adolescence* (New York: Fawcett Columbine, 1998), 206–8.
2. Ibid., 207.
3. Personal conversation with Brent Benton, Brian Hughes, and Julie Kim, Princeton seminarians who reported on the reactions of their churches' youth to moshing (April 14, 1999).
4. Hersch, *A Tribe Apart,* 209.
5. George Barna, *Virtual America* (New York: Regal, 1994), 58–59. Another 24 percent say they "rarely" or "sometimes" experience God's presence in worship, while 27 percent said they "always" experience God's presence in worship.
6. David Elkind and Sally Elkind, "Varieties of Religious Experience in Young Adolescents," *Scientific Study of Religion* 2 (1962), 102–12.
7. George H. Gallup, Jr., *The Spiritual Life of Young Americans: Approaching the Year 2000* (Princeton, N.J.: George H. Gallup International Institute, 1999), 3.
8. Bill Moyers, "Of Myth and Men," *Time,* April 26, 1999, 94.
9. Bernhard Lang, *Sacred Games: A History of Christian Worship* (New Haven and London: Yale University Press, 1997), 1.
10. *Rolling Stone,* April 15, 1999, cited in *Youthworker Journal,* July/August 1999, 14.
11. See Matthew McAllister, *The Commercialization of American Culture: New Advertising, Control and Democracy* (London: Sage, 1996).
12. See Rex D. Matthews, "With the Eyes of Faith: Spiritual Experience and the Knowledge of God in the Theology of John Wesley," in *Wesleyan Theology Today,* ed. Theodore Runyan (Nashville: United Methodist Publishing House, 1985), 406–15; Martin Luther, "Preface to the Romans," in *Martin Luther: Selections from His Writings,* ed. John Dillenberger (Chicago: Quadrangle Books, 1961), 24; Jonathan Edwards, "A Treatise Concerning Religious Affections," in *The Works of President Edwards,* vol. 4 (New York: Burt Franklin, 1968).
13. Joseph Kett, *Rites of Passage: Adolescence in America, 1790 to Present* (New York: Basic Books, 1977), 64ff.
14. I am indebted to Douglas Strong, professor of American church history, Wesley Theological Seminary, who pointed me to this thesis. See William McLaughlin, *Revivalism, Awakenings, and Reform* (Chicago and London: University of Chicago Press, 1978), and Richard Riss, *A Survey of 20th Century Revival Movements in North America* (Peabody, Mass.: Hendrickson, 1988).
15. Jay Howard, *Apostles of Rock,* cited in *Life,* July 1999, 81–82.
16. See Michael S. Hamilton, "The Triumph of the Praise Songs," *Christianity Today,* July 12, 1999, 29–35.
17. Among Christian youth in North America, "practices" of faith are proving a route to religious revival as teenagers take part in ancient Christian rituals (rosaries, contemplative prayer, fasting, service to the poor, sacraments, and singing, to name a few) that identify them with a community of faith defined by practices more than by territory.
18. Wade Clark Roof, "Today's Spiritual Quests," in *1997 Princeton Lectures on Youth, Church and Culture* (Princeton, N.J.: Princeton Theological Seminary, 1998), 93–102. Roof cites current models of automobiles as evidence of the pervasiveness of the "journey" metaphor in North American culture. Advertisers promote cars

named Trek, Voyager, Explorer, Quest, Pathfinder; Nissan recently advertised under the slogan: "Life is a journey. Enjoy the ride."

19. See Tom Beaudoin, *Virtual Faith: The Irreverent Spiritual Quest of Generation X* (San Francisco: Jossey Bass, 1998); Kenda Creasy Dean, "X-Files and Unknown Gods," *American Baptist Quarterly* 24 (March 2000), 3–21.

20. See Johan Huizinga, *Homo Ludens: A Study of the Play-Element in Culture* (Boston: Beacon Press, 1970, c1950). The intrinsic relationality of play is described by D. W. Winnicott, *Playing and Reality* (London and New York: Routledge & Kegan Paul, 1971), especially chapters three and four, 38–64.

21. Wolfhart Pannenberg, *Anthropology in Theological Perspective* (Philadelphia: Westminster Press, 1985), 332–33.

22. Erik H. Erikson, *Identity, Youth and Crisis* (New York: W. W. Norton, 1968), 189–191.

23. Lang, *Sacred Games,* 371.

24. Ibid., 369–70.

25. Erikson, *Identity, Youth and Crisis,* 243.

26. Sharon Daloz Parks, "Faithful Becoming in a Complex World: New Powers, Perils, and Possibilities," in *1998 Princeton Lectures on Youth, Church and Culture* (Princeton, N.J.: Princeton Theological Seminary, 1999), 45.

27. Augustine, *Confessions,* trans. Henry Chadwick (Oxford: Oxford University Press, 1991), 24.

28. Tom Beaudoin, *Virtual Faith,* 96–120.

29. Walter Brueggemann, "Passion and Perspective: Two Dimensions of Education in the Bible," *Theology Today* 42 (July 1985), 180 (italics original).

30. For a thorough treatment of the role of passion in Christian education, see Kenda Creasy Dean, "Youth Ministry as the Transformation of Passion" (Ph.D. diss., Princeton Theological Seminary, 1996).

31. Lang, *Sacred Games,* 431.

Chapter 10

"Multicultural" Worship

A Careful Consideration

GEDDES W. HANSON

Introduction

"*First thing, we've got to clear away the underbrush and deal with those big limbs up there. We have to be careful." This was the watchword of the more experienced coworker who had offered to help me clear a fairly well-wooded lot, preparatory to building a house. I wanted to cut down trees, to get the chain saw into the trunk. He had us taking out small shrubs with machetes and trimming as high up tree as we could, cutting off as many long branches as we could, before we got around to doing what I considered the real object of our being out there—getting trees down on the ground.*

Unless we did the clearing and trimming, he argued, we stood a chance of ending up with a tree that was cut through the trunk but "hung up" in another tree's upper reach of limbs. That would complicate the task of downing both trees. Eliminating the underbrush was a good investment of time because we could get more secure footholds in the cleared earth. We would then have safer positions from which to approach a tree, and a safe exit path in case the tree began to fall toward us.

Cutting to the heart of multicultural worship is a bit like clearing that overgrown lot: there is the urge to reach out and just take the saw to the trunk. I want to argue that a more careful approach of clearing and trimming might be more helpful. In this case that means coming clean on our assumptions and clarifying principal definitions.

Care is particularly important in this instance because, despite the recent popularity of the concept "culture" and its relation to the study of organizations, there has been an unfortunate lack of

/145

precision its use. In many instances one cannot reasonably assume what another person means when the word is used. The concept "worship" presents a similar problem. Coming clean on what we mean by both will lead to a more fruitful conversation.

It is my operative assumption here that worship is an activity that is the definitive expression of a religious culture. For most American Christians it is experienced in a congregation,[1] the most basic corporate element of the church. In our aggressively voluntaristic society, there is decreasing enthusiasm for prescribed religious forms and an increasing determination to worship according to the dictates of one's own preferences, not all of which (for example, racial, national, ethnic, or class background) are primarily religious.[2] Congregations have become communities of *choice* as well as of remembrance.[3]

Culture

In the arena of worship, the use of "culture" is made problematic by (1) the imprecision of the definition, (2) the tendency to be overly simplistic when identifying different cultures of different types, and (3) a lack of consensus regarding how the concept is related to the concept of organization.

The word "culture" has had a long and complex use in Western civilizations. Its meanings have changed in interesting ways. Originally a verb (to culture), having to do with the raising of and caring for crops, the word settled into primary linguistic use as a noun, referring to the sum of the artistic, philosophical, social, political, economic, and religious practices of a particular group (a referent). The variety of practices considered in determining the culture of the group varied with the user. Eventually, nonsocial aspects were set aside. The definition that appeared in the 1940s focused attention on the ephemeral aspects of a particular group's life:

> The *essential* part of culture is to be found in the patterns embodied in the social tradition of the group, that is, in knowledge, ideas, beliefs, values, standards and sentiments prevalent in the group.[4]

This narrowing of the definition allowed the word "culture" to do a better job of distinguishing between and comparing particular groups. Still, it was left to the imagination of the researcher to determine which of the ideas, beliefs, values, standards, and sentiments in question were sufficiently important, or salient, to be used in such an analysis. It is possible to distinguish broad-leaved from needle-leaved trees because *all* trees have leaves and they are *either* broad- *or* needle-leaved. In the same vein, careful treatment of the concept of culture depends on the ability to identify social traditions that are *common* to all groups, and demonstrably *varied among* them.

The difficulty in speaking about culture carefully is compounded by the problem involved in identifying the groups whose cultures we wish to study and distinguish. The treacherous condition of the ground on which we stand is evidenced by the wide range of referents on which we base our distinctions: biology, as, for example, "black," "white"; geography, such as African American, Asian American, Euro-American; language, as Hispanic American, Latin/Latino; history, for example, Native American, indigenous aboriginal; and age—generation "whatever"—are routinely mixed as signifiers of cultural identity.

The more closely we examine these signifiers, the more obvious become the variations, nuances, and particularities within the group that are functions of specific historical, social, political, and economic factors. Many African American clergy serve marvelously diverse congregations. West Indian immigrants, their children, and their grandchildren, members of families that trace their lineage through those who immigrated from the South to the North in search of "the Promised Land," African immigrants, and those who trace their roots through the experience of Northern free blacks and slaves sit side by side in the pews and around the table at meetings of the official board. Those pastors serve best who understand the congregation in its *varieties* of African-Americanness. Although each of these parties is part of the African diaspora, the worship they practice together might reflect a greater similarity to that of Euro-American coreligionists than to other congregations of African Americans.[5] Pastors serving "Pan-Asian" congregations or those serving congregations in which language is the social "glue" find themselves in similar situations.

Speaking carefully about culture is made even more treacherous by the fact that cultural analysis—to say nothing of *cross*-cultural analysis—is itself a culture-bound activity. Observers describe others in terms of their similarity/dissimilarity to the observers' accepted norms. In order to speak with any authority of the life of any other group it is necessary for observers to have a firm grasp on the particularities of the life they take for granted. This firm grasp is difficult to achieve, because the observers' lives are as much in flux, in often-unpredictable ways and along as many vital indexes, as those they scrutinize. Those who seek to make definitive judgments about "cultures" find themselves in a position analogous to that of a TV police hero in a thrilling car chase. There she is, driving at excessive speed, dodging this and that and the other urban obstacle (potholes, pedestrians, etc.), whipping the steering wheel back and forth with her right hand while, with her left, she takes shots with her service revolver at the vehicle of an escaping "perp," systematically shooting out the tires of the other wildly gyrating car. Possible, yes, but not plausible, and nothing on which to depend very heavily.

In addition to arriving at some satisfactory set of dimensions on the basis of which to identity and distinguish between cultures, the task we have set for ourselves requires that we stipulate the relation we see between the concept of culture and that of organization. A cursory overview of the emerging literature, however, reveals a noteworthy lack of consensus on how that is to be done. A careful look at the literature suggests that there are three major points of view on the culture-organization relationship. One point of view can be called the *and* school. From this perspective the organization and culture in question are seen as separate entities. Culture is essentially outside the organization. Whatever the organization is/becomes is determined by the degree to which the dominant elements of its cultural context are imported into it or rejected by its members. Another point of view, identifiable as the *of* school, focuses on culture as a product of the organization. The focus of investigation here is the socioritual commodities that are produced as the organization goes about its business of providing goods and services. Culture is seen as one of the variables employed by the collective as a tool for relating effectively to its environment.

Adherents of the third perspective adopt a metaphorical view of the organization *as* a culture: an organism that exists to celebrate/reflect/embody a particular set of values. In a partial reverting to the classical roots of the word, the organization can be viewed as a plant, in the sense that it exists to bear particular fruit. The fruit of the collective, which can be understood as political, intellectual, economic, social, artistic, or religious artifacts, take the shape they do because they are fruit of that particular vine. To the degree that there is "cultural integrity," the fruit on every branch grows out of common commitments to the particular values that the culture exists to embody. With sufficient exposure to the artifacts, a sensitive observer will be able to make judgments about the nature of the organization and the values it incarnates. Months spent in sequence with the congregations of a Roman Catholic parish, of the Church of God in Christ, and of a Presbyterian denomination will provide ample data from which to draw both cultural descriptions and discriminations. The examination of the issue of "multicultural" worship will proceed from this perspective on the culture-organization relation.

Happily, in the midst of this thicket of interlocking upper branches and treacherous undergrowth, there is help in the work of a scholar who has given serious attention to the question of distinguishing between cultures. Geert Hofstede provides a careful way of thinking about social traditions that are universal among groups and that vary between them. The essence of Hofstede's work is most accessible in the report of a study done by a major multinational corporation with regard to significant variables within an international workforce. The population involved was "extremely well-matched subsets from each country's population. . . . [Because of this] cultural differences among countries outside the corporation should be larger than they would be inside, so the national cultural differences found by the study . . . should be a conservative estimate of those existing for the countries at large." The studies revealed that, with regard to values, the characteristic that is the basis of *cultural* distinction, members of national groups from fifty-three countries—European, North American, South American, East African, West African, Arabic-speaking, Asian—differed mainly along only four dimensions.[6]

A brief statement of each dimension will suffice here. *Power distance* refers to the degree to which members of a culture accept and endorse the level of inequality implicit in their relations. *Tolerance for ambiguity* is the degree to which the things that the culture makes and does reflect the tolerance of a perceived lack of structure in situations that are novel, unpredictable, and not amenable to precise meaning or control. Hofstede's third dimension of cultural significance, *the tensive opposition of "masculine" and "feminine" behaviors,* explores gender roles and values operating in an organization. The polar opposites are identified with the stereotypically traditional gender roles of northwest Europe of the middle of the twentieth century. Of critical importance also is the degree to which prescribed gender roles are assigned to persons of each sex. And in the fourth dimension, Hofstede discusses cultural understandings of *individualism* and *collectivism.* He defines individualism as the tendency to predicate one's identity on one's own individual achievement and acquisitions. Collectivism, by contrast, refers to the situation in which identity is derived from one's participation in the group. In the first instance, persons are individuals who might choose to *invest* themselves in particular relationships. In the second instance, persons *are* networks of relationships and have no identity apart from them.

Hofstede's cultural grid gives us a device of the sort I spoke of above. It provides for the description of cultures that is not tied to simplistic referents or limited to particular specific salient dimensions. It also allows for relative differentiation and comparison.

The ways in which these culturally significant dimensions create worship behaviors and the attitudes toward them will be suggested in the next section. First, however, care requires that we isolate the concept of worship from entanglements, as we have with regard to culture.

Worship

It is characteristic of religious collectives that they each reconceive "everyday" reality in their particular way. The everyday phenomenal world that is available to all creatures is understood to be only one dimension of a greater whole. In addition to the phenomenal, reality is understood to encompass a transcendent dimension that has been discovered or revealed. Being religious is, therefore, an exercise in attribution. Religious people strive for consistency by attributing aspects of the phenomenal world to the will/activity of the transcendent dimension of their reality. The degree to which one is religious is reflected by the extent of one's disposition to make extraphenomenal attribution.

A Muslim who maintains confidence in the will of Allah is attributing the shape of "historical" and "natural" phenomena to a transcendent will in a reality that allows for limited human agency. The evangelical Protestant whose understanding of the transcendent-phenomenal relationship presupposes a larger space for human agency says of her religion, "You can't be nonchalant." The Rastafarian, reminded that he and his brothers have a reputation for sternly "reasoning" about the way of Jah with Babylon, retorts, "We take everything seriously!" To a "genuinely" religious person, "nothing is spiritually meaningless."[7]

Christians are those who have been persuaded of a triune God who is author and end of creation, and whose self-disclosure is in the incarnation, crucifixion, and resurrection of Christ. They see their place as those who, by the grace of God, have been blessed to know of these acts, who look forward to participating with Christ in God's future, and who seek to live as a sign of that future.[8] By virtue of the missionary energy of its adherents, the church has been transplanted to every corner of the globe. Communities that accept the Christian experience of the Divine continue to do so in ways that reflect the conviction that Jesus is Lord. They follow the apostolic tradition of expressing that conviction in ways that are, if only in part, particular to their historical, political, social, economic, artistic, and philosophical contexts. As religious cultures, these communities (ecclesia) have developed theological and ethical commitments and styles of worship that they claim as their own and which they identify as the normative means for their being Christian.

The authenticity of an ecclesia's worship is a function of two variables. The first of these is *the degree to which members of the ecclesia recognize it as an appropriate response to the individual and corporate experience of the transcendent.* The believer has a religious experience—one in which aspects of phenomenal reality (a) are attributed to a divine agency (b)—then worship takes place (c).

> O Lord my God! When I in awesome wonder
> Consider all the worlds Thy hands have made,
> I see the stars, I hear the rolling thunder, (a)
> Thy power throughout the universe displayed. (b)
> Then sings my soul, my Savior God, to Thee: (c)
> How great Thou art! How great Thou art!
> Then sings my soul, my Savior God to Thee:
> How great Thou art! How great Thou art![9]

> © Copyright 1953 S. K. Hine. Assigned to Manna Music, Inc., 35255 Brooten Road, Pacific City, OR 97135. Renewed 1981. All Rights Reserved. Used by Permission.

Particular initiatives/behaviors/acts/rites impress themselves on believers as especially appropriate responses to the Divine presence in their lives. Initially these responses to the Divine are spontaneous: cries of anguish and of joy, gestures of humility, glorification, and petition, the impulses to silence and meditation, springing unsummoned from depths of which the believer(s) might not have been aware.

At some point a particular combination of rhythms, expressions, acts, and attitudes receives the imprimatur of those to whom the community grants the prerogative to be arbiters in these matters, for example, the elders, the intellectuals, the political leaders, or those who can claim the closest relation to the source of faith—a text, an event, or a person. A liturgy is established for the sake of order, clarity, and predictability, and, perhaps, to establish and justify the prerogatives of the arbiters. Embedded in the liturgies will be such items as hymns, prayers, invocation, benedictions, verbal explorations of a sacred text, processions, prostrations, genuflections, manual acts, and dance. Tastes, sounds, sights, and movements are enlisted and formed into a drama that articulates the collective's vision and identity.[10] Laws will be enforced that regulate the manner in which emotion is displayed.[11] Those who make a decision on these matters go to lengths to invoke the worship practices of those believers whose experience is considered the classical expression of the religious tradition. Everyone pays homage to "the old-time religion."

A liturgy might be specific to a revivalist sect meeting at a Midwestern crossroads. It might have the ecumenical claim of liturgy fixed among Eastern Orthodox Christians or among their cousins in the Roman Catholic Church. The record of the attempts of Christian believers to enact the mystery of God's initiative and the variety of their response is the history of the worship of the Christian church. The elements of these practices may be neither unique nor idiosyncratic to the community in question; they are, however, to be *normative* for it.

I remember spending some time with a congregation in one of the prairie provinces of Canada. Some of these folk had trekked west from established settlements and were among the first to set plow to soil in that part of the commonwealth. There was a particular gusto in the way they sang:

> Guide me, O Thou great Jehovah,
> Pilgrim through this barren land;
> I am weak, but Thou art mighty;
> Hold me with Thy powerful hand;
> Bread of heaven, bread of heaven,
> Feed me till I want no more.[12]

In a very special way, this was *their* hymn. It was a testimony to their confidence in a God who continually recapitulated succor and strength to those on the way to a Promised Land. It was their legacy to their children—now established and comfortable—a remembrance and a reassurance.

Sometimes the elements are quite specific, although often encrypted.

> Let us break bread together on our knees;
> Let us break bread together on our knees.
> When I fall on my knees, with my face to the rising sun,
> O Lord, have mercy on me.[13]

Here is another religious community dreaming of a Promised Land, this one to the east, on the other side of the middle passage—Home.[14] In each case the community worships by lifting up part of the canon of religious experience as claimed by Christians and witnessing to it in a way that speaks of phenomenal life within the context of a larger reality to which it is particularly privy.

> My Lord delivered Daniel,
> My Lord delivered Daniel,
> Oh, my Lord delivered Daniel,
> Then why not every man?[15]

On occasion the worship element reflects a condition for which there is no canonical precedent: the caller asks, forte,

> Do you want to find Jesus? . . .
> be a Christian? . . .
> get religion? . . .
> expect to be converted?

To each query the chorus responds, piano,

> Go in the wilderness,
> Leaning on the Lord.

An African American congregation that has been schooled in the history of its forebears' endeavors to be faithful in slavery will recognize the allusion to the risks involved in being part of the "invisible institution," which met in secret to worship out of sight and earshot of the owners.[16]

A worship practice that is not indigenous to a religious community will be openly embraced and immediately meaningful to the degree that it reflects a recapitulation of the same values and a rehearsal of the same attributions to divine action as does the one into which it is implanted. Short of a significant degree of commonality, the alien practice is exotic, a curiosity, and, perhaps, a reminder that there are others than ourselves who are a part of the church. Renditions of African American spirituals, Latin, German, or Russian liturgical music, gospel music, or untranslated texts from cantatas and oratorios have the power to fascinate and impress us, emotionally and musicologically. They do not, however, contribute to our worship unless we are able to recognize in them the manner in which the transcendent is on the move in the phenomenal circumstances that surround us.

The second variable on which the authenticity of a congregation's worship depends is *its cultural vocabulary*. Attention must be paid to the degree to which the experience with transcendence is couched in behavior and action that reflect the values attached to *power distance*, the *tolerance for ambiguity*, the *tensive opposition of masculine and feminine behaviors*, and the degree to which the member's identity is derived from *membership in the collective*.

In terms of the *power distance* dynamic, an ecclesial collective might be led in worship by clergy who are significantly separated from their fellows by physical distance, by an architectural device such as pulpit, table, or iconostasis, by use of archaic language, by anachronistic dress, by distinctive physical gestures, or by a particular sophistication in the interpretation of sacred texts. To the degree that phenomena that distinguish between parts of the collective are built into its normal worship life, it is reasonable to suspect that worship is manifesting the values of a culture constituted in part by a disposition toward significant power distance. The community accepts and endorses the inequality it has liturgically instituted.

However, in another worship context different cultural values regarding power distance might be evidenced. Clergy are viewed as functionaries serving at the convenience of their fellows. Places of worship are designed to incorporate all the actors in the worship service—choir, congregation, clergy—in a common space. The liturgy allows for the participation of individuals who are not of the clergy "class." Those who serve without benefit of ordination perform vital roles in the drama. Worship leaders wear the ordinary dress of the day, speak the vernacular of the day, and are accorded respect in the area of religious practice like that accorded to doctors and lawyers in the areas of health and legal practices. Each person's appreciation of the sacred texts' meaning is equally valid. Obviously this collective would be constituted, in part, by a disposition to a relatively narrower span of power distance.

In terms of their *tolerance of ambiguity*, some ecclesial collectives worship with liturgies that they consider inviolate. Regardless of the origin of the worship practices, they must be repeated in exactly the same way each and every time. Inflections of voice and posture are considered necessary to preserve and perpetuate the meaning of the behavior. Ecclesial collectives for which this is of high value will use manuals for worship, with rubrics for leadership carefully spelled out. Orders of worship will be distributed to facilitate the participation of congregants. For some communities, any deviation from the established form—including the manner in which the offering is received—threatens to compromise the worship.

In other ecclesial collectives this sort of precision would be suspect at best. In these congregations, the object is to open the community to the experience of the direct and *immediate* presence of the Holy Spirit in prayer, song, dance, and sermon. The unpredictability of the Spirit, which blows where it will, is evidence of the power of the transcendent. Valuing the unpredictability of God's advent, the culture crafts a religious artifact, its worship service, in which the elements are calculated to open congregants to an ecstatic experience of the Spirit.

By virtue of their position on Hofstede's hypothetical continuum between "femininity" and "masculinity" as cultural values, congregations behave in ways that emphasize an assertive revision of the phenomenal world—in its political, social, economic, artistic, and philosophical aspects—in line with their vision of the transcendent, their dictates, and imperatives. There are African American congregations that find scriptural reasons for interpreting the prevailing racial priorities in the United States as a power distance unauthorized by the transcendent realm of their experience. Not only that, their disposition toward the stereotypically "masculine" pole of the "masculinity–femininity" dimension motivates them to become involved in structuring patterns of resistance and opposition. Theirs is an assertive, even aggressive ministry. Worship will be characterized by extensive use of prophetic texts, reiterations of the social justice commitment of the church, and exhortations to the congregation to become "involved" in helping to revise a phenomenal world out of "synch" with the divine realm.

Other congregations might abhor the same discrepancies between the phenomenal realm and the transcendent. They will be constituted, however, by a commitment toward the other, stereotypically "feminine," pole of the "masculinity–femininity" dimension. The witness of these congregations will reflect the primary concern to succor their constituencies. Unlike their more "masculine" neighbors, these congregations will not be motivated to create aggressive or confrontational social justice ministries to redress the social ills they discern. They will often be active, however, in ministries to social needs. Artifacts—by way of worship and social and economic devices—will be constructed to provide emotional and material support for congregants and others in need. They will seek to provide their members with the means to lead more comfortable lives. These lives will be in harmony, but in a minor key, with those of the dominant power in the society.

In like manner, differences can be observed on the individual/collective cultural spectrum. Worship that emphasizes the need to "get right with God" reinforces the parishioner's sense of the self as a child of God (rather than as a part of God's people) and otherwise encourages a "privatized" relation with the Deity and reinforces a primary commitment to strengthening each worshiper as an autonomous individual. Relation to the ecclesia as the source of religious identity is a decidedly recessive theme. In an extreme case, a parishioner might be satisfied to come, commune, and leave without being involved with any other parishioner. On the other hand, a neighboring congregation, committed to the polar virtue, exists to provide opportunities for believers in Christ to be of mutual support and growth. Everyone is brother or sister, and children are considered a corporate gift and responsibility. In terms of the theme and focus of worship, dominant images include "the nation," "the people," "the family," and "the congregation." The individual has identity by virtue of participation in a common life. The goal of individual involvement is the strengthening, enriching, and perpetuation of the community as a whole.

Conclusion

When the long and often tedious work of trimming and clearing was done, the task of felling the trees became significantly simpler. It had become obvious that the bend in a forty-foot tulip poplar tree would incline it to fall in a particular direction. Surface roots that would restrict movement had been exposed and marked in our memories.

Merely substituting worship elements that are not indigenous to the congregation for those ordinarily in use does not necessarily affect the *cultural* nature of the worship experience. The invocations "Kum ba Yah" and "Veni Creator Spiritus" might be *experientially* interchangeable; a congregation that feels free to use one or the other might find itself with an expanded repertoire for planning worship experiences. However, such a situation does not necessarily result in the creation of worship that reflects another culture. What will be *culturally* important is the degree of tolerance for uncertainty with which the congregation entreats the Deity. Either prayer might call for the visitation of a very orderly, well-disciplined, and carefully enunciated presence. Either prayer might also call for the visitation of a presence that is indifferent to order, empowers the people in the pew to control the service, and moves all to ecstatic, unintelligible outbursts.

Given the terms in which this discussion has been framed, the concept "multicultural worship" is oxymoronic. Worship is specific to a particular religious collective's determination to act out its experience with the transcendent in ways that reflect its essential cultural commitments. Mixing elements of worship from different cultures in the same experience compromises it. The mix might result in something aesthetically pleasing but it raises questions about its authenticity as worship.

What, then, about those occasions when members of different racial groups, or persons of different national origins or with family roots deep in widely separated parts of the globe, do gather for mutually enriching worship? These are occasions in which people of widely differing racial, ethnic, and geographic backgrounds have come to celebrate a common experience and a common religious culture—however improbable that might seem to those who use the term "culture" without care. There *are* congregations within which persons of different racial, ethnic, and national backgrounds enact the same religious experiences and the same values. Racial-ethnic minority members of predominantly Anglo Protestant denominations, Roman Catholicism, and, increasingly, Eastern Orthodox churches often worship in ways that are indistinguishable from the majority members of those ecclesiae. Worship services in these congregations might be multiracial, multiethnic, or multinational, but they are not multicultural—which does not deny their being signs of the oneness of the church.

There might be cases in which the use of worship tools that are indigenous to several communities become vehicles by which the experiences of each are altered and expanded to *include* the experiences of the other—or by which a community finds more vivid expression of the experiences it has already celebrated. This experience is not primarily worship. It is primarily pedagogical. It will become worship when Canadians on the Saskatchewan prairie come to supplement their remembrance of their God's steadfastness with a complementary confession of human faithfulness—

> We've come this far by faith
> Leaning on the Lord;
> Trusting in his holy Word,
> He's never failed me yet,
> Oh, can't turn around,
> We've come this far by faith[17]
>
> © Copyright 1965. Renewed 1983 by Manna Music, Inc., 35255 Brooten Road, Pacific City, OR 97135. All Rights Reserved. Used by Permission.

—and recognize it as an expression of *their* corporate experience. In like manner, middle-class mainline communicants might come to recognize, in the Communion spiritual, the reality of their own alienation from the kingdom in which they claim citizenship.

Congregations of the same denomination enact different values. Congregations of different denominations enact the *same* values. These phenomena are reflected in what has been called the restructuring of religion in the United States. Charismatic Roman Catholics will worship with values regarding the expression of emotion in worship that coincide more with those of some of their Protestant neighbors than with those common among their coreligionists. This coincidence suggests that the charismatics and the Protestants in question are united in a degree of tolerance for uncertainty that separates them both culturally from the entirely predictable drama of the traditional Roman Catholic Mass or the orderliness of much mainline worship.

Given the lack of care with which the concept of culture has been used in popular parlance, the notion of multicultural worship can be expected to appeal to those who are moved by Jesus' prayer that "they may all be one," while laudably resisting the impulse to achieve that oneness by establishing an ecclesial hegemony.

Christians are of a religious expression that describes itself as both *one* and *catholic*. The persistence of congregations that wish to continue to worship in ways and using hymns and prayers that grow out of the historical realities of those with whom they identify on racial, ethnic, or national terms need not be problematic. Neither does anyone's worship experience profit from the incorporation of elements that are opaque. The worship of several congregations is enhanced when the elements that each brings come to be helpful in expressing the experience they have come to *share* in *ways* that reflect fundamental values. As they shape and are shaped by resources born of experiences from multiple strains of the faith, congregations are reconstituted—creating new congregations and an authentic worship of greater fullness.

In horticultural terms, we seek to develop *cultivars*. A cultivar—that is, a cultivated variety—is the product of the grafting together of two varieties of the same species whose characteristics are deemed to be valuable supplements of each other. In congregational life this synthesis might occur spontaneously and informally as congregants resonate with hymns, prayer, gestures, and responses with which they have become acquainted through other venues—radio, television, movies. It might be the conscious choice of a liturgical arbiter to change an age-old manner of doing liturgical business in order to create an artifact that more closely mirrors an emerging experience or a shift in a value of cultural significance.

Careful leadership in this area of a congregation's life recognizes the need to produce a new cultivar, not as a device for positioning the congregation more advantageously in the ecclesial marketplace, but as a means of altering the *essence* of the congregation—increasing its sensitivity to the gifts of experiences and responses to the sacred that are among the experiences of their coreligionists and couched in new cultural terms that have become persuasive.

The role of the horticulturalist/clergy is important. Cultivars are not created because the roots of one variety are buried with those of another in the same hole. One variety must be grafted onto the other. To be authentic, the new liturgical configuration will require a revised articulation and interpretation and evaluation of each event, past, present, and future, of the congregation. If the revision places the witness or history of the congregation in an unpleasant light—as will be the case in some multiracial or multiethnic ventures—it might become a stumbling block to the congregation's ability to accept the reconfiguration. In order to enhance and enrich the worship of either congregation, the cultures must merge to the extent that each recognizes itself—history, witness, and mission—in the other and is able to express that recognition in cultural terms to which both are committed.

A congregation needs to know what it is doing. Its parishioners will appreciate what it will mean to relate to another variety of the faith only to the degree that they appreciate who they are and what they are doing and why. No attempt at multi-anything in the church will be more than superficial if it focuses on the forest exclusively, and gives short shrift to the trees. An exploration of how and why we come to do worship *this* way might, in some congregations, contribute to a healthy determination to explore the resources that are peculiar to us more deeply and exhaustively.

People of goodwill continue to chip away at the *isms* of race, gender, national loyalty, age, and class (among others) that humans have constructed to bedevil themselves. Of the segregators, the most intractable will be culture. The experience of numbers of multiracial, ethnic, and national congregations teaches us that many people can learn to accept others with whom they feel they share a common experience. They will have a harder time accommodating themselves to folks who act in ways in which they have no confidence—be that in a worship service they consider an austere, sterile repression of the human spirit that is entirely inadequate to express the mystery of God; or in an entirely undignified, raucous display of human emotion entirely inadequate as a sacrifice of heart *and* mind—to speak of differences along only one dimension of cultural significance. As long as this is the case, attempts at multi*cultural* worship will falter. We need not lament that. So what if we don't have "multicultural worship"? The oneness of the church is not compromised by the catholicity implicit in its embrace of and by different cultures. Nothing is lost and much is gained by the use of more than one language—cultural or otherwise. There is still a lot to be said for Pentecost.

160 Geddes W. Hanson

NOTES

1. It was the practice of early Christians to refer to their gatherings as *ekklēsia,* a term borrowed from the secular, primarily political, groups with which they were familiar. I will use the words ecclesia and congregation interchangeably. For a discussion of the relation of ecclesia and the church, see Francis Schüssler Fiorenza, *Foundational Theology: Jesus and the Church* (New York : Crossroad, 1984); Joseph Bracken, S.J., "Ecclesiology and the Problem of the One and the Many," *Theological Studies* 43 (1982): 298–311; and Kevin Giles, *What on Earth Is the Church?: An Exploration in New Testament Theology* (Downers Grove, Ill.: InterVarsity Press, 1995), 230–43.
2. Nancy Ammerman, "Organised Religion in a Voluntaristic Society," *Sociology of Religion* 58 (1997): 203–15.
3. Penny Long Marler and David A. Roozen, "From Church Tradition to Consumer Choice: The Gallup Surveys of the Unchurched American," in *Church and Denominational Growth*, ed. David A. Roozen and C. Kirk Hadaway (Nashville: Abingdon Press, 1993); R. E. Prell, "Communities of Choice and Memory: Conservative Synagogues in the late 20th century," *Conservative Synagogues and Their Members: Highlights of the North American Study of 1995–1996*, ed. J. Wertheimer (New York: Jewish Theological Seminary of America, 1996).
4. A. L. Kroeber and Clyde Kluckhohn, *Culture: A Critical Review of Concepts and Definitions* (Cambridge, Mass.: Peabody Museum of American Archeology, 1952), 34.
5. Brenda Agahahowa, *Praise in Black and White: Unity and Diversity in Christian Worship* (Cleveland, Ohio: United Church Press, 1996).
6. Geert Hofstede, *Cultures' Consequences: International Differences in Work-Related Values,* abr. ed. (Beverly Hills, Calif.: Sage, 1984).
7. That is to say, humans are "genuinely" religious to the degree that "nothing is spiritually meaningless, in which no important part of the general functioning brings with it a sense of frustration, of misdirected or unsympathetic effort. It is not a spiritual hybrid of contradictory patches, of water-tight compartments of consciousness that avoid participation in a harmonious synthesis" (E. Sapir, *Selected Writings in Language, Culture and Personality,* ed. D. Mandelbaum [Berkeley: University of California Press, 1985]). I have used here a description by which Sapir spoke of culture in his essay "Culture: Genuine or Spurious," originally published in 1919. His subsequent essay, "The Meaning of Religion," also published in the Mandelbaum volume, provides my warrant for making the substitution.
8. Juan Segundo, *The Community Called Church* (Maryknoll, N.Y.: Orbis, 1973).
9. Carl Gustav Boberg, 1885; English version Stuart K. Hine, 1953, in *The Presbyterian Hymnal* (Louisville, Ky.: Westminster/John Knox Press, 1990), #467.
10. Kieran Flanagan, *Sociology and Liturgy: Representations of the Holy* (New York: St. Martin's Press, 1992); Elochukwu E.Uzukwu, *Worship as Body Language: Introduction to Christian Worship* (Collegeville, Minn.: Liturgical Press, 1997); Bernhard Lang, *Sacred Games: A History of Christian Worship* (New Haven, Conn.: Yale University Press, 1997).
11. Timothy J. Nelson, "He Made a Way out of No Way: Religious Experience in an African-American Congregation," *Review of Religious Research* 39 (1977): 5–26; H. Hochschild, "Emotion Work, Feeling Rules and Social Structure," *American Journal of Sociology* 85 (1979).

12. William Williams, 1745; trans. Peter Williams, 1771, in *The Presbyterian Hymnal* (Louisville, Ky.: Westminster/John Knox Press, 1990), #281.

13. African American Spiritual, n.d.

14. A. Raboteau, "African-American, Exodus, and the American Israel," in *African-American Christianity,* ed. P. Johnson (Berkeley: University of California Press, 1994).

15. African American spiritual, n.d. For a discussion of the appropriation of canonical themes in the spirituals of African American slaves, see Lawrence Lavine, *Black Culture and Black Consciousness: African American Folk Thought from Slavery to Freedom* (New York: Oxford University Press, 1977).

16. A. Raboteau, *Slave Religion: The Invisible Institution in the Ante-bellum South* (New York: Oxford University Press, 1978).

17. Albert A. Goodson, in *The New National Baptist Hymnal* (Nashville, Tenn.: National Baptist Publishing Board, 1977), #222; © 1965 Manna Music, 2111 Kenmere Ave., Burbank, Calif., 91504.

Chapter 11

Music

The "Universal Language" That's Dividing the Church

MARTIN TEL

One might expect celebration at the beginning of a chapter dealing with multicultural music in worship. The images that come to mind are worship experiences at the assembly of the World Council of Churches, with colorful songs and garb from six continents and countless islands. Some dance freely to rhythmic drumming or spring to the powerful strumming of guitars. Others move in very controlled and stylized ways to the haunting melody of the bamboo flute. Most find themselves somewhere between the extremes, but all are basking in the rich musical foretaste of the feast to come.

But such occasions are rare, and if the truth be told, rather than bringing Christians together, music is driving them apart. The new divisions are based not so much on what we believe as on how we worship. Congregations that were once able to come together as one now divide their worship according to preferences of defined sub-cultures. Some celebrate. Others lament.

Worship Wars: "In Time of War, Truth Is Always the First Casualty"

It is difficult in the midst of such division and conflict to deter-mine what responsibility we ourselves bear for this state of affairs. Nevertheless, I think it is time to seek truth once again. Perhaps in the common quest we may be able to walk away from the conflict and turn in a more charitable direction.

There are two aspects of truth that I would like to explore prior to addressing directly the issue of multicultural music in worship. The first is the aspect of truth manifested in excellence. "Finally, beloved, whatever is true, whatever is honorable . . . whatever is pleasing, whatever is commendable, if there is any excellence and if there is anything worthy of praise, think about these things" (Phil. 4:8). One could "think about" any of these qualities at length and to great profit. My concern here is excellence. It seems that we have lost touch with what it means for our music and worship to be excellent. Harold Best gives a pithy definition of excellence when he writes that excellence is excelling, our becoming better than we once were.[1] Though few would have a problem with this definition, many become uneasy when we begin to unpack the word "better."

"Becoming *better* than we once were": suddenly we have on the table a concept that does not jibe well with secular culture and many popular approaches to multiculturalism. Best calls it "better-than-ness," that is, hierarchy in goodness. Such a way of thinking was part and parcel of traditional cultures and was expressed in Christianity particularly through the distillation of both Jewish and Greek thought. Not only was there agreement on "better-than-ness," but there was also general agreement as to the criteria for determining it, objective qualities like unity, variety, proportion, and clarity.[2]

Can such a construct and understanding of excellence have a place in the dialogue concerning multicultural church music? Or are such philosophies that arise out of Christian culture so embedded in Western, Greco-Roman culture as to "stack the deck" so that artifacts that arise out of traditional Western culture come out ahead? I don't know. My inclination is to say that insofar as standards of excellence are rooted in a Judeo-Christian understanding of God and the revelation of scripture, they are still viable for the church today.

To a greater or lesser extent these objective qualities of excellence to which the Christian philosophers referred are embedded in the musics of other traditional religions as well, whether consciously or unconsciously. The Hindu raga, for instance, with its many permutations of a single melodic formula over a sustained drone, demonstrates with clarity qualities of both unity and variety. Much of the same can be observed in other traditional religions. In their artifacts and music one detects unity, internal richness, and clarity. Often one of these qualities is subdued in order to highlight another. Though a Palestrina motet sounds very little like a single bamboo flute playing in a traditional Japanese gagaku mode, both might be considered excellent in objective ways.[3]

In the more recent past, and within some fundamentalist circles today, arguments and attitudes supported the notion that the exotic, the syncopated, the highly charged or hypnotically ethereal, were qualities antithetical to Christianity. Looking back, most agree that rather than having arrived at such conclusions from solid theoretical, theological, or historical grounds, such judgments were reactions against the unfamiliar and rejections of cultures other than one's own. Indeed, any appropriation of multicultural music in the church must be distinctively Christian. The qualities of music that resonate with Christianity, however, are not the provenance of any single culture. Goodness, wherever we find it, is a reflection of the divine Creator.

Why delve into such obtuse and ancient philosophizing when all we really want to do is celebrate multiculturalism? It is important to at least consider the place that truthfulness in excellence plays in multicultural church music. Popular ideas of multiculturalism are based on thinking that there is none better than the other. Multiculturalism becomes a euphemism for the modern assumption that all things are equal and all should be accepted. This spirit is readily adopted by many, if not most, in the church, and truthfulness suffers. By not caring for truthfulness and excellence in our ministries, we stoke the flames of our conflicts. And, as we shall see, by not including excellence in the equation of multicultural worship music considerations, we betray a disrespect for and, in some cases, an abuse of traditions other than our own.

But excellence has its necessary counterpart. The second aspect of truth I will explore is relevance. Relevance must also fit into the equation. A pursuit of excellence alone can lead to an idolatrous elitism. All music, including music from another culture, must have significant meaning for those who are worshiping. Cross-cultural artifacts often require a formal initiation of some sort in order for them to be relevant for the worshipers. Saint Augustine is one of the early fathers who writes about beauty (excellence) in the objective line of the Greek philosopher Plato. Augustine agrees with the Greeks that unity, variety, and clarity help us to determine what is most excellent. But Augustine does not stop here. Whereas Plato would have nothing on this earth stand between himself and the contemplation of perfect forms, Augustine, speaking in the Christian tradition, counters that love for neighbor must interrupt such pursuits.[4] Christ demonstrated through the incarnation a concern to be relevant to those he encountered. Christ instructs Christians to do likewise.

But to pursue relevance without a heart for excellence is also problematic. Many of the divisions in the music ministries of the church can be found in a contentedness to live with only half of the truth. Excellence without concern for neighbor can lead to elitism. Conversely, those who emphasize only relevance will tend to focus on results. After all, if it ministers, if it brings people in, should this not be the criterion for determining the worthiness of the songs we sing in worship? No. The end cannot be the sole determining factor for justifying the means. Christian worship must not settle for mediocrity or disobedience simply because it is effective.[5]

Seeking the truth in the church's song is important. However, we must all remember that as long as we are on this side of the veil, we will see dimly. As we search for and speak about truth, we must do so with humility. Secular society's rejection of truth may owe much to the church's arrogant and careless wielding of "truth" language. We must not speak of such truth as if we can know it fully. We must not argue as Job's friends.

The Overarching Culture

The word "culture" can have many meanings. The contributors to this book are using the term as a reference to "social, linguistic, national, ethnic, and theological realities that locate and identify who we are and what we believe and value." This can be understood as the primary culture we are born into. But the definition needs to be set against an overarching culture which, in North America and more and more throughout the world, is influencing how we think of primary or traditional cultures. This overarching culture characteristically places a high value on market capitalism, consumerism, and the industries of technology and entertainment. The culture relies heavily on television's communicative power and presence to promulgate these values.[6]

It is important for the church to understand as accurately as possible the matrix the church finds itself in today. In seeking to understand the church's position within the overarching culture, Quentin Faulkner suggests that we must acknowledge the presence of a new secular religion.[7] If it is correct to think of mass culture manifesting itself in a new religion (and I am inclined to be convinced by Faulkner), then it is a religion with awesome power indeed, enormously vital and attractive. "Traditional indigenous cultures are powerless against it." Any effort to keep old ways alive "inevitably results either in dilution or in ossification."[8] The church has yet to dialogue in an honest way with such a religion. Perhaps the dialogue has not happened because mass culture is really not interested in the church. But it does not help that the church has not owned up to the immense vitality and persuasiveness of the overarching culture.

This power is partly manifested in the mass culture's assumptions. Whereas traditional religions have tended to operate with doctrine and dogma, this new culture replaces them with assumptions that are appropriated informally and embedded deeply. One does not question assumptions lightly.[9]

In light of all this, we have to wonder why the church should be concerned with formal introduction to traditional cultures if we could more easily (that is, informally) participate in the larger umbrella culture. After all, such a culture seems to be in the powerful position to subsume all traditional cultures anyway. We are closer than ever to having a unified global culture under the banner of North American mass culture. Many evangelically minded people see this as an opportunity to create a uniform musical language for worship, a language that is powerful and seemingly winning international acclaim. But while the zeal is evangelical, could one ascertain whether or not the medium is evangelical? (I mean evangelical in the sense of fittingness with the gospel of Christ.) What are the costs of adopting (or succumbing to) this popular, sweeping form?

Some would see the North American umbrella culture as a form of multiculturalism. However, mass culture is in many ways intolerant of traditional cultures. Mass culture will not put up with the necessary formal introduction that crossing a culture boundary requires. When the umbrella culture comes into contact with a traditional culture it tosses aside genuine internal richness and reduces it to aspects that can be fed through the meat grinder and served up for easy consumption. "'Multiculturalism' (as it is preached today) then becomes a smokescreen that obscures the gradual reduction of many cultures into a unified secular culture. The smorgasbord approach characteristic of today's popular multiculturalism (a bit of Black here, a bit of Latino there, resting on the remains of a rejected quasi-Judaeo-Christian world-view) is in fact a hallmark of the new secular religion."[10] We in North America all stand under the shadow of this umbrella culture.

Why Should the Church
Cross Cultures Musically?

Cornelius Plantinga, in his book *Not the Way It's Supposed to Be: A Breviary of Sin*, gives us a vision of shalom: "Above all, in the visions of Christians and other theists, God would preside in the unspeakable beauty for which human beings long and in the mystery of holiness that draws human worship like a magnet. In turn, each human being would reflect and color the light of God's presence out of the inimitable resources of his or her own character and essence. Human communities would present their ethnic and regional specialities to other communities in the name of God, in glad recognition that God, too, is a radiant and hospitable community, of three persons. In their own accents, communities would express praise, courtesies, and deferences that, when massed together, would keep building like waves of passion that is never spent."[11]

To break shalom is sin. To not seek shalom is sin. If this vision of worship is shalom, or when enthusiastic worshipers at the World Council of Churches in Zimbabwe perceived the new Jerusalem breaking into earth from heaven, is neglect of such goodness an option? Is division not sin? Crossing cultures in our worship music is not an easy task. Why should we take such pains? Because Christ desires unity in the church.[12]

Music, the mythical universal language, is more and more being used as a fence to keep people apart. In Michael Hamilton's words, "Our new sectarianism is a sectarianism of worship style. The new sectarian creeds are dogmas of music."[13] Some of this has to do with ethnic or linguistic aspects of culture, some has to do with other subcultures. To quote Plantinga's book title, this is "not the way it's supposed to be."

If we can have a vision of shalom, of the way it's supposed to be, we must pursue it. *Lex orandi, lex credendi*—the rule for prayer is the rule for belief. Each month I look forward to celebrating the sacrament of Holy Communion at the local church I attend. Time and time again I am profoundly moved by the words of the post-communion prayer: "O Savior God, look upon your Church in its struggle upon the earth. Have mercy on its weakness, bring to an end its unhappy divisions, and scatter its fears. Look also upon the ministry of your Church. Increase its courage, strengthen its faith, and inspire its witness to all people, even to the ends of the earth."[14] We must actively work out our prayers and visions. It is incongruent for us to pine for a future when all nations will be united in praise if we have no intention of making it true in our own communities, crisscrossed by cultural lines and barriers.

And why musically? Not because it's easy or fun (for often it is the opposite), but because music can connect us to the lives of others. As Mark Bangert writes, "Music has staying power; more than any other cultural characteristic it conveys and enfleshes the uniqueness of a people. In a very profound sense music is social text, the place where we can 'read' the community."[15] Cultures pour out their souls in their art. Here we may find a bridge for cross-cultural connection. And when we begin to listen to and in time sing one another's songs, we may have a new and renewed ecclesiology which will favor more and more unity in our unhappily divided church.

Crossing cultures musically can also help us to name and remove idolatries. Trained church musicians in North America are no less susceptible to the mass culture than are other people. Though obviously many leaders are more influenced by popular culture, most conservatory- and university-degreed musicians are trained in the "institution of high art." Of course, high art is not sin. Elitism in "high art" is a sin, because it treats what is a limited good as if it were an ultimate good.[16] Church musicians shoot themselves in the foot when they vilify music for its simplicity or toss aside a song because it is "repetitive."

Of course, other cultures also have their classical traditions. But often when we sing multiculturally in worship we by necessity gravitate to what is most accessible, at least initially. What we first appreciate are the folk songs, which are often simple and, at least in some cultures, very repetitive. We discover too that these songs of the people are excellent in their form, and excellently suited to their purpose—to carry the people's prayer and praise. There is no denying the beauty of the simple Zimbabwean hymn "If You Believe and I Believe."[17] Cross-cultural singing experiences can assist in dismantling idolatries. This is not license to deny or ignore the richest of our arts. Indeed, each culture should excel to its ability. But part of excellence in the congregation's song is that it truly is the people's song. There are reasons to be wary of the pop packaging of much of the "praise" music on the market today, but the problem cannot be pegged solely on qualities of repetition and simplicity, qualities that have always been integral to the people's song. Multicultural music has reminded us of this.

Pitfalls in Cross-Cultural Musical Endeavors

It seems that whenever we are handed something good we have a predilection for abusing the gift. Of course this is what idolatry does (treating a limited good as if it were an ultimate good), and that is why it is so deceiving. Yes, multicultural music in worship can help us debunk our old idols, but we must be careful not to institute new, replacement idols. A commitment to multicultural music holds great promise for renewed hospitality and unity in the church. But when multicultural music is treated as an ultimate good, the church is deceived.

Again, the umbrella culture in which we live and breathe sets us up for misappropriations of music from other cultures. Many churches have bought into the assumption that communication should be entertaining and must be easy. In this preselection process, gone are all the songs that offer lament or protest of injustice. Gone are any songs that defy our Western notational system. Traditional East Asian and Middle Eastern genres are deemed to be too cerebral or stylized and are summarily written off. Some of the African and Hispanic songs are attractive to us, but they need to be "adapted" to fit our style. And so on and so forth. And this is not only what pop culture does to music of other traditions. The same fencing is going on around the tables of church music committees.

Many delegates to the 1999 General Assembly of the Presbyterian Church (U.S.A.) returned with a pre-publication sampler of a songbook. The foreword touts: "All the music is easy to sing."[18] One multicultural inclusion is a setting of a traditional Zulu song, "Siyahamba." In the presentation of this Zulu artifact, no deference is given to the original singers of this folk song. The improvised harmonies integral to the song (best learned by rote) are reduced to a unison melody line. There is no suggestion as to how percussion might be employed, but rather a pop piano accompaniment with guitar chords has been contrived. In the end, the African chant is robbed of its "Zulu-ness" to such an extent that it differs only negligibly from other songs in the collection. Is this how the church is to be multicultural? The sampler states that all the texts are "in accord with Reformed theology and inclusive language about people." Is it not fair to ask whether or not the music, the medium of the text, has something to say about theology and inclusivity as well? If our songs on earth are to be a foretaste of the riches of heaven, it is no wonder that some are rethinking whether they indeed want to be "in that number."[19]

And then there is that aspect of the umbrella culture which I referred to earlier as the "institution of high art." This institution, by making aesthetic contemplation the noblest use of all art (including music), has enabled us to take artifacts from other cultures and disregard their original function. The multicultural song is displayed or objectified for self-musing. We are invited to promenade past these acquisitions as we would through the "Slippers of the Ming Dynasty" exhibition at some renowned museum of art. Such must not be said of the multicultural music offered in our worship. Karen Ward writes: "In the present milieu of 'cultural enthusiasm,' it is especially important to remember that cultural, ethnic, or racial idioms are employed in worship to serve the gospel."[20]

And, finally, multicultural singing can be used as a camouflage to hide the angst of distrust and the sin of division. A friend of mine worked in a parish in a suburban area in the Midwest. There was clamoring in this fairly traditional parish for the inclusion of African American and Hispanic-style songs, though neither of these cultures was represented in their community. There was a perception that some "lighter" styles would ease the boredom of their routine worship. My friend relented, but only with the understanding that there would be efforts made to make connections with the culture from which they were borrowing. There happened to be a large Hispanic population in the city, and arrangements were made for the parish youth group to meet together with an urban Hispanic youth group. Friendships were made as these youth crossed the invisible borders separating their neighborhoods. It was the parents who brought the program to an abrupt conclusion. Singing multiculturally can be dangerous because it can give the false satisfaction of actually being and living multiculturally. Obviously this parish had no such aspirations. "Give us your guitars and your tunes, but please don't cross our lines." Like the Babylonians, we can be adept at demanding songs. Our skill for acquiring songs is not equaled by our concern for justice.

Prepare the Way

I have written more here about theory and philosophy than about the "how to" that everybody claims to really want. However, I believe that the theory, the theology, must precede the practice (or at the very least develop alongside it). John Dewey said that there is nothing more practical than a good theory. And so we must all give thought to the philosophies and theologies from which we work out our worship. An unarticulated theory of multicultural worship music is still a theory, but it is more dangerous than the one that is probed. By putting aside such inquiry and dialogue, we stoke the fires of our worship wars.

To sum up, I have distilled some of what I have written above into five ideas about how we might prepare ourselves and our congregations for the use of multicultural music in our worship.

1. Commit to excellence and relevance. To attempt one without the other will lead to further division. Learn to enjoy the dynamic counterpoint of these seemingly opposite demands. Consonance without dissonance remains only a concept, not a reality.
2. Commit to contemporary worship. Here at Princeton Theological Seminary, we once conducted a vesper service in a seventeenth-century North German Lutheran tradition, complete with a Schütz Magnificat accompanied by period instruments. Before the service

began, liturgical musicologist Robin Leaver formally introduced us to the culture from which this liturgy and music came. We practiced some of the chorales and chanted litanies. And then Robin Leaver said something that startled many: "This evening we will have a contemporary worship experience"—for, as he went on to explain, contemporary worship is not determined by when or where or in what culture the music or liturgy was composed. Contemporary worship happens when we worship God now. In silence we prepared ourselves to meet God in worship, and God was present among the worshipers. Many in the chapel that evening may have come to the event for a merely aesthetic experience of high art. Robin Leaver, in a very Lutheran fashion, preached the idols out of our hearts.[21] Just as here, all the multicultural music in our church services should be committed toward contemporary worship experiences.

3. Listen for the voice of the other. In order for there to be true multi-cultural dialogue, each culture must have a voice. On the first level this must be a human voice. We learn best by listening to the natives of our cultures. We gravitate so quickly to the printed page of musical notes and symbols. The music is not there. I love to watch composer Alice Parker hold the hymnal to her ear and exclaim: "I don't hear a thing!" The song is in the human voice.

And on another level, there is our cultural voice. Sometimes we have the music of our own culture turned up so loud that we fail to hear the songs of our neighbors. In fact it is possible that we have drowned out the voices of some of our cultural neighbors so that they must now rediscover their own voice. Although we have romanticized the idea of music as the universal language, it is, as Mary Oyer points out, "far more likely an exclusive language, communicating only with those who are initiated. It must be learned in much the same way a spoken language is learned."[22] Dialogue requires that everyone has a voice. Listen.

4. Cross-cultural sharing must go both ways; otherwise it is cross-cultural taking. Ever since the Abyssinian Baptist Church of Manhattan made it into European travel brochures as the place to experience African American worship, the church has been inundated by hundreds of tourists vying for their pew space. They want to experience the black gospel tradition. Indeed, this church is rooted in its African American heritage and culture. Yet many are surprised to learn that their choir also sings Handel's "Messiah." Churches and denominations that are of dominantly European extraction have

benefited richly from the treasures of the African American culture of spiritual and gospel song. But rather than taking, there should be exchanging, and rather than being surprised by such genuine sharing and acceptance of gifts, we, of whatever culture, should be concerned when the artifacts are traveling in only one direction.

5. Commit to justice and love. Christian worshipers often do not consider how multicultural music can be a vehicle for injustice. The word multicultural for many connotes a quasi-magical aura of "everything's allright." However, "If going about multicultural worship begins to look like a liturgical version of a world food court, then does it not elevate us to a privileged consumer caste while others are compelled to satisfy our needs?"[23] The prophet Amos brings a clarion word from God:

> I hate, I despise your festivals,
> and I take no delight in your solemn assemblies. . . .
> Take away from me the noise of your songs;
> I will not listen to the melody of your harps.
> But let justice roll down like waters,
> and righteousness like an ever-flowing stream.
> (Amos 5:21–24)

In love and justice may our communities reflect the triune God we adore, that radiant and hospitable, most excellent community of three Persons. Together may we piece together a Te Deum of the nations. Together may we hold fast to the vision of God's shalom. *Soli Deo gloria.*

NOTES

1. Harold M. Best, *Music through the Eyes of Faith* (San Francisco: HarperSanFrancisco, 1993), 108.
2. For further explanation and application of "objective qualities" of excellence, see Nicholas Wolterstorff, *Art in Action: Toward a Christian Aesthetic* (Grand Rapids: Wm. B. Eerdmans Publishing Co., 1980), particularly pt. 3, chap. 4, "Norms in Art: Artistic and Aesthetic Responsibility."
3. To argue that there are universal objectives that manifest themselves in traditional music from all cultures (unity, variety, proportion, clarity) is not to say that the objectives are reducible to the same terms. In very broad strokes, Western music is more likely to be evaluated according to harmony, while Eastern music may focus more on melody, and an African musical aesthetic may be approached more with an ear toward rhythm.
4. See Augustine, *City of God* 22.20 and Robert J. O'Connell, S. J., *Art and the Christian Intelligence in St. Augustine* (Cambridge, Mass.: Harvard University Press, 1978), 138–39.

5. It could otherwise be stated that often the means does equal the end. If the means lacks real depth or excellence, one may expect that the end will be found correspondingly lacking. One could list exceptions to this principle, but exceptions should not determine practice. For more on the balance of both excellence and relevance, see Best, p. 118. See also my article "Truthfulness in Church Music," *Princeton Seminary Bulletin*, n.s., 19, no. 1 (1998): 26–39.

6. See Neil Postman, *Amusing Ourselves to Death: Public Discourse in the Age of Show Business* (New York: Viking Penguin, 1985), Marva Dawn, *Reaching Out without Dumbing Down: A Theology of Worship for the Turn-of-the-Century Culture* (Grand Rapids: Wm. B. Eerdmans Publishing Co., 1995), esp. pt. 2, "The Culture Surrounding Our Worship"; and Thomas Shattauer, "How Does Worship Relate to the Cultures of North America?" in *Open Questions in Worship: What Does "Multicultural" Worship Look Like?* ed. Gordon Lathrop (Minneapolis: Augsburg Fortress, 1996), 13. There are many ways in which this characterization of mass culture needs to be nuanced, and one should acknowledge that there are positive aspects of mass culture from which we have all benefited. However, it is interesting that some Christians see such a characterization as an "assault" against mass culture and would refute it, while the industries of mass culture by and large seem to be at peace with it.

7. Quentin Faulkner, "Cult and Culture at the Millennium: Exploratory Notes on the New Religion," *Soundings* 79, no. 3–4 (1996): 399–420.

8. Ibid., 405.

9. One *assumes* that there is no objective basis for excellence. "I am no better than anyone else and no one else is better than I." If this were doctrine, one might sooner venture to challenge it. As an assumption, many will consider such a statement to be above dispute.

10. Faulkner, "Cult and Culture," 417.

11. Cornelius Plantinga, Jr., *Not the Way It's Supposed to Be: A Breviary of Sin* (Grand Rapids: Wm. B. Eerdmans Publishing Co., 1995), 12.

12. Unity is our goal, but unity must be understood as something other than uniformity. Uniformity can be seen in aspects of our modern culture, whether it is the elitism present in institutions that dictate that aesthetic contemplation is the end of all art, or popular culture, which seeks to bend all art to common denominators of ease and entertainment, or uniformity as manifested in fundamentalism, which seeks to protect a particular culture through isolation and rigid rules of conformity.

13. Michael S. Hamilton, "The Triumph of the Praise Songs: How Guitars Beat Out the Organ in the Worship Wars," *Christianity Today* (July 12, 1999): 30.

14. *Rejoice in the Lord,* ed. Erik Routley (Grand Rapids: Wm. B. Eerdmans Publishing Co., 1985), 570.

15. Mark Bangert, "How Does One Go About Multicultural Worship?" in *Open Questions in Worship: What Does "Multicultural" Worship Look Like?* ed. Gordon Lathrop (Minneapolis: Augsburg Fortress, 1996), 30.

16. I take this definition of idolatry from Wolterstorff, *Art in Action.* See p. 83.

17. In *Sent by the Lord: Songs of the World Church,* vol. 2, ed. John L. Bell (Chicago: GIA Publications, 1990), 51.

18. *Lift Up Your Hearts: Songs for Creative Worship. Pre-publication Sampler Edition.* ed. Linda White (Louisville, Ky.: Geneva Press).

19. Recent attempts in denominational hymnals to include global hymns are to be applauded. We need to see these examples as initial steps. But when these songs are difficult to distinguish from the songs of the dominant tradition of the collection, red flags should be raised. While the example cited from the sampler sounds a discouraging note, there is encouragement in other collections, most notably in the Mennonite collection *Hymnal: A Worship Book* (Newton, Kans.: Faith and Life Press, 1992). For the most part this hymnal avoids imposing Western harmonizations on musical genres that were conceived as unison or improvised harmony. The *Hymnal Accompaniment Handbook* (Newton, Kans.: Faith and Life Press, 1993) is an excellent source for leaders in preparing to introduce the multicultural examples to the congregation.

20. Karen Ward, "What Is Culturally-Specific Worship?" in *Open Questions in Worship: What Does "Multicultural" Worship Look Like?* ed. Gordon Lathrop (Minneapolis: Augsburg Fortress, 1996), 36.

21. In his treatise "Against the Heavenly Prophets," Martin Luther rebukes Andreas Karlstadt for his espousal of radical iconoclasm. Luther contends that idolatry is in the heart: "I approached the task of destroying images by first tearing them out of the heart through God's word." See *Luther's Works: American ed., vol. 40,* ed. Conrad Bergendoff (Philadelphia: Muhlenburg Press, 1958), 58.

22. Mary Oyer, "Global Music for the Churches," in *Music in Worship: A Mennonite Perspective,* ed. Bernie Neufeld (Newton, Kans.: Faith and Life Press, 1998), 74.

23. Bangert, "How Does One Go about Multicultural Worship?" 27.

Chapter 12

Navigating the Contemporary Worship Narrows

Channel Markers for Deep Waters

LEONORA TUBBS TISDALE

*M*y husband Al loves to sail, and in recent years has taught our family to love it too. The first sailing trip our family ever took with him was on the Chesapeake Bay, where the warm June breezes, the sounds of water lapping against the sides of the boat, and nights spent stargazing in secluded coves quickly converted even the most skeptical among us.

One of the things we learned early on, though, was that in sailing water depth is critical. Especially when sailing through the "narrows"—those bodies of waters that are, as the name implies, narrower and more treacherous than the wide open waters of the bay—there is always the danger of running aground on the shoals that jut out into the water on either side of the channel. And nobody, but nobody wants to run aground. At its best, running aground can turn a delightful day's sail into an instant lesson in frustration, as would-be sailors sit idly for hours waiting for a tow. At its worst, running aground, especially against rocky shoals, can cause debilitating damage to a boat's hull.

Consequently, one of the first things my husband taught our family of novice sailors was vigilance in watching for the red and green channel markers of the bay, which signal where the deeply dredged channels lie. As long as we stay between them, and do not veer outside them on either side of the narrows, we know we are in sufficient depth to keep us from running aground.

Worship: Sailing the Deep

Throughout its history, the church has been likened to a ship, sailing the seas of this world with Christ as its captain. The World

Council of Churches, one of the most ecumenical and multicultural bodies of Christians on earth, has as its symbol a ship sailing the seas of the *oikoumenē* (the whole inhabited earth), with a cross as its mast. And worship—whether at the World Council of Churches level or the local church level—has often been one of those venues where the church has sailed at the greatest depths.

It is in worship that the church has encountered the holy Creator of the universe, who fashioned the seas and all that is in them, and who gives breath to every living thing. It is in worship that we have returned to the waters of our baptism, dying and rising anew with the Christ who calls us to faithful discipleship. And it is in worship that the church has sensed anew the refreshing winds of the Spirit, filling its sails for new ventures in faith and witness. At its best, worship takes us to the deepest places of existence, where our lives find their true rhythm and flow, and where our entire beings give glory to the one who upholds, guides, and sustains us on our voyage.

Contemporary Worship Wars

Yet in recent years, as congregations have been tossed about by the many "worship wars" that have plagued their common life, the dangers of running aground or of steering too close to the shallows have also increased. The wars of which I speak are numerous and common in congregational life today:

- Wars over whose cultural style and taste and preferences in music will predominate in worship

- Wars over which hymnal or order of worship to use

- Wars over whether worship should focus primarily on evangelistic outreach to nonbelievers (as in many "seeker" or "seeker-oriented services") or on the ongoing nurturing of believers

- Wars over whether we should gear our worship planning and design toward first- or second-generation immigrants, toward baby boomers or Generation Xers, toward youth or the aging

- Wars over how "traditional" and how "contemporary" our worship should be.

In the midst of all these wars, which cause tremendous upheaval in local congregations, and in the midst of the arguments made pro and con on both sides of the battles, I am increasingly concerned by the question that is all too often ignored in these debates, namely, *How do we keep worship "deep" theologically*? How do we steer a course in our common worship—whatever its style or form or substance—that avoids steering too close to those theological shallows on either side of the narrows that can rob worship of its deepest meaning, mystery, and joy? How do we steer a course that avoids either frustrating its worshipers or doing damage to the very essence of who and what the church is, and that takes our ship into the deep waters, where we encounter the fullness of the God revealed to us in Jesus Christ?

The Quest for Theological Channel Markers

In order to assist us in that quest, I want to suggest four theological channel markers that can guide pastors and worship planners as we reflect on the nature of worship in our own unique and diverse contexts. Let me say at the outset that I do not believe there is any one "right" way to worship God deeply (although I, like you, have my personal preferences). One of the things I learned through worshiping with the church universal during my eight years of involvement with the World Council of Churches is that there are many, many ways in which to worship God deeply. Though my own tradition is solidly Reformed (having been a lifelong Presbyterian), I have also had the opportunity in my life to sail deep worship waters with Russian Orthodox believers in Russia, with Roman Catholic Christians in Venezuela, with black Baptists in Georgia, with Pentecostals in Korea, and with Quakers in Rhode Island. My experience of worship in the church universal and ecumenical leads me to be very cautious about thinking any one way to worship is the "right way" or that any one denomination sails the deeps alone.

But I also know that any cultural or denominational expression of worship that does not attend to its theological purposes can also end up in the shallows, leaving worshipers sensing that the whole experience has been, at best, an exercise in frustration or, at worst, an experience that, if not checked, just might do serious structural damage to the nature, purpose, and mission of the church itself.

My goal then is not to advocate for any one right way to worship (though I am sure that my own biases will inevitably shine through), nor is it to prescribe a set way to navigate through the various worship wars we experience in our unique and diverse congregational contexts. I'm enough of a sailor by now to know that there are many safe courses a boat can take and still "stay the deep." Rather, what I hope to do is to provide some questions—theological questions—that can be "channel markers" for us as we find our way through the worship narrows: markers that can tell us where the shoals lie on either side of the bay, and that also guide us toward the deeper waters to be found in their midst.

Four Channel Markers for Worship Leaders

1. Deep worship is focused both on the praise and glory of God and on the edification of the worshipers.

One of the debates that is frequently engaged during today's worship wars involves the question of whether worship will focus primarily on being *soli Deo gloria* ("to the glory of God alone"), or will focus primarily on attending to the needs and preferences of the worshipers. Often those who emphasize the former remind us that we were created to worship God, and consequently we need to offer God our best in worship: our best music, our best preaching, the best prayers of our traditions. Drawing on Kierkegaard's theater image for worship, these folk remind us that in worship we are not the audience, God is. And the purpose of true worship is not our edification, but the glory and praise of the God of the universe. If we want to truly praise God, they say, then we bring God our best. And we don't allow worship to be interrupted by elements (such as announcements) that might detract from the praise and glorification of God alone.

On the other end of today's worshiping spectrum are those who argue that if the church is going to engage contemporary people in its life of worship and praise, then it must attend more closely to their needs, desires, and preferences. Contemporary people are bored with our traditions, these folk say, and often find them either irrelevant to their own lives, or unintelligible, or downright boring. Witness, in this regard, the significant decline in worship attendance most mainline churches have suffered in recent decades. If we want to meet the needs of contemporary people, especially the unchurched, then we have to meet them where they are. We need to sing hymns that have familiar tunes or whose rhythms and melodies are reflective of local culture. We need to translate our prayers into the vernacular of the people, avoiding language that is archaic or lofty. And our worship needs to incorporate a strong teaching function so that those who are unschooled in the faith may learn its ways easily.

John Buchanan, pastor of Fourth Presbyterian Church in Chicago and editor of the *Christian Century* magazine, has written an article in which he likened some of the worship wars he witnessed in local congregations during his year as moderator of the Presbyterian Church (U.S.A.) to the tensions between two Italian brothers struggling to keep their restaurant open in the motion picture *Big Night*. Writes Buchanan:

> The older brother, Primo, is a magnificent chef, an artist, committed to purity, faithfulness, and integrity. The younger brother, Secundo, is a businessman, an entrepreneur who has to negotiate a loan extension with the bank and figure out how to pay bills. Primo makes wonderful risotto that nobody will buy. "What is this stuff? Where's the meatballs?" a disgruntled diner complains. Primo loves his art, gives his elegant concoctions away, and ultimately doesn't care if anyone will pay money for his food. Secundo looks longingly across the street at a very successful Italian restaurant/nightclub that does not aspire to purity and integrity, serves lots of spaghetti with meatballs (no risotto), plays phony but popular Italian music, and has lots of customers.

Buchanan comments that this movie reminds him for all the world of the current debates within local congregations over worship: "Shall we continue with the Prayer of Confession or substitute a dramatic skit? Employ J. S. Bach or praise songs? Use a pipe organ or a synthesizer?"[1]

But Buchanan also contends that these arguments are the wrong arguments.

> What we have to ask ourselves are basic questions: What's the purpose of worship? Is it transformation? Really? Is it proclamation? Is it celebration? Can we do it all and can we do any of it without becoming ponderous and boring? How many meatballs do you keep on the menu in hopes that a customer will try risotto?[2]

The question Buchanan raises is critical: What is the purpose and focus of worship? My own tradition, the Reformed tradition, clearly comes down on the side of worship that is aimed toward the glory and praise of God. Our chief end as human beings, says the *Westminster Shorter Catechism*, "is to glorify God and to enjoy [God] forever." We were created to give glory to our Creator.

But that does not, of course, answer the question that haunts most worship committees and worship leaders: namely, in whose language and styles and forms will we express our praise of God? Nor does it acknowledge the reality that knowledge of God and knowledge of self are also integrally related in Reformed theology. In worship we not only discover who God is, we also discover who we are and who we are called to become. Worship, in the final analysis, is both celebrative and transformative. It is, as David Newman puts it, both praise of God and empowerment of humanity.[3] And the two cannot be separated, lest we end up on dangerous shoals on either side of the narrows.

If we steer too hard toward the *soli Deo gloria* side of the waters, we can end up with a worship elitism that is so absorbed in its own traditions and rituals that little notice is paid to those who are struggling to understand why we do what we do, or how they too might participate in the praise and glory of God. Especially troubling are those occasions when the church's worship becomes inaccessible to those on the margins of society—children, the poor, the less educated—worship that de facto excludes their participation because it assumes an insider knowledge not broadly shared, or a monocultural definition of what offering God "our best" means.

Despite my deep appreciation and love for the worshiping tradition of my own Presbyterian denomination, I am also judged by the fact that the poor have not come to our worship services in great droves. Nor have children or youth or people of other cultures always been made to feel welcome and included in our worshiping communities. Somehow, in our quest for *soli Deo gloria* we have also communicated a style of glorifying God that has not made that praise accessible to all.

Yet worship can also run onto shoals when it becomes too focused on the edification of humanity. Worship that is more concerned with marketing than with glorifying God, that flattens all sense of awe and mystery and wonder in the name of accessibility, that eschews all tradition in the name of the "new" and the "innovative," and that reduces God by making God more palatable to the tastes of the worshipers, is equally problematic. Increasingly we are falling prey to a market mentality in church promotion that offers consumers as many options as a shopping mall, or that seeks to draw them into the church with something that is not even called "worship" in the traditional "word and sacrament" sense of the term.[4] What becomes dangerous when the ship of worship sails too close to these shoals is the supplanting of God as the center of worship, an individualism that focuses more on "what worship does for me" than on how it empowers and unites the whole body of Christ for service in the world, and (at its worst) a reduction of God to a size and type that fits human needs.

To sail the deep waters, worship needs to chart a path between these two extremes, bringing people into the presence of a God who alone is worthy of our adoration and praise, but also providing them with a language and forms for worship that allow them to address God authentically, and in ways that can transform and renew the particular local community gathered in God's name.

2. Deep worship is Trinitarian in nature, giving witness to the fullness of God's nature and attributes as attested in Scripture.

Many observers of the contemporary worship scene caution that there is a growing tendency in today's church to "reduce God to our size" in worship, rather than allowing worship to express the fullness of who God is and what God desires of us. Certainly one of the classic theological checks against such reductionism is to ask the question: *Is our worship genuinely Trinitarian in nature?*

Lutheran liturgical scholar Frank Senn reminds us that "long before Trinitarian dogma was defined by ecumenical councils, expressed in ecumenical creeds and preserved in ecclesiastical canons, Christian were worshiping the [Triune] God. . . . Orthodox Christian worship is explicitly Trinitarian, and church canonical structures have existed to preserve its Trinitarian substance."[5]

While the invocation of the Trinity in prayers, hymns, creeds, and other liturgical formulas contributes to shaping worship that is Trinitarian in nature, I would contend that these formulas alone do not make it so. At issue is a deeper question: Are all three Persons of the Trinity regularly explored, invoked, and represented in the sermons we preach, the hymns we sing, the prayers we make, and the way in which we speak of God in worship? Or do we, without even realizing it, fall prey to an unconscious unitarianism in which one person of the Trinity is regularly celebrated and lifted up, to the exclusion of the other two?

One of the critiques Senn makes of some contemporary worship services is that they tend toward a unitarianism of one Person of the Trinity in their selection of hymns. Neoevangelical services, for instance, tend to offer worshipers a steady diet of Jesus-hymns. Neo-Pentecostal services, on the other hand, favor a diet rich in Spirit-songs. Because such services also often eschew the use of traditional creeds, preferring the use of personal testimonials or of freshly written contemporary "statements of faith," worship becomes skewed toward one Person of the Trinity.[6]

One of the byproducts of such worship is what theologian Edward Farley describes as a loss of "a sense of the terrible mystery of God, which sets language atremble and silences facile chattiness. . . . If the seraphim assumed this Sunday morning mood," he says, "they would be addressing God not as 'holy, holy, holy,' but as 'nice, nice, nice.'"[7]

On the other hand, however, it is also the case that Protestant churches have, at times, fallen prey to a unitarianism of "God the Transcendent Wholly Other" in their worship practices, and have failed to give equal emphasis either to the incarnational presence of the loving and healing Christ or to the surprising, charismatic inbreakings of the Spirit in today's church and world.

I was a youth in the church of the '60s and still remember the worship wars that were fought in that era over the charismatic movement that emerged within many so-called mainline denominations. On the whole, congregations in that day tended to respond to the challenges posed by the charismatic movement in one of two ways (often depending on their pastoral leadership): either they embraced it, enthusiastically supporting more Spirit-centered forms of worship, or (more commonly) they resisted it with their whole beings, maintaining worship as they had traditionally practiced it. The problem was that in opting for either of those routes, many congregations chose to stay closer to the shoals of unitarianism of one form or another rather than moving toward a more deeply Trinitarian channel.

Peter Marty, a Lutheran pastor in Davenport, Iowa, urges mainline congregations to get beyond the language of "contemporary" and "traditional" when speaking of our worship differences, and to move toward a place where all people, regardless of their worship tastes, are more open to being surprised by God's grace in worship. God, he implies, is far bigger than any of our expectations, and people who come to worship want "more than the transcendent glory of God in a neat package. They want expressions of faith that have some size."[8] Genuinely Trinitarian worship can help move us toward a faith that "has some size."

3. Deep worship acknowledges both the "already" and the "not yet" dimensions of God's reign.

Christian worship is inherently eschatological—calling us to hope in God's present and coming reign, even as we name the realities that distort and oppose that reign in our world. The *Baptism, Eucharist and Ministry* document of the World Council of Churches reminds us that the Eucharist is "the feast at which the Church gives thanks to God for the signs [of God's reign present in the world today], and joyfully celebrates and anticipates the coming Kingdom in Christ."[9]

One of the things I have long appreciated about worship that is birthed in situations of oppression is that it tends to steer a deeper course between the "already" and the "not yet" than some of the worship I experience elsewhere. When worshiping in situations of oppression, lament and celebration, brokenness and healing, mourning and resurrection hope, praise and empowerment for action come together in ways that deepen and enrich worship.

I think in this regard of the worship I experienced twenty years ago in a small church in South Korea during the days of the Park Chung Hee regime (a dictatorship of the right), where the families of political prisoners gathered each Sunday under the watchful eye of the Korean CIA to pray for a restoration of democracy in their land, to hear from the scriptures words of hope and comfort, to sing their protest hymns, and to feast at the Table of the coming reign of God. Most especially I remember how the "concerns of the church" took on a whole new depth and dimension for me there, as the "already" and the "not yet" united in worship.

I think in this regard of worship I experienced in Buenos Aires, Argentina, with the World Council of Churches, where after an afternoon spent walking with the Mothers of the Plaza de Mayo—women who for over twenty years marched each week in the center of that city to protest the disappearance of their children during the brutal years of political and military dictatorships—we Christians of the world gathered for worship that embraced both weeping and hope, both acknowledgment of the fierce power of evil in this world and anticipation of God's coming reign of justice and peace.

I think in this regard of the worship I experienced at Riverside Church in New York City on the occasion of the first visit of Nelson Mandela to the United States after his release from many, many years in prison under apartheid rule in South Africa. That service was as joyous and celebrative a gathering as I have ever experienced in a Christian church. We literally danced in the aisles at its conclusion to the beats and chants of South African rhythms. But the celebration was also deeper, more profoundly joyous, because it was rooted and grounded in a radical awareness of the power of racism and evil in this world, and in a sure belief in the reign of a sovereign God who in the "already" and the "not yet" is breaking the chains of oppression and setting the captives free.

But let me bring it closer to home, for worship does not have to take place on some foreign shore or in a place of political oppression to be eschatological in nature. Recently I have worshiped on several occasions with a congregation in my own community where there is a great deal of brokenness due to addiction to drugs or alcohol. The congregation has a number of twelve-step programs meeting in its building, lights a candle at the beginning of each worship service as a sign of its solidarity with those in recovery, and lists each week in its bulletin the names of every person who has requested prayer. I have been struck by the fact that in each of the pews of this church are packages of tissues, and it is clear that they are not simply intended for children with runny noses! It is the expectation here that people will mourn as well as rejoice when they come to worship, and that tears will be shed as they are brought face to face both with their own shortcomings and with the hope that God alone offers them.

But what has also struck me about this congregation is that the concern for personal healing is also yoked with a more cosmic concern for the healing of the whole creation and an intentional inclusivity that welcomes all—regardless of race, economic class, or sexual orientation—in the name of Christ. This church is involved in advocacy for many who are marginalized or ostracized in society. The preaching, the prayers, the sacraments, and the hymns—which actually embrace a wide diversity of styles and types, ranging from African American spirituals, to contemporary scripture choruses, to responsorial psalms, to traditional hymns of faith—all serve the larger purpose of moving people into the presence of a God who alone has power to heal all the broken places of our lives and of our world. And worship, in a profoundly eschatological way, regularly acknowledges both the "already" and the "not yet" of God's reign.

Some of the questions I fear we are losing in the midst of the worship wars that plague local congregations are these: Is our worship, in our own local community of faith, eschatological in the fullest sense of the term? Or does it veer too closely to the shoals on either side of the worship narrows?

Does our worship allow space in which people can name and mourn the sinful realities of the world in which we live, and mourn the radical power of evil, even as we hope in God's coming reign? Or have we fallen prey to a chirpy, trite hope that cheapens sin and glosses over evil?

Does our worship allow space for embracing both the personal and the cosmic dimensions of God's coming reign, or does it veer too closely to the shoals on either side of the channel—either focusing primarily on personal salvation and pastoral care, or focusing almost entirely on cosmic redemption and social action?

To stay in the deep waters, worship needs to chart a middle way. And when it does, I daresay that many of the questions that divide us in worship will move toward the background, as the more significant question becomes: What music, liturgical forms, and prayers can move the people of God toward a deeper understanding of God's reign, which promises resurrection power in the face of every evil we encounter in this life?

4. Deep worship enables people to love and praise God with their whole beings: heart, soul, mind, and strength.

Long ago Augustine said that the goals of preaching should be "to teach, to delight, and to persuade," in order that the gospel might "be heard intelligently, obediently, and willingly."[10] In other words, preaching should speak to the totality of a human being, engaging the mind, the emotions, and the will in responding to God's gracious acts in Jesus Christ.

Deep worship does the same. Holding together the mysterious and the mundane, deep worship appeals to the senses as well as to reason, to the emotions as well as to the will, to the deep recesses of human consciousness as well as to those aspects of human consciousness of which we are more readily aware. Deep worship helps the worshiper express love as Jesus commanded us to do: with our heart, soul, mind, and strength.

Just as worship planners might be helped by asking which part of the Trinitarian God is emphasized (or deemphasized) in worship, so we might also be helped by asking which part of the human being is lifted up or ignored. How well does our worship encourage us to praise God with the mind? with the emotions? with the will? with the body? Are we, in our worship, veering too close to the shoals of one of these markers, causing frustration for some worshipers because we are not steering a deeper course that engages the whole person more fully?

One of the great rewards of holding together and valuing in worship both word and sacrament, speech and silence, visual symbols and embodied gestures, prose and poetry, easily singable music and music that gives praise in melodies we could not begin to emulate, is that by so doing we also enable people to give homage to God more fully and more deeply than they could with any one form alone. Deep worship is born out of intelligibility and unfathomable mystery, out of prayer that easily erupts from the lips and out of that sighing within us that is too deep for words, out of speech that illumines and silence that draws us deeper into the realms of the Spirit.

When my daughter was a little girl—about five years old—I remember saying prayers with her one Saturday night at bedtime, as was our custom. As a part of my prayer, I asked God (in good Reformed fashion) to prepare us to receive the Lord's Supper in worship the following day. Suddenly, in the midst of my praying, I was interrupted by what sounded for all the world like clapping. Startled, I opened my eyes, and, sure enough, my daughter was clapping her little hands for all she was worth. "Why, Leonora!" I said, rather startled, "Why are you clapping?" "Because," she answered, "you said we're going to have Communion, and I love Communion!"

I learned a lot about sacraments by worshiping with my children. Both of my children, when they were very young, loved sacraments and would sit through a service of any length in anticipation if a sacrament was to be celebrated. Why? Because sacraments communicated mystery and wonder and gospel to them in a way that did not require them to have linear logic, proper doctrine, or well-developed verbal skills. Sacraments involved visible, audible, sensory things that they could see and touch and feel and taste. Sacraments invited them to participate with their bodies in worship, and to allow their imaginations to run free. Sacraments caught them up in rituals that conveyed love and mercy and grace to them, before they ever had language to name those realities.

I worry sometimes that in our quest for worship that is "accessible" and "intelligible" to different types of folk—be they believers or nonbelievers—we are also running up against the rocky shoals where didacticism and rationalism rob worship of its sacramentality and mystery. And I confess to being troubled by services that evangelize without also inviting nonbelievers into the presence of sacramental mystery where they, like my children, can first experience a mystery they then spend the rest of their lives beginning to fathom.

Several Easters ago I sat in church behind a couple of visitors. Just before the service began, I overheard one whispering to the other as she pointed to the eucharistic table spread with the resurrection feast, "What do you suppose those symbols on the table mean?" My first response was to be startled once again by the post-Christendom age in which we live, and by the fact that these were folk who had never observed Communion elements before. But then I heard the other responded in a whisper, "I don't know. I guess it has something to do with the rituals this religion observes. We'll have to learn more about it."

Yes, I thought to myself, you will. And we will help teach you. But one of the best ways to learn is the way in which my children have learned about those mysteries: by being in worship where they are celebrated, interpreted, and experienced; by participating in the rituals that surround their observance, and by drawing close to the Table and to its mysterious

Host, who always extends grace and love before any of us are ever able to explain, analyze, or rationally appropriate it.

Conclusion

In his book *Worship Theology*, Don Saliers says that liturgical celebrations that have "deep souls" always yield new discoveries. "They continue to be luminous, even revelatory. They are occasions where the doxa of God is at the center, and the pathos of human beings is truly prayed and sung. Perhaps," he says, "we could use the term 'holy' to characterize liturgical celebrations with deep souls. Encountering the holiness of God fills the forms we employ with what cannot be manufactured."[11]

My own suspicion is that if we concentrated more of our time and energy in local congregations on steering a course toward worship with "deep souls"—worship that is concerned both with the glory of God and the edification of the worshiper, worship that is genuinely Trinitarian in nature, worship that is eschatological in the fullest sense of that term, and worship that addresses the whole person (heart, soul, mind, and strength)—we might find ourselves avoiding some of the shallows on which other vessels have run aground. To be sure, paying more attention to these channel markers will not solve all the worship wars in which our churches are engaged. We will continue to struggle in worship, as elsewhere in life, with issues related to gospel and culture. But if we at least attend to these theological markers as we plan, I suspect we might find ourselves heading toward deeper waters, where, with the winds of the Spirit stirring around us, the waters God created for our renewal undergirding us, and Christ, our captain, at the helm, we will know the unfathomable wonder and praise true worship can afford.

NOTES

1. John M. Buchanan, "Reflections on Worship in the Middle of the Moderatorial Year," *Reformed Liturgy and Worship* 31, no.1 (1997): 12.
2. Ibid.
3. David R Newman, *Worship as Praise and Empowerment* (New York: Pilgrim Press, 1988).
4. Witness, in this regard, the Willow Creek Church phenomenon, in which Sunday morning "seeker services" are separate and distinct from the "worship services" of word and sacrament engaged in by believers on weekday evenings.
5. Frank C. Senn, "'Worship Alive': An Analysis and Critique of 'Alternative Worship Services,'" in *Worship* 69 (1995): 215.

188 Leonora Tubbs Tisdale

6. Ibid.
7. Edward Farley, "Sunday Morning: A Missing Presence," *Christian Century*, March 18–25, 1998, 276.
8. Peter W. Marty, "Beyond the Polarization: Grace and Surprise in Worship," *Christian Century* (March 18–25, 1998): 284.
9. *Baptism, Eucharist and Ministry* (Geneva: World Council of Churches, 1982), 14.
10. Saint Augustine, *On Christian Doctrine* (Indianapolis: Bobbs-Merrill, 1958), 4.17. 142.
11. Don E. Saliers, *Worship Theology: Foretaste of Glory Divine* (Nashville: Abingdon Press, 1994), 205.